RULE *the* WEB

RULE *the* WEB

How to
Do Anything
and Everything
on the Internet—
Better, Faster, Easier

MARK FRAUENFELDER

 ST. MARTIN'S GRIFFIN ⚜ NEW YORK

Book Design by Maura Fadden Rosenthal

www.stmartins.com

Library of Congress Cataloging-in-Publication Data

Frauenfelder, Mark.
    Rule the Web : how to do anything and everything on the Internet—better, faster, easier / Mark Frauenfelder.—1st ed.
        p.   cm.
    ISBN-13: 978-0-312-36333-8
    ISBN-10: 0-312-36333-8
    1. Internet—Handbooks, manuals, etc.   2. Computer network resources—Handbooks, manuals, etc.   I. Title.

TK5105.875.I57F7697   2007
004.67'8—dc22

                                                                2007009002

10 9 8 7 6 5 4 3

To Carla, Sarina, and Jane
You rule my world

CONTENTS

INTRODUCTION

When Tim Berners-Lee created the first Web site in 1991, at the European Organization for Nuclear Research in Switzerland, he was hoping it would become the standard way for researchers to share data with each other. Little did he know that, fifteen years later, his invention would be the foundation of a media revolution with over a billion avid users (and growing—check internetworldstats.com/stats.htm for the latest figures). From its humble origins in a nuclear research facility, the World Wide Web has swayed elections, created a new class of telecommuters, generated billions of dollars of wealth, destroyed old business models, built new business models, and changed the way people shop, read the news, choose doctors, listen to music, plan vacations, watch TV and movies, share family photos, get answers to questions, find directions, do homework, learn new skills, communicate with each other, find long-lost friends, invest in the stock market, distribute propaganda, publish recipes, pay bills, auction off unwanted stuff, start online businesses, find a new place to live, and alleviate boredom. In short, the World Wide Web, more than any other technology, has changed the way we live more profoundly than any other technology invented in the last fifty years.

Rule the Web isn't a directory of useful Web sites (though there are plenty to be found here). Nor is it a guide to using the Web; there are many such books available. What is *Rule the Web*, then? **It's a guide to getting stuff done with the Web.** I wrote *Rule the Web* to help you get things done in your life, both online and offline, by using useful (and mostly free) Internet resources. The hundreds of tips, tricks, techniques, tutorials, and workarounds here will help you unleash your creativity, manage your time, collect a massive library of movies, music, books, podcasts, and games, get the best deals on just about everything, plan an unforgettable vacation, improve your health, find answers to all of your questions, avoid online scams, and much more. If you've been online for any length of time, you already have favorite sites and preferred ways of doing things that have given you a glimpse of the real power of the Web. *Rule the Web* unlocks the Web's potential, opening up a richer, nimbler, and more useful trove of online resources and services. The book is organized into sections that correspond to different aspects of your life: Creating and Sharing, Searching and Browsing, Shopping and Selling, and so on. There's also a Toolbox section designed to help you keep your computer operating spyware- and virus-free and at peak capacity, along with a selection of Internet tips from some of my favorite bloggers.

Because the Web is a fast-moving medium, and print, well, isn't, I encourage you to visit *Rule the Web*'s companion Web site at ruletheweb.net. In addition to chapter updates and my blog about the latest Web services, you can listen to podcast interviews with guest experts, view screencast tutorial videos, and participate in live call-in talk shows. I hope you'll join us!

IMPORTANT NOTE: I'm not advising you to do anything that may be illegal. It is your responsibility to use the information in the book in a safe and legal manner. Use of the information in *Rule the Web* is at your own risk. It is your responsibility to make sure that your activities comply with applicable laws, including copyright, and with any contractual terms you may have agreed to (remember, every time you click on an "I agree" button, you're entering into a contract). In this book, you'll find information about Web sites that offer medical advice, financial advice, legal advice, and advice on other subjects that could cause harm to you or your property, privacy, or bank account. Before making use of any of the information contained in *Rule the Web*, you should consult your doctor, financial advisor, lawyer, and spiritual advisor. The author and publisher disclaim all responsibility for any resulting damage, injury, or expense.

RULE the WEB

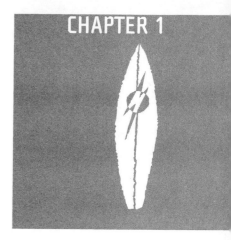

CHAPTER 1

CREATING AND SHARING

I think my favorite thing about the Internet is the way it lets anyone with a computer and a $20-a-month connection create and distribute their words, sounds, images, and movies to a potential audience of a billion people. This kind of broadcasting power would have cost millions in equipment fees and licenses twenty years ago. (Thank goodness the Web happened below the government's radar, or you'd probably need a license to blog now.) Today, the barriers to entry have been all but obliterated. You no longer need money to have your voice heard by a large audience; you just need to be interesting.

In this section, you'll learn how to cheaply and easily set up your own Web site, blog, podcast, video podcast (a.k.a. vodcast), and wiki (don't worry, I'll explain all these terms in the book), along with tips for getting the most out of them. You'll also learn how to meet like-minded people through social networking services, and how to upload and download files that you want to share with other people.

⏩ WEB SITES

▶ How Do I Set Up My Own Web Site?

Design and publish your own Web site for free and in minutes with Google Page Creator

Web sites used to be hard to make. After registering a domain name (such as ruletheweb.net) and paying a service provider to host your Web site, you had to learn HTML (HyperText Markup Language, used to create Web pages) and then figure out how to upload your pages and images to your host.

Today, you can design and publish simple Web sites quickly and easily. One way to do this is by getting a MySpace.com account, but the tools are limited and the results are pretty ugly. Also, your visitors need to register at MySpace in order to see your page. I greatly prefer Google Page Creator. The pages it produces are much more elegant looking, and are viewable by anyone.

>Here's how to create a Web page with Google Page Creator

Visit pages.google.com and log in (you'll need to sign up if you don't already have an account with Google).

If this is your first visit to Google Page Creator, a page that looks like the one on page 3 will greet you.

Start entering text wherever you see a "Click here to enter your pages . . ." placeholder. See page 4 for an example.

To add a link to text, highlight the text and click the "Link" button. You can link to other Web pages (including other pages you've made using Google Page Creator), email addresses, or downloadable files.

Add photos by clicking the "Image" button and then choosing them from your hard drive or from the Web.

Use the formatting buttons on the left to change the font size and styles.

You can change the overall style of your page by clicking "Change Look" and "Change Layout."

The "Add Gadget" link lets you spice up your page with a calendar, local weather conditions, a clock, a stock chart, and other widgets.

Once you're satisfied with the result, click "Publish." It is now available for the entire world to see at yourusername.googlepages.com /home (where yourusername is your Google user name.) It took me all of six minutes to create the image at the bottom of page 4.

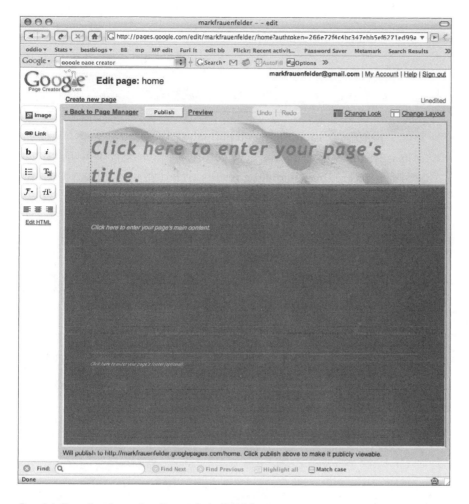

Google's Page Creator makes it easy to build Web pages.

▶What's a Domain Name?

Domain names are human-readable Internet addresses

Every computer connected on the Internet has a unique address assigned to it, called an IP (Internet Protocol) address. For example, 66.74.73.191 is the IP address for the computer I'm on right now. This number lets the network know where my computer is. (You can look up the IP address of your computer by visiting cqcounter.com/whois.)

A Web page created in just a few minutes.

IP addresses are akin to postal addresses: each one is unique, and that's why someone in Newport, Rhode Island, can scribble an address on a postcard and be assured it will arrive at its destination in Portland, Oregon. The computers that store and serve Web pages—called hosts, because they house the files that make up Web sites—also have IP addresses associated with them. If you want, you can visit Web sites by entering the IP addresses of the host machines. For instance, 204.11.50.136 is boingboing.net's IP address. Enter it in your browser and it will load right up. But who can remember IP addresses? That's where the domain name system comes in. Around the world there is a network of computers called Domain Name Servers. These computers contain databases with the IP addresses of every registered Web site in existence. Whenever you enter the name of a Web site into your computer, say boingboing .net, your computer sends a request to a Domain Name Server to translate the name into the IP number so your Web browser can load the Web site.

When you register a domain name and sign up for a hosting service, the hosting service gives you an IP address, which you must provide to the domain name registrar so the domain name and IP address can be linked together.

Getting your domain name registered is just the first step in setting up a Web site. You will also need a Web host to serve your Web pages to your eager audience. There are hundreds of hosts out there, and you can find reviews of many affordable ones at CNet (reviews.cnet.com/Basic_hosting/7026-6541_7-0.html). My first choice for hosting is Laughing Squid (laughingsquid.net). Based in San Francisco, Laughing Squid specializes in small customers, and its rates start at just $6 a month.

Once you register a domain name and sign up with a host, your host will provide instructions on how to put your Web site on the host's server.

▶ How Do I Buy a Good Domain Name as Soon as It Becomes Available?

Use a "drop catcher" to snap up a domain name as soon as its registration expires

You don't actually own a domain name, you just rent the right to use it. Domain names must be re-registered regularly or the domain will stop working. That means that any Web sites or email accounts using that domain will stop working, too. You typically have seventy-five days after the expiration date to renew your domain. If you fail to renew it within the grace period, someone else can register the name and put up whatever kind of Web site he or she wants. You'll lose all access to it.

Every day, about 20,000 domains are lost due to non-payment. I lost a domain that way. In 1995, I registered the name boingboing.com. But I failed to renew my registration, and as soon as it expired, a design firm called Boing! Boing! snagged it. I suppose I could have tried to get it back by taking the firm to court, but I wasn't interested enough to pay a lawyer to find out. Instead, I grabbed boingboing.net, which I now dutifully re-register every year. Today, most registrars will allow you to set your domain to auto-renew with the credit card on file.

Has someone "stolen" your domain name? Or is there a domain name registered to someone else that you want for yourself? If you're willing to pay more, you can hire an online "drop catcher" to pounce on a domain name as soon as it expires. These guys exploit the three-hour "drop" period (between 11 AM and 2 PM Pacific time) on the seventy-fifth day after a domain expires. At some point during the three-hour drop period, the domain will be removed from the master database at ICANN (Internet Corporation for Assigned Names and Numbers, which oversees the domain name system) and made available for registration to the first person that grabs it. If it's a name that a lot of people want, then it's almost a sure bet that the domain will go to a person who has hired a drop catcher such as pool.com or snapnames.com. Both services charge $60 to backorder a domain name, but if you're after a domain that had a lot of traffic going to its Web site, or one that has a memorable name, chances are good that you aren't the only one trying to snatch it up. So even if the drop catcher service you used to grab the domain is successful, if that service has been retained by anyone else in addition to you, you'll have to bid against the other person to get the domain. The bidding process for each company is different, but they're engineered in such a way to extract as much money from you as possible. Be prepared to pay at least a few hundred dollars to get the domain.

▶ How Many People Visit My Web Site?

Use a free counter to find out how many people visit your site and where they came from

Trust me: once you build your Web site, you'll become incredibly curious about how many people are visiting it, and how they found out about it in the first place. All you have to do is install a counter on your blog. Counters are programs that keep a log of the number of visitors that come to your site, when they visited, what site they linked from, how long they stayed, which links they clicked on, what browser and operating system they used to read your blog, and even what country they're from. Most good counters store daily, weekly, and monthly statistics so you can see how quickly your popularity is growing. There are dozens of companies out there offering free counters. I like StatCounter (statcounter.com) because it doesn't have ads and it looks unobtrusive on a Web page.

StatCounter also gives you the option of hiding your stats from your readers, but I've always enjoyed making Boing Boing's stats public to share and compare with other bloggers.

Another option: If you're already using Feedburner (feedburner .com) to manage your blog's RSS feeds, you might be interested in Feedburner's Web page stats tracking capability.

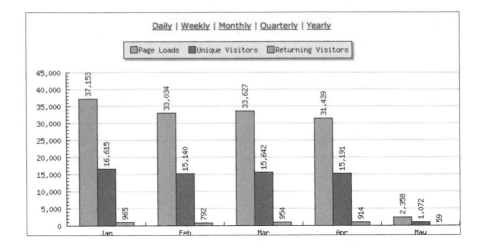

▶ How Do I Increase My Web Site's Popularity?

K.I.S.S. it, Digg it, and Optimize it

You've probably heard the acronym K.I.S.S., for "Keep It Simple, Stupid." Here, it stands for "Keep It Scintillating, Stupid." You can promote all you want, but if your content stinks, nobody will visit more than once. You need consistently killer content and you need to update it regularly. The sites that get tons of traffic tend to be ones that post new material throughout the day. Even if you only have a relatively small following, if you post juicy stuff all day long, your regulars will hit your pages repeatedly. The traffic of these repeat customers can add up to big numbers over the course of a month.

"Digg it" refers to digg.com, the social bookmarking and site-recommendation service. It's a place where people can discover the most popular sites and, in turn, recommend worthwhile sites to others. If something on your site gets "dugg" by enough users, it will rise in the popularity rankings, driving significant traffic to you. The first thing you want to do is submit stories from your site to Digg that you think people will, well, dig. You can also add a Digg submit button to all of your stories so that anybody who so desires can recommend a link with one click. And don't stop at Digg. There are dozens of similar social bookmarking sites. You can add "Submit" icons to your content that link to the submit forms of all the major bookmarking sites. If you use the blogging software WordPress (wordpress.com), there's a plug-in called Sociable (push.cx/sociable) that will add icons and links at the ends of your blog posts for the bookmarking sites you specify. Another WordPress plug-in called ShareThis allows visitors to share the links on your blog via email and social bookmarking. You can also get icons and linking code at the respective bookmarking sites (besides Digg, try del.icio.us and reddit.com). Elamb.org has a nice tutorial on adding social bookmarking icons to various types of blogging software at www.elamb .org/howto/servicelinks.htm.

"Optimize it" refers to "Search Engine Optimization" (SEO), something that's become serious business now that most users rely on search engines to find just about everything on the Web. As the name implies, SEO involves using various techniques to ensure that your content not only gets noticed by search engines like Google, but appears at the top of the results. For instance, if you blog about Japanese baseball teams, you would use SEO to make sure that anyone searching for the phrase "Japanese baseball" on Google would be directed to your site first. The first thing you need to do is to make sure that your site has been submitted to all of the major search engines. Wikipedia.org has a comprehensive list of search engines (en.wikipedia.org/wiki/List_of_search_engines) and Web directories (en.wikipedia.org/wiki/List_of_web_directories). Visit each engine and follow their directions to submit your site—each one's rules are different. Next, make sure that the titles of all of your Web pages are fully descriptive (which will make them rank higher in results). Don't write "Introduction" when you can write "Introduction to Sock Monkey Collecting" instead. Also, Web pages have what are called "meta tags," which are keywords and site descriptions that are factored into search results (although less so than they used to be). Look at the "head" section of your page's HTML code and fill out the meta

DEEPER

Choose popular words. You can also optimize your word choice. Search for "keyword tool" on Google. Keyword tools allow you to enter words to see their ranked popularity on various search engines and suggest related words that might draw more traffic.

tags with words that best describe your content. Also, if you use images on your site, use the "alt=" tag to label them. Search engine software can't interpret images, only the descriptions you give of them.

In the end, the best way to optimize is to heavily promote through social bookmarking service like Digg, submitting links of your content to high-traffic sites, and, best of all, through visiting and commenting on other people's Web sites. If they're like most bloggers, they'll more than likely return the favor, and even link back to you. The more you get linked to by sites with high Web credibility, the higher your star will rise in the search engine universe.

Search engine optimization techniques could (and do) fill volumes. To take your optimization to the next level, check out the free tools and resources at seologic.com/guide.

▶ How Do I Create a Discussion Board for My Site?

Set up a message board where visitors can post comments

There's an old saying about the Internet: "The quickest way to get a right answer online is by posting the wrong one." It's true. On countless occasions, I've posted something I considered a fact only to receive a blizzard of emails from people with the correct information. While I'm always embarrassed about disseminating bogus news, I'm glad that the truth prevails online. One of the easiest ways to get feedback on your blog is by activating your comment system. All modern blog services have built-in comments. To activate them in Blogger, log onto your account at blogger.com, click "Settings," and then "Comments." Look at page 11 to see how I set up my comments on Blogger.

I selected "Show Comments" because I want everyone to be able to read what others are saying. I allow anyone to comment, although you can limit the ability to comment to people who have registered at Blogger or only to members of your blog. I show backlinks, which are automatically generated links to any blog that references my blog entry. That way, readers can see what other bloggers think about

DEEPER

Use numbered lists. People have a strong attraction to numbered lists ("Top Ten Reasons Why Kevin Federline Is Whiter Than Vanilla Ice," "The 25 Dumbest USB Devices of All Time"). Create such lists and the Blogosphere will beat a hyperlink to your door. Numbered list stories are consistently among the most popular on the Web.

Customizing comments settings in Blogger.

what I'm writing. I set the comment entry box to appear in a pop-up window, and I require "word verification," which means that anyone who wants to leave a comment must type in the randomly generated characters displayed in a graphic like the one on page 12.

Word verification (also known as a "captcha") is an effective way

Using "captchas" to prevent blog comment spam.

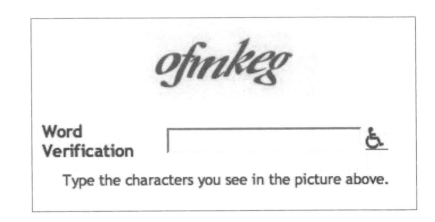

to combat comment spam, because spam software can't read the swirly characters. (It's sometimes difficult for humans to read, too!)

I also enabled comment moderation. This means that, when someone leaves a comment, it doesn't get posted right away. Instead, Blogger sends me an email with the text of the comment for my approval. That way, abusive emails get deleted without ever appearing on my site.

>Message boards for non-blog Web sites

If you have a non-blog Web site, try QuickTopic (quicktopic.com) to add message boards to your Web site where visitors can comment and discuss. After you've registered at the site, you can create a board for any topic by giving it a title and clicking "Start Topic." QuickTopic will generate an address like this: http://quicktopic

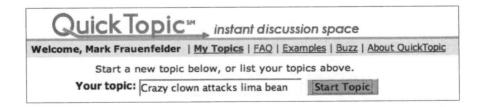

QuickTopic is a very easy way to add comments to your blog on a Web site.

.com/37/H/Y3UZECgfUSb (see page 12), which you can paste into your Web site to give your visitors a place to discuss.

For a more traditional message board, the free (ad-supported) ProBoards (proboards.com) is very easy to set up and use. After filling out a short form, you'll get a Web address you can add to your site that links to a full-featured message board.

▶▶ BLOGS

▶ What Are Blogs and Why Should I Read Them?

Blogs (short for "web logs") are regularly updated Web sites with entries posted in reverse chronological order—in other words, newest entries on top

Web logs are regularly updated Web sites that provide a continuous stream of content, whether that be links to other stuff or just stuff of the author's own creation. To me, a good blog is a log of "interesting stuff." I think of a good blogger as a "pre-surfer"—a trusted person who spends a lot of time online looking for interesting things from the Web and the rest of the world to write about.

Technorati.com, a blog indexing site, tracks over 57 million blogs and adds a staggering 100,000 new blogs to its index every day. All those blogs produce 1.3 million new entries every day.

With this many blogs online, it's a sure bet that there are many blogs out there that you would be interested in, if you only knew about them. So how do you find out which blogs are a good match for your interests? Start by visiting Technorati's page of popular blogs at technorati.com/pop (see page 13). Here you can peruse the most linked-to blogs, the top search terms on Technorati (that is, the most common keywords used by readers to find content on the millions of blogs that Technorati indexes), and the favorite blogs of Technorati readers.

DEEPER

Installing a full-featured commenting system on your blog. If you're willing to roll up your sleeves and install software on your Web server, give phpBB (www .phpbb.com) a try. This free bulletin board system is very powerful and customizable, making it your best choice for a message board for your Web site.

Find interesting blogs by visiting technorati.com/pop.

Click the "100 Top Favorited Blogs" link to read short descriptions of blogs and visit the ones that pique your interest. Many blogs have something called a "blogroll," which is a list of recommended blogs. If you like someone's blog, you'll probably enjoy some of the ones on their blogroll.

▶ How Do I Create My Own Blog?

Building a blog from scratch is a lot easier than you might think

Why would you want to start a blog? Here are a few reasons: 1.) You want to share photos and anecdotes with family members who live far away. 2.) You're an artist and you want to show off your work. 3.) You have a hobby and you want to connect with people who share the same interest. 4.) You want to keep a record of all the cool Web sites you visit so that you and you friends can go back and visit them. 5.) You work in a company that needs to stay on top of research and develop-ment news in your industry. 6.) You know a lot about a particular subject and you enjoy sharing your knowledge and opinions with other people, and want to engage in debate and conversation with them. 7.) You're a budding comedian and want to try your jokes out on the public.

Blogs are so popular because they make it easy for anyone to publish on the Web. Before blogging software was developed in the late 1990s, posting fresh material to your Web site was a complex and tedious task. That's why so many sites read: "Under Construction." Usually, the sites weren't really under construction; the person maintaining the site was just tired of the rigmarole required to keep it current, and gave up. (For a funny gallery of "Under Construction" logos, visit cs.utah.edu/~gk.)

The history of blogging can be traced back to 1996 when a site called Xanga.com launched a service that allowed people to maintain online diaries. But blogging didn't really take off until 1999, when a company called Pyra Labs introduced a service that would change the landscape of the Web. It was called Blogger, and it allowed anyone with an Internet connection to create Web pages that were very easy to update with fresh content. Blogger organized the content into reverse chronological order (so the most recent content would always be at the top of the page, where it should be), and automatically generated a browsable archive and a searchable database. It was nothing short of a revolution on top of a revolution (the Web) on top of a revolution (the Internet).

Today, there are lots of different ways to make and maintain a blog, but Blogger (now owned by Google) and Vox (owned by SixApart, makers of the venerable Movable Type blogging software) are both excellent places to begin. With either service you can create a blog and start publishing to the Web in under ten minutes flat.

Should you use Vox or Blogger? That depends. Vox is slightly easier to use than Blogger, and with it you can create a very nice-looking blog in minutes. It integrates well with Flickr, YouTube, and other media sites, making it easy to add photos, videos, and more to your blog. On the other hand, Blogger offers greater customization. You can run your own ads on a Blogger blog, add a visitor counter, and even dig into the guts of the HTML and edit them to your heart's content. Because I like to twiddle with my blog, and I already know HTML, I prefer Blogger. But for a newcomer who wants to make an attractive blog without having to worry about any technical issues, Vox is the way to go.

>Creating a blog using Blogger

1. **Go to blogger.com and create a free account.** Just enter a user name, a password, a display name (the name that will appear on your blog posts; it can be your real name or a pen name), and your email address. That's all you need to create your account. Click "Continue."

2. **Give your blog a name.** Provide a blog title, like "Mark's New Blog," and a blog address, like marksblog.blogspot.com. Blogger will let you know if the address you want is still available.

3. **Choose a template.** You don't need to be a professional designer to make a pretty blog. Blogger offers a bunch of pre-designed layouts you can use.

That's it. You now have a blog and a Web site address that you can print on a business card or email to your friends.

Now that you have your own blog on Blogger, you can start publishing your entries. If you aren't logged into your Blogger account, go to blogger.com and sign in.

1. **Create a new entry.** Click the image of the green cross, labeled "New Post," and you'll see a window like the one shown on page 17.

2. **Give your entry a title.** When you title a blog entry, don't be clever at the expense of clarity. Think like a newspaper editor and summarize your entry in a single descriptive sentence. People skim blogs the same way they skim newspapers—they're on the lookout for something that catches their interest. Also, an RSS newsreader (see page 27 to learn about RSS) may not display anything but your headline, so that may determine whether or not a reader clicks through to the entire entry.

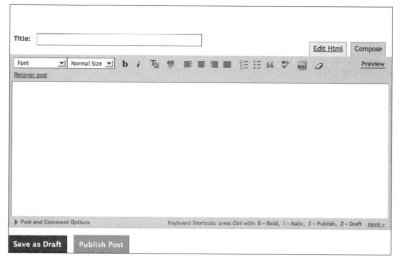

Creating a blog post on Blogger.

3. **Write your entry.** If you're writing about another Web page, always summarize whatever is on that page. For instance, if you're writing a blog entry about a video of a skateboarding dog, describe the video in your blog entry. The worst thing you can do is write something like: "Check out this amazing video—you'll be blown away!" You shouldn't force people to click a link to learn what it is. A much better approach is to say: "Here's a video clip of a bulldog riding a skateboard. It knows how to steer, push with one leg, and how to jump on and off the board at curbs." Your readers will really appreciate the effort and come to rely on you as a curator of cool stuff.

4. **Add images, links, and formatting to your entry.** The icons on the top of the Blogger draft window allow you to add bells and whistles to the text of your entry. You can highlight any portion of the text and make it italicized, boldface, or colored. You can turn any text into a link by highlighting that text and clicking on the icon of the globe with a chain link. If you want to add a picture, click the icon of the photograph. Note that there are two ways to add photos to your blog entry. One is by

selecting an image that's already on your computer. You do this by clicking "Browse" and navigating to the image you want. The other way is by entering the URL of an image already on the Web.

The problem with the latter method is that Blogger will simply point to the URL of the image in your blog entry. Why is that a problem? Because the owner of the URL might become angry that you are "hotlinking" to an image on his or her site, which uses some of his or her monthly data transfer allowance. Also, sometimes images become unavailable on other Web sites, which will leave an unsightly broken link in your blog post. That's why I recommend you use the first method—selecting an image on your computer. When you do this, the image is stored on Blogger's own image server, and it's perfectly OK to use Blogger's bandwidth!

5. **Preview your entry.** Click "Preview" to see what your entry looks like before you publish it. Now would be a good time to proofread your entry for any spelling or grammatical errors.

6. **Publish your entry.** Click "Publish Post." Congratulations! You're now a bona fide blogger.

>Creating a blog using Vox

Vox is a relative newcomer to the "instant blogging" arena. In some ways it's the easiest blogging service to use, and in others, it's one of the more confusing—mainly because of all it has to offer. SixApart designed Vox for showcasing audio, photos, and videos, making it easy to incorporate them into your blog entries. Like Blogger, Vox can generate your blog in a matter of minutes.

1. Sign up for a free account at vox.com.

2. Click on "Design" to choose a layout and a theme. You can also edit the name of your blog here (see page 19). Click on "My Vox Blog" at any time to see what the result looks like.

VOX's interface for setting up a blog.

3. In the upper-right corner, you'll see a silhouette of a head with a question mark in it. Roll your cursor over it and a small menu will appear. Choose "Edit your profile" and enter as much personal information about yourself as you care to share with the public. You can also upload a photo of yourself.

4. If you'd like to post messages to your blog using your mobile phone, click "Mobile Settings." You'll be given an email address you can use to send messages from your phone. Be sure to click the "Create Post" link and choose "Yes (create post for items sent to this email)" from the pull-down menu.

VOX allows you to add multimedia "items" to your blog entries.

5. Click "Outside Services" if you'd like to integrate your Flickr or Photobucket account with your Vox blog, or if you'd like to cross-post with a TypePad account that you already have.

6. Click "Privacy Notifications" and "Posting Defaults" to set defaults for who can visit your blog: friends, family, or the public. You can also fine-tune the privacy of each entry when you post.

7. Now that you've designed your blog and finished the other set-up details, you can start writing entries. Click on "Compose" and enter text in the window. You can format your text by clicking on the buttons along the top of the text entry window, and add links by clicking on the chain icon. The icon of two people lets you link to other people in your Vox "neighborhood," which consists of other Vox users you've added to your list.

Note the row of buttons directly above the formatting buttons. (See above.) These let you insert "items" into your blog entries. You can add photos, books, audio, videos, and something called "collections." Let's look at them one by one.

Photos: When you click on the Photo button, Vox gives you the option of adding photos from your computer, your Flickr account, your Photobucket account, or iStockphoto. Click one of the tabs running along the top of the photo window to choose the source. iStockphoto is a stock photography house with thousands of photos that you can use for free on your blog. Search by keyword to find a photo to add some color to your text entry.

Audio: You can add audio from your computer or from Amazon. Actually, when you choose Amazon as your source, it doesn't

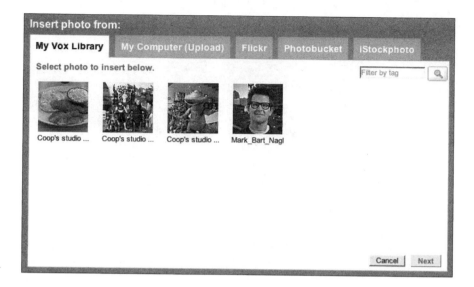

With VOX you can add photos from a variety of sources.

add a song link to your site. Instead, it adds an album cover graphic and a link to Amazon. If you choose "My Computer," you can upload MP3s (or audio in a variety of other formats) when you save the blog entry. Vox posts the audio with an embedded player, so that visitors can listen by clicking a play button. File size for audio is limited to 25 MB.

Video: Vox lets you add video from your computer, Amazon, YouTube, and iFilm. Again, with Amazon you can't add actual video—only links to DVDs that Amazon sells. Vox allows you to upload videos up to 50 MB.

Books: You can only add books from Amazon and, again, Vox simply inserts a cover image of the book and a link to the Amazon store.

Collections: Before you can insert a "collection" of sounds, images, and videos into a blog entry, you will need to create one. To do that, click "Organize" at the top of the window, and then "Collections" from the list on the left. Click "New" and give your collection a name, such as "Hawaiiania," or "Hot Rod

Adding photos to a VOX collection.

Hootenanny." A folder will appear with a small blue button below it. Now you can add items from your Vox library to the collection. To do that, click on one of the item categories, like "Photos." Roll your mouse cursor over the item you want to add and, when the small arrow appears below it, click it and select "Add to Collection" (see above). Now people will be able to access your entire collection from your blog entry. It's a fun way to capture the sights and sounds of a vacation or event.

8. Even after you've started publishing blog entries, it's a piece of cake to change the layout of your blog. Just click "Design," select a theme, and apply it to your blog.

▶What Are Some Tips for Running a Popular Blog?

Follow a few simple rules to ensure your blog gets the readership it deserves

I love blogging. The idea that anyone with a cheap computer and a $20-a-month Internet connection can publish words, pictures, videos, and audio to a potential audience of a billion people never fails to excite me. This kind of media broadcasting power would have cost millions of dollars just a decade or two ago. I've been posting to my own blog, Boing Boing (boingboing.net), since January 2000, after I wrote an article about blogging for a business magazine called *The Industry Standard* and fell in love with this form of self-publishing. (The *Standard* killed the article because the editors thought blogs were a passing fad! *The Whole Earth Review* ended up publishing the article in its Winter 2000 edition. You can read it here: (kk.org/tools/page52-54.pdf.)

With over half a decade of blogging under my belt, I've learned a lot about publishing a successful blog. Today, Boing Boing is the most popular English-language blog in the world, according to the blog-ranking service Technorati (technorati.com). It's won Webby awards and Bloggy awards for several years running, and has over one million daily readers (including people who subscribe to it via RSS). I edit Boing Boing with three friends: Cory Doctorow (a science fiction author), David Pescovitz (a researcher at the Institute for the Future), and Xeni Jardin (a freelance journalist and regular technology contributor to National Public Radio). Boing Boing's business manager, John Battelle, was the founder and publisher of *The Industry Standard*—oh, the irony! In all fairness, though, John didn't deal with editorial content for the magazine and had no idea I'd written the article. Today, Boing Boing has turned into a profitable business, thanks to advertising revenue.

Through all of this, I've thought about what it is that has made Boing Boing (and other blogs) successful and interesting. Here are some tips that should come in handy:

1. **Write about what you're interested in.** The cardinal rule of blogging is to write about the things that fascinate you. It may sound obvious, but I'm surprised at the number of people who post things just because they think they will attract more readers to their site. Nothing is further from the truth. If you aren't passionate about the things you're writing about, readers will quickly become bored and never return. If you happen to love

collecting vintage guitar-string envelopes, then by all means start a blog about it. I promise you that the other thousand people around the world who share your interests will find you and become loyal readers. In short, create the kind of blog that you would like to read yourself.

2. **Don't worry about being the first person to post something.** Some bloggers think it's crucial to be the first to blog a story. Chasing after scoops is foolish. With literally millions of blogs out there, and thousands of new ones appearing every day, it's unlikely you'll be the first one in the blogosphere to cover a news event. Instead, focus on finding things that interest you (rule #1, again) and adding your unique perspective. And remember, if a piece of news is new to you, then it's going to be new to a lot of other people as well.

3. **Limit the number of links you have in an entry.** On Boing Boing, we usually try to include just one link per entry, and place it at the bottom of the entry. That's because each entry should be about one idea, not a bunch of scattered thoughts with links going in all different directions across the Web. There are exceptions to this rule, of course, and sometimes you really do need to have two or more links in an entry for comparison purposes, but the "one-entry/one-link" restriction is a good starting point.

4. **Write at least one entry every day (weekends excepted).** Think of your readers as laboratory animals in an experimental cage that's equipped with a bunch of levers. The levers are blogs. If the lever you control dispenses a tasty morsel each time it's pushed, the animals will keep coming back for more. If you forget to provide a treat for the animals' effort, the animals will stop pressing your lever and look for a more reliable source of nutrition. That's why it's good to post at least one blog entry a day, because people will get used to the idea that your blog will deliver a treat each time they visit.

5. **Use pictures.** If you own the rights (or have the permission from the rights holder) to a photo or illustration that pertains to the subject you're writing about, by all means use it. Images are the quickest way for people to determine whether or not a blog entry is worth the time to read. I always include the cover of any book, DVD, CD, or comic book I'm reviewing because it makes the blog page look more interesting. (I don't worry about securing permission to use images in these cases, because I feel confident that my use of them in a critical review constitutes "fair use"). A few good places to find photos that you can use for free are Open Photo (openphoto.net), Flickr (flickr.com /creativecommons), and Creative Commons (search.creative commons.org).

   Another option is paying to use photos on your blog. iStockphoto (istockphoto.com) is a royalty-free stock photography community where you can buy the rights to use over a million images on your blog for as little as $1 each and videos for $5 and up. The quality of most photos is excellent, and I guarantee that if you use images that illustrate your writing in a creative and appropriate way, it will make your blog more successful. (If you're a photographer or illustrator, you can upload your work to iStockphoto and collect royalties when other people use your images.)

6. **Include a way for people to suggest links for you to write about.** Boing Boing has a "Suggest a Link" form to let readers send us ideas for things to write about and link to. We get lots of good leads from this suggestion form. If you're interested in setting up a form, you can either install a Formmail script (like the one here: nms-cgi.sourceforge.net/scripts.shtml), which requires some technical know-how, or you can use a form service like Formmail.to (which charges $1 a month) to handle everything for you. Of course, you can also include your email address on your site (or use a Gmail address especially for handling link suggestions), but if you go that route, you should

"mask" the address from email-harvesting software used by spammers (see page 363 to learn how to foil email-harvesters).

7. **Credit your sources.** When someone tells you about an interesting link, or you write about something you discovered while reading another blog, credit that source by providing a link to it. Your source will appreciate it, and will repay you in kind the next time they blog something they came across on your blog.

▶ Can I Blog Anonymously?

If you want to be heard but not seen, blog anonymously

I always attach my name to anything I write online, because I feel that it's important to stand behind what I say in public. But I also understand that anonymous speech is sometimes necessary. Corporate whistleblowers and political dissidents living under oppressive regimes have a right to be heard without getting fired or imprisoned.

For example, in 2004, a young Internet journalist from Tunisia, Zouhair Yahyaoui, wrote an entry on his popular TUNeZINE blog asking his readers to vote on whether Tunisia was a "republic, a kingdom, a zoo, or a prison." Soon after, six Tunisian secret policemen arrested him while he was in a cybercafé. Yahyaoui was held without charges and tortured until he revealed his blog password, after which the Tunisian government removed his blog from the Internet. He was held in prison under appalling conditions, and died there in 2005.

That's one reason I like the idea of anonymous blogging. BlogSafer (anoniblog.pbwiki.com) is a guide for blogging in countries that frown on free speech. It offers guides for bloggers in Saudi Arabia, Iran, China, Malaysia, Zimbabwe, and other countries where bloggers must live in fear that they'll suffer the same fate as Zouhair Yahyaoui.

Does anonymous blogging have a potential for abuse? Sure it does. But to me, the benefits of anonymous speech outweigh the dangers.

▶ What Is RSS and How Do I Use It?

Get fresh blog entries automatically delivered to your computer

You've probably heard the term RSS, but you might not know what it means. In fact there are several different explanations for what RSS stands for, though the most common is "Really Simple Syndication."

Basically, RSS is a way to "subscribe" to a blog. With RSS, you can sit back and have blog entries delivered to you, instead of using your Web browser to visit a blog to see what's new. In RSS jargon, a subscription is called a "feed," because it's a stream of information that your RSS reader "consumes" and displays for you to read. It's a bit like receiving email messages.

Here's an example of an RSS feed: I have a blog, called Mad Professor (madprofessor.net), where I review books, tools, toys, software, movies, and music. One way to read the blog is by visiting the Web site, which looks like the screenshot on page 28.

Another way to read Mad Professor is by subscribing to its RSS feed. The image on page 29 shows what Mad Professor looks like in an RSS reader.

I'm a devoted RSS user. I have RSS subscriptions to a couple of hundred different blogs, and I can go through them very quickly using my RSS reader program. Instead of having to visit all those sites individually, I can browse a list of headlines from all my subscribed feeds in one window. If I'm not interested in a headline, I don't bother reading the post. (Most RSS readers also allow you to browse complete posts, but keep in mind that some blogs only publish their headlines to RSS to keep you clicking through to their sites—and bring in some ad revenue while you're at it.) And I prefer the clean, spare look of RSS to the many over-designed, slow-loading blogs out there. (Why do so many bloggers think yellow text on a purple background is cool?)

A typical blog, as viewed in a Web browser.

>What RSS reader should I get?

To use RSS, you need a program called a feed reader or aggregator. You tell the application which Web sites you want to subscribe to, and the program will visit those sites on a periodic basis. If it finds new content, it will download the latest entries for you to read at your leisure. In addition to subscribing to blogs, you can also subscribe to non-blog RSS feeds, like FedEx or UPS package tracking updates (see page 132), weather alerts, Flickr photo streams, automated eBay auction search results, and much more.

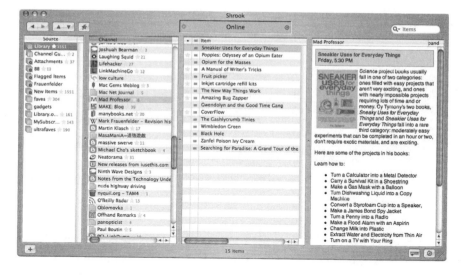

The same blog viewed in an RSS reader.

There are two kinds of RSS readers: standalone and Web-based. I use a standalone reader because it stores the feeds on my hard drive, allowing me to read them offline. But Web-based readers are popular too. The advantage of a Web-based reader is that you can read your feeds from any online computer, not just your own.

So which RSS reader should you get? For the Mac, I like Shrook (utsire.com/shrook), a free reader that has plenty of bells and whistles, such as the ability to download podcasts and videos. The free FeedDemon for Windows and NetNewsWire for Macs (both at newsgator.com) are very popular. My favorite Web-based RSS reader is Google Reader (google.com/reader), which lets you subscribe to and read RSS feeds from the Web.

>How to subscribe to an RSS feed

To subscribe to an RSS feed, your RSS reader needs the feed's address, which is different from the address of the blog itself. The feed address for Mad Professor is madprofessor.net/index.xml. It looks like an ordinary Web address. If you enter this into your Web browser, however, you'll probably be greeted with a page of ugly-looking code.

The standard RSS feed icon.

DEEPER

Subscribing to a blog that doesn't have an RSS feed. Some blog publishers don't offer RSS feeds. But don't let that stop you from creating a feed for that site. Go to Ponyfish (ponyfish.com) and enter the address of the Web site you're interested in. Ponyfish will then display the Web page and ask you to click links you want to see in your RSS field. Look for the permalinks (links that display individual blog's entries) because these will yield a cleaner, more accurate feed. Click at least two links; more is better. Ponyfish will create an RSS feed based on your input, which you can copy into your RSS reader.

This is because an RSS isn't designed to be read as a Web page. Your RSS reader knows how to translate this code into a human-readable form.

Most Web sites that offer RSS feeds publicize the fact somewhere on the home page. Unfortunately, there isn't any one standard way to do it. Some sites have a button (often orange colored) that says "RSS" or "XML" (XML is the language RSS feeds are written in). Some have a button that looks like the one at left. Some have a text link that says "Subscribe to this site." It's not always easy to find a feed!

To subscribe to a feed, you can't just click the feed link—you'll just bring up the aforementioned ugly-looking page of code. Right-click the link and select "Copy link location" from the pull-down menu. Then, open your RSS reader application, select the function that lets you subscribe to a feed, and paste the address into it. However, if you're using Firefox 2.0 or later, you can configure the browser to subscribe to an RSS application when you click on a Web feed. To set up this option in Firefox, go to "Preferences" → "Feeds" and click "Subscribe to feed using:" to choose your RSS reader application. See page 31.

▶ How Can I Give My Blog an RSS Feed?

Grow your readership by creating an RSS feed for your blog

As more and more people wake up to the advantages of RSS (see previous question, "What Is RSS and How Do I Use It?" on page 27), bloggers who don't offer an RSS feed risk being left behind. I know this, because Boing Boing has 350,000 daily Web site visitors and over 1,000,000 RSS subscribers! It's clear that people prefer the speed and convenience of RSS over Web-based blogs.

>Adding a feed to your blog

Most blogging services, such as Blogger, Vox, TypePad, WordPress, and Movable Type, can create RSS or Atom feeds for you.

If you use Vox for blogging, then RSS is on by default. If, for

Setting up Firefox to handle RSS feeds.

DEEPER: ADDING THE STANDARD FEED ICON TO YOUR BLOG

If you'd like to add the standard feed icon. Feed Icons (feedicons.com) has a free, downloadable folder containing the icon in different sizes and background colors. To upload the icon to Blogger's server, click "Posting" in the Blogger window and then click the snapshot icon. You can select the feed icon you've chosen by clicking "Browse" and then "Upload Image." Add the icon's address to the HTML in your Blogger template, so it looks like this:

```
<p><A HREF="http://myblog.blogspot.com/atom.xml"><img src="
http://photos1.blogger.com/blogger/6043/0/320/feed-icon-12x12
.jpg" border="0">Subscribe to this site's feed</a></p>
```

some reason, you've deactivated RSS and want to switch it back on, click "Design" at the top of the vox.com page, click "Customize your sidebars," check "Subscribe Module," then click "Apply." You're done.

If you have a Blogger account, log into it at blogger.com, click the "Settings" tab and then click "Site Feed."

Click the pull-down menu next to "Allow Blog Feed" to choose "None," "Short," or "Full." If you choose "None" only the headlines will appear in RSS readers (along with a link to the blog entry, of course). If you chose "Short," feed readers will display the first 255 characters (or first paragraph, whichever is shorter) of each blog entry. "Full" will send entire blog entries to feed readers. I highly recommend the "Full" option, because it is a drag for readers to have to click the link to go to a Web site to read the rest of a blog entry. Partial entries ruin the RSS experience.

▶ How Can I Post Entries to Blogger Via Email?

Add new entries to your blog by sending an email from any computer

The usual way to add a new blog entry to your Blogger-based blog is to go to blogger.com, click the "Posting" tab, click "Create new post," write your blog entry, and finally, click "Publish Post." But there's an easier way to do it—by email. Here's how:

From the Blogger page, click "Settings," then "Email."

1. In the field that's marked "Mail-to-Blogger Address" you'll see a partially completed email address that looks like that below.

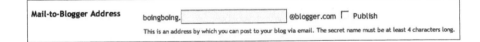

Mail-to-Blogger Address   boingboing.[   ]@blogger.com ☐ Publish
This is an address by which you can post to your blog via email. The secret name must be at least 4 characters long.

Blogger lets you set up a private email address so you can blog by sending an email message.

2. Enter a secret word (at least 4 characters long) in the blank between your Blogger user name and blogger.com.

3. Now you're set. When you want to post something to your Blog, just send a message to your secret blogger.com email address (don't let anyone know what it is or they will be able to post entries on your blog!).

Vox offers the same blog-by-mail service. Go to (vox.com/account/profilc/), click "Mobile Settings," and copy the email address that Vox generates.

▶ How Can I Blog Using My Mobile Phone?

Post photos and captions with your mobile phone

Today, most cell phones come with decent built-in cameras. One of the best ways to share the photos you take with your phone is by posting them on a blog. But instead of downloading the images to your computer and then uploading them to your blog, you can use Blogger Mobile to streamline the process. Blogger makes the process ridiculously easy:

1. From your mobile phone, send a photo and a message to go@blogger.com. Blogger will send an automated text message to your mobile phone, containing a "claim token."

2. Copy it down for the next step.

3. Enter the claim token at go.blogger.com to claim your blog.

Now you can customize your blog template. Anytime you send photos from your phone to go@blogger.com, they will be automatically posted to this blog.

If you already have a blog that you'd like to post images to, you can switch to that blog when you claim your mobile blog.

Vox offers the same blog-by-mobile service. Go to vox.com/account/profile/, click "Mobile Settings," and copy the email address Vox generates.

▶ How Can I Prevent My Blog or Web Site from Showing Up on Google?

Keep your blog a secret between you and your friends by telling robots to bug off

Search engines like Google use software programs called "crawlers" that move from link to link, indexing the content of the Internet. When you search Google, you are actually searching the index, not the Web itself.

If you have a blog you don't want Google to know about (maybe it's a gallery of family pictures, or a vacation journal you want to share with your co-workers but not the Web-reading world at large), you can put up a virtual "no trespassing" sign on your blog.

Here's how:

1. Open your blog's template file. In Blogger, do this by clicking the "Template" tag on your blog dashboard at blogger.com.

2. Near the top of the template, find <head>.

3. Right below <head> enter the following:

   ```
   <meta    name="robots"    content="noindex,
     nofollow">
   ```

This tells any crawlers that come across your site not to index it, and not to follow any links on it, either. In other words, it tells crawlers to turn around and go back to where they came from. Of course, email spam harvesters that crawl the Web looking for email addresses ignore these messages, so if you want to prevent any posted email addresses from being slurped by sleazy spambots, you'll have to mask them. (See page 375, "How Can I Prevent My PC from Becoming a 'Spam Zombie'?")

▶How Can I Blog So That Some or All of My Entries Are Only Visible to Friends?

Your blogging software may already have a private posts feature built in or there may be a third-party plug-in

Most popular blogging programs have some way of controlling user access to your content. Some let you mark certain people as "friend" or "family," which allow them to read posts that others can't see, for instance. Check the support documentation on your program's Web site to find how to access and control these features. If the program does not offer such control, there may be a third-party plug-in that does.

Let's look at a few popular blogging services to see some of the different ways that this is handled.

WordPress (wordpress.com) has many levels of user access, allowing you to control who is allowed to modify and access what on your site, but this does not include barring some users from seeing select content. Luckily, someone has created a plug-in, called Post Levels (fortes.com/projects/wordpress/postlevels), which handles this. The latest version even works within RSS feeds of WordPress blogs (prompting the reader for name and password when they access a restricted post).

TypePad (typepad.com) allows you to either password-protect your entire site or a blog section within your site. If you want to have public and private content, you basically have to have two blogs, one non–password protected and one password protected.

MySpace (myspace.com) allows you to make your page only accessible to your friends. You can also set permissions for who can comment, who can ask to be your friend (e.g. no bands trawling for new fans), and other privacy settings.

LiveJournal (livejournal.com) lets you set the security level of any of your postings from private to friends-only to public.

Blogger (blogger.com) offers no form of password protection. You can choose not to have your blog listed in their blog directory, but you have no way of keeping your content completely private.

*Control who can read your blog
posts at VOX.*

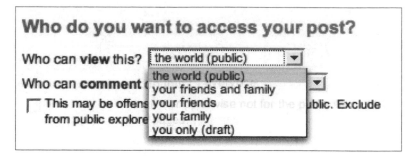

Vox (vox.com) gives you complete control over who can see individual posts: everyone, friends, family, friends and family, or just
you. (See above.)

▶▶ PODCASTING

▶ What Are Podcasts and How Do I Listen to Them?

*Subscribe to thousands of self-produced audio programs and
listen to them on your PC or MP3*

Simply put, a podcast is an audio program that you can listen to on
your computer or MP3 player. It's a bit like listening to the radio, but
the difference is that you can subscribe to a podcast and, whenever a
new program becomes available, it'll download automatically and be
waiting for you to listen to on your own schedule.

The best way to explore podcasts is with iTunes. (It's free and
works on Mac or Windows, so there's no reason not to download it
from apple.com.) iTunes is the ultimate application for managing
podcasts because you can use it to find, subscribe to, download, and
listen to thousands of podcasts being produced by professionals and
amateurs. You can also use iTunes to transfer podcast episodes to
your iPod for listening on the go.

>Searching for podcasts

First, click the purple Podcasts icon in the Source column on the left side of the iTunes window. Then, click "Podcast Directory" near the bottom of the screen. You'll be taken to the iTunes Podcast Directory page, where you can browse by subject, search for keywords, or choose from the Top Podcast list. For now, all podcasts offered through iTunes are free, but I imagine some podcast producers will eventually start selling subscriptions to their podcasts, given that Apple has put its Podcast Directory in its iTunes Music Store.

You can find out more about any podcast in the directory by clicking on its link. You'll get a program description, a list of individual episodes sorted by the date, and the option to subscribe. If you want to sample before downloading, just double-click the title of an episode to listen to. If you want even more information, click the "Web site" link for the Web site of the podcast's producer.

>Subscribing to and downloading podcasts

Once you've found a podcast that piques your interest, you can either subscribe to it by clicking on the "Subscribe" button near the top of the screen, or download an individual episode by clicking on the "Get Episode" button next to the episode you'd like to download.

While iTunes has thousands of podcasts in its directory, it doesn't catalog every single one on the Web. If you want to subscribe to a podcast that isn't in the directory, copy the address of the podcast into your clipboard, then select "Advanced" → "Subscribe to Podcast . . ." from the iTunes menu bar and paste in the address, as shown on page 38.

When you subscribe to a podcast, it appears in the Podcasts window. A speaker icon in the first column means that the episode is currently playing. A blue dot indicates that you have at least one unplayed episode of that podcast. If you click the little gray triangle next to the blue dot, you can reveal the complete list of episodes. Episodes in gray haven't been downloaded. Click "Get" next to any gray episode and the download will begin. An exclamation point means iTunes has stopped

DEEPER

Finding podcast archives.
Sometimes, iTunes displays only the most recent episodes of a podcast. To browse the podcast's entire archive and download older episodes, click iTunes "Web site" link to be taken to the podcast producer's Web site.

Subscribing to a podcast in iTunes.

downloading episodes to your computer either because you haven't listened to any of that podcast's episodes for a while, or because there are technical problems with that podcast's feed. If downloads have stopped because of a listening hiatus, click the icon for a pop-up box as shown above. You can choose to download more episodes by clicking "Yes," or continue to keep the subscription in suspension by clicking "Cancel." An orange dot with two animated arrows going around in a circle means that an episode download is in progress. If you want to visit the description page for any of your podcasts, click the gray arrow icon next to its name. In the lower right corner of the podcast subscriptions window, there's a "Refresh" button. Click it to download the latest episodes of your podcasts.

Click the "Settings" button in the lower right corner of the podcast subscriptions window to control how iTunes manages your subscriptions. You can set it to check for new podcast episodes once an hour, once a day, once a week, or manually (i.e., only when you click the "Refresh" button). You can also specify which episodes to download, which ones to keep on your computer, and which ones to copy to your iPod, if you have one. Note the "Keep" option. If you have it set to "Keep: All unplayed episodes," iTunes will delete episodes after you've listened to them. For some reason, iTunes tags an episode as "played" even if you haven't listened to it in its entirety, so you might want to change it to "Keep: All episodes." In any case, you can always re-download an episode if you need to. Once you have everything set up the way you want it, you can sit back and let the free content start pouring in.

It's just as easy to unsubscribe from a podcast as it is to subscribe to one. Just highlight the podcast you no longer want, and click "Unsubscribe" in the lower left corner of the window. You'll notice that the name of the podcast doesn't go away, and that a "Subscribe" button now appears next to it. All of the previously downloaded episodes are available when you unsubscribe. If you really want to get rid of the podcast and all the episodes for good, then take the nuclear option by clicking on the podcast title and pressing your computer's delete key. You'll have the option of keeping the episodes or moving them to the trash, but in either case, the podcast will be wiped off your list of subscriptions for good. Similarly, you can delete single episodes by clicking on them and pressing "delete."

>Playing podcasts on your iPod

If you have an iPod connected to your computer, you'll see an icon for it in the left column of the iTunes application. Click it to open the preferences that allow you to manage podcasts on your iPod. Click the "Podcasts" tab to set the sync options. You can select which podcasts iTunes copies to your iPod and which programs within each podcast you want to store on your iPod. To make sure you have the latest version of the iPod software on your player, visit apple.com/ipod/download.

▶ How Can I Record My Own Podcast?

Broadcast your own radio show on the Web using a simple, free online service.

Podcasts are online audio programs that you can subscribe to and listen to on your computer or portable MP3 player. If you use iTunes (and you should, because it's excellent, free, and available for Mac and Windows), it's easy to subscribe to thousands of podcasts being produced all over the world including cooking shows, language lessons, interviews, comedy programs, music showcases, and more. See page 36, "What Are Podcasts and How Do I Listen to Them?" to learn how to use iTunes to manage your podcast subscriptions.

Would you like to produce your own podcast? It's not difficult. In fact, with today's online podcasting services, it's a breeze. One of the easiest is Odeo Studio (studio.odeo.com), which lets you record audio using several different ways: using Odeo's recorder, uploading audio stored in your computer, or linking to audio that's already on the Web.

Here's how to create a podcast using Odeo.

1. **Choose a name for your podcast.** After signing up for an account at studio.odeo.com, go to studio.odeo.com/channel/

Podcast pick: "The Diner"

I don't know how newspaper columnist James Lileks manages to write so many words every single day and be so consistently witty, funny, and profound. On top of that, he produces a regular podcast called "The Diner" (web.mac.com/lileks/), which features his ruminations on the decline of food, the service industry, design, cars, art, music, manners, and just about everything touched by human hands. He deserves a Nobel and a Pulitzer for his stories of growing up in North Dakota, where his father owned a service station.

I listen to "The Diner" while I exercise at the gym, and I'm sure I have been branded the village idiot because I chuckle and grin the whole time.

Use Odeo Studio to create your own podcast.

create/ and create a name for your podcast. This is where you'll add a description of your podcast along with keywords so it can be found in a search and the URL of your blog you plan to publicize the podcasts on. (See above.)

2. **Record your podcast episode.** Next, you'll want to create the audio of your first podcast episode. If you want to record live audio using your computer, go to studio.odeo.com/create/studio. (See page 41.)

This browser-based recorder can use your computer's built-in microphone, or you can connect a microphone to it for better sound quality. (Before recording the episode, check the sound level by recording a 10-second test. You can adjust the sound levels with the slider bar on the right.) Odeo's recorder limits your recording to 60 minutes, which is more than enough

With a microphone and Odeo Studio you can record the audio for your podcast.

for a podcast. (If you have something longer to record you can break it up into two podcast episodes.)

When finished recording, click "Stop" and "Save Recording." This will save the audio file to Odeo's servers and bring up a page where you can add a title, a description, and an image to the podcast. This page also provides a snippet of HTML code that you can add to your blog that embeds an Odeo player right into the blog entry. People who visit your blog can play the podcast by clicking the player.

Recording audio directly to the computer is just one way to create a podcast with Odeo. You can also upload audio files that you've recorded and edited using an audio application such as GarageBand or link to audio files from Web sites (make sure you have permission from the copyright holder first!).

Be sure you visit the Podcasting Survival Guide (odeo.com/channel/95450/view), which features excellent podcasting tips, including how to pre-produce your podcast, how to record live events, how to get the most out of different kinds of microphones, how to publicize your podcast, and more from veteran podcasters such as Dough Kaye from IT Conversations and Franklin McMahon of the CreativeCOW podcast.

3. **Add the audio to your podcast.** Once you've recorded or linked to your podcast episode, you need to place it into your podcast feed. That's easy. Click on "Saved Audio" and then click the audio file you want to work with. (See below.) Here, you can add information about the episode and upload a photo that will appear in iTunes and on an iPod when your listeners play the episode. Near the bottom of this window you'll see a pull-down menu titled: "Place in:" Select the name of the podcast you wish to add the episode to and click "Save."

4. **Publicize your podcast.** You can let people know about your podcast in a number of ways. Click on the name of your blog in the "My Podcasts" window. You'll see something called an "RSS URL" that you can embed as a link on your blog. You

Any audio files you record or link to can be placed into one of your podcasts on Odeo.

can also copy and paste the "Podcast Badge" HTML code into your blog template to add a button that your visitors can click. Odeo also has a nifty Flash player that you can add to your blog so that visitors can listen to your podcast episodes right from your blog. Click on "Saved Audio" and copy the HTML code at the bottom of the page, under "Put this Audio on your Web site." Odeo has several different embedded players to choose from. Click the "Try these new players" link at the bottom of the page.

▶ How Do I Broadcast a Live Podcast So That People Can Call into My Show?

The easiest and cheapest way to do it is to use Skype, the free Internet phone service

Skype (skype.com) is the popular Internet phone program discussed in the "Internet Phones" section (see page 272). It's not only a way to make free and cheap phone calls, worldwide, but it's also a favorite among podcasters for recording phone conversations for their podcasts. To record a conversation, install Skype and set up a new account (see page 272). Each of your guest callers will need Skype too, or you can call them on a regular phone using the Skype-Out feature, which costs a small fee and doesn't offer the same audio quality as a PC-to-PC connection. For an annual fee, you can also get a SkypeIn number that guests can use to call you. Make sure to test the call quality beforehand to make sure that it sounds okay. Your PC-based callers will need a microphone.

There are a number of free recording apps out there, but if you get serious about your podcast you might want to spring for a full-featured commercial application. Free apps on the PC side include HotRecorder (hotrecorder.com) and PowerGramo Recorder for Skype (powergramo.com). Both of these have free versions with limited compression and other record options and inexpensive commercial versions for under $20.

Mac users should also check out Audio Hijack Pro, a powerful

DEEPER

Submitting your podcast to iTunes music store. Because so many people use iTunes to subscribe to podcasts, it's important to have your podcast listed in the iTunes store. Apple has provided a set of step-by-step instructions for doing this at apple.com/itunes/store/podcaststechspecs.html.

audio recording program that costs $32 from Rogue Amoeba (rogueamoeba.com). It will capture audio from Skype, iChat, and Gizmo and you can add a number of sound-enhancing effects to the recording. If you're doing pre-recorded podcasting, you don't have to deal with the issues of streaming your signal to listeners in real-time. But if you do want to create a true live show, there are two great live podcasting services: BlogTalkRadio and TalkShoe.

BlogTalkRadio (blogtalkradio.com) offers a one-stop shopping solution for creating "talkradio"-style podcasts. When you sign up as a host for the free service, BlogTalkRadio issues you a dedicated phone number that listeners can use to call into the show, as well as a phone number that you use to call into the service to host the show. Up to five other people can talk at one time, and you can monitor a Web page to see the list of the callers on hold.

Once you sign up, you'll have access to a "Host Dashboard" where you can schedule show segments and control other aspects of your podcasts. BlogTalkRadio automatically records your shows as MP3s and archives them so people can listen anytime. BlogTalkRadio is easy to use, and the live call-in aspect is a lot of fun, but remember: since it's live, there's no editing—everything you and your guests utter will be broadcast.

TalkShoe (talkshoe.com) works much like BlogTalkRadio, but it's designed more like a giant conference call, in which certain people can be designated as talkers and hundreds of others as listeners. To make a live podcast, sign up (it's free) and click on "Create Public Talkcast." Unlike BlogTalkRadio, however, TalkShoe requires a Mac, and you have to download the TalkShoe Live! client to use it.

If you want to improve the sound quality and other production values of your podcast, M-Audio (m-audio.com) has a really nice (and cheap!) hardware/software package called Podcast Factory. You get a decent desktop mic, a USB-based audio interface (for connecting microphones or musical instruments to your PC), and a suite of audio recording, mixing, editing, and MIDI software. All for only $180.

▶ **How Can I Create a Vodcast?**

With an inexpensive camera and an Internet connection, anyone can create an online video show

Today, the most inexpensive computers and handheld devices can play video. They can even be used to create, edit, and broadcast your own video podcast (a.k.a. vodcast, which stands for video-on-demand 'cast). It's not hard to make a vodcast—one of the most popular ones, "The Show," created by Ze Frank, consists entirely of headshots of Ze Frank saying wacky things and making goofy faces at the camera (zefrank.com). Rocketboom (rocketboom.com) episodes, on the other hand, appear on a set consisting of a table and a world map for a backdrop, alternating with on-the-scene interviews and event coverage.

Vodcast production consists of four steps:

1. **Pre-production.** To make a great vodcast, you need to plan your show in advance. Start by thinking of a one-sentence description of your episode. For example, "A look at the funny people who buy stuff at yard sales." Now, imagine that you've completed the show and you're watching the finished result. What elements would it contain? Write it down and make a list of the kinds of footage you'll need. For a funny-people-at-a-yard-sale show, you might need interviews with yard sale habitués (what kind of questions are you going to ask them?), interviews with the people holding the yard sales (perhaps asking them to share stories of the strangest yard sales incidents they can remember), and pan shots down tables filled with knickknacks and other "color" or "B-roll" shots that you can add to the show during voice-overs (so that the show doesn't consist entirely of talking heads).

Use these lists and notes to develop a final checklist of what to shoot and what kinds of interview questions you should ask. Keep in mind that things will happen once you are out in the field that might cause you to deviate from the script. That's fine. For instance, if a meteor crash-lands into a box of

DEEPER

Podcasting tutorials. This answer only scratches the surface of issues involved with live podcasting, recording, and Internet audio. To find out more, check out these two tutorials on recording and streaming Skype-based podcasts:
1. labnol.blogspot.com/2006/06/how-to-record-skype-conversations.html
2. radiofreefinland.net/2006/02/18/how-to-create-a-live-online-radio-show-podcast-using-your-computer-and-skype-skypecasting-that-can-take-live-callers-from-a-telephone.

Bee Gees and REO Speedwagon LPs while you're at a yard sale, it might be interesting to capture the event and its aftermath on video.

It's also helpful to create a storyboard of the video using a digital still camera and Flickr that you can share with your "crew."

A list of excellent videography tips and a "talent release" script can be found at videomaker.com/learn/tips-to-get-started.

2. **Shooting the video.** Yes, high-definition video cameras are becoming more affordable by the month, but you don't really need them for vodcasts. The gargantuan files they produce will need to be heavily compressed for online delivery. The only things you really need to concern yourself with are sound quality and camera movement. An external microphone is a must. The built-in microphones on video cameras are inadequate for interviews or capturing environmental sounds, and they tend to pick up the sound of the camera's motor.

To use an external microphone, your video camera must have a microphone jack. Most low-end camcorders don't have them, but a few do, and can be picked up for $300 or less. A shotgun camcorder mic, which mounts on the camera and points towards the subject you're shooting, is a good choice for videos that require interviews with lots of people at an event. They cost as little as $30 (search froogle.com for "shotgun camcorder microphone"). But if you're interviewing someone in an indoor "studio" setting, a $25 clip-on lavalier mic that attaches to the interview subject's shirt or jacket lapel provides the very best sound quality.

Just as important as the sound quality is the stability of your camera shots. Nothing looks more amateurish, in the 1960s-dad-with-the-8mm-camera-at-Thanksgiving sense, than a video shot that jerks and pans all over the place. Also, pans, zooms, and jitters greatly increase the size of your final, compressed video, making it more of a hassle for your viewers to download and watch. If it's not inconvenient, use a tripod for stability as much as possible. It will make a huge difference in the quality of your show.

To add some fancy shooting techniques to your video, learn by studying TV shows and movies: you'll start noticing neat little tricks that can add energy to your show, if used judiciously. For example, when setting up a new shot, you might focus the camera on a colorful object, such as a parrot or an ice-cream sundae, then zip the camera quickly to your subject.

For action shots, professionals use a contraption called a Steadicam, which allows the camera operator to run and shoot without any jitter. The effect is wonderful, but a Steadicam costs thousands of dollars. You can build a camcorder stabilizer that's 90 percent as good as a Steadicam for $14. Invented by a college student, Johnny Chung Lee, it's made from steel plumber's pipe and a weightlifter's weight disc. Complete instructions are available at cs.cmu.edu/~johnny/steadycam.

Even though your final vodcast won't be longer than five minutes or so (and I think most vodcasts are better when they're under two minutes), you'll probably want to shoot a lot more video than that, so you'll have plenty of material to choose from when editing.

3. **Editing and post-production.** Taking your raw video and turning it into a short, tight show can be the most time-consuming, challenging, and enjoyable part of the process. I won't go into the details of how to edit your video (you can use iMovie, Windows Movie Maker, Final Cut Express, or any other video-editing program), but I will offer a few tips to keep it mind:

Keep it short and sweet. Video consumes a lot of storage space and bandwidth, and people will be more reluctant to download a 200 MB video than they would a 40 MB one. Also, it is very difficult to create a video longer than four or five minutes that can hold a viewer's attention. Keep only the very best stuff, and don't hesitate to throw everything else on the cutting-room floor.

Don't use fancy titling and transition effects. Besides looking ridiculous, all those swooping, spinning, and morphing effects end up fuzzy and pixilated due to the heavy-duty compression your file will have to undergo when you prepare to upload it to the Internet. Simple dissolves and plain old cuts are easer to render, and they look classier too. As for titles, simple is better, and remember to make the text large enough to be read on the screen of a video-capable iPod or mobile phone.

Use your B-roll to maintain interest. When your subject speaks for more than a few seconds, alternate the interview footage with shots that help describe what they are talking about.

Add a soundtrack. Your vodcast will look better if you add some music to it. Visit podsafeaudio.com to browse through songs by artists who've licensed their work under a Creative Commons (creativecommons.org) license. There are several different types of Creative Commons licenses, and most of them do not allow you to use works for commercial purposes. If your vodcast isn't something you intend to earn money on, then you can safely use any of the songs on podsafeaudio.com (provided you credit the song's artist). For vodcasters who are looking to make a buck from their shows (perhaps through the sale of advertisements on their vodcasts), check out slicktracks.com, which sells downloadable royalty-free music for as little as $1.99 per track. Once you buy a track, you can use it as often as you want in any and all of your vodcasts and podcasts.

Mac users can easily generate background music loops with GarageBand, a music editing application that comes with Apple's $79 iLife suite (http://www.apple.com/ilife/). Windows users can do the same with m-audio.com's $49.95 application, Session.

Use a text-prompting program. To give a more professional delivery when recording in-studio vodcasts, use a teleprompter application to scroll your lines across your computer's display. Videocue for Mac ($39.99) (varasoftware.com) and Ultra-Light Prompter for Windows ($89.99) are both good options.

4. **Distribution.** To compress the final video to a size suitable for online use, nothing works better than QuickTime Pro (apple.com/quicktime), which costs $29 but is worth every penny.

Open your video in QuickTime Pro and select "File → Export" and then chose the ". . . to iPod" setting from the "Export:" menu. The exported video will have a file type of .M4V. If your video is longer than a couple of minutes, you'll probably want to tweak the "Export Settings" to reduce the file size. Change the "Frame Rate" to 15 frames per second, and the size to 240×180. Click the "Audio" tab, select "Mono" in the "Channels" menu and choose an output sample rate of 32 kHz.

Now you need a place to upload your compressed video online, so other people can gape in awe at your masterpiece. If you're willing to assign a Creative Commons license to your blog, consider uploading it to Archive.org (See page 73). If you have your own Web site, you can upload the files to your host server using FTP, but keep in mind that video files are large, and if your video "goes viral" and millions of people start watching it, you could end up with an astronomical bandwidth bill.

Once your video is online and waiting to be viewed, you can get the word out that it's there. Set up a blog for your vodcast at vox.com (or try Libsyn.com for a more complex but powerful solution). See "How do I create my own blog?" (page 14) and "How can I give my blog an RSS feed?" (page 30) to learn how to generate an RSS feed.

Now you can publish the link to the RSS file on any Web site or send it via email. Don't forget to submit your vodcast to the iTunes video podcast directory, either. Apple has a site that explains how to do it: apple.com/itunes/store/podcaststechspecs.html.

▶ How Can I Listen to Three Hours of Podcasts in Two Hours?

Speed up playback of your podcasts in QuickTime

I learned this trick from Phil Windley's Technometria blog (windley .com). If you like listening to podcasts, but don't have enough time to listen to all of them, you can speed up the playback using Quick-Time (which comes with Macs and can be downloaded for Windows at apple.com/quicktime). Here's how:

1. In iTunes, select the podcast you want to listen to and right-click it.

2. Select "Show song file" from the contextual menu.

3. Right-click the file and select "Open with . . . QuickTime Player."

4. Select "Show A/V Controls" from QuickTime's Windows menu (see page 52).

5. Adjust the Playback Speed slider while playing the podcast until you find a speed that still allows you to understand what's being said. Note that the pitch of the recording remains the same at different speeds, which prevents the narrator from sounding like a chipmunk.

Windley says that a 1.5-times increase in playback speed usually works, but when he really needs to think about what's being said, he will slide it back to 1.2.

You can also speed up audiobooks and podcasts on your iPod. Select "Settings" → "Audiobooks" → "faster."

Speed up playback of podcasts and audiobooks in QuickTime.

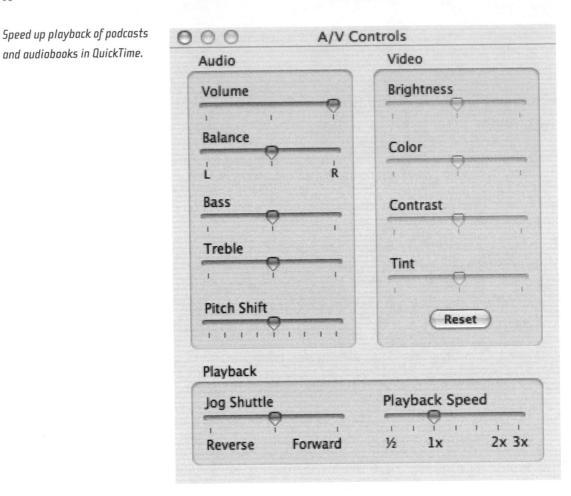

WIKIS

▶What's a Wiki and What Can I Use It For?

A wiki is a type of Web site that can be edited on the screen by any user, making it a great way for people to collaborate

Wiki is a Hawaiian word that means "quick." On the islands, you might hear people shout "wiki-wiki," meaning "better hop to it." On the Internet, wiki-based Web sites (named so because they take almost no time to implement and make changes to) have become one of the fastest growing corners of cyberspace. The most famous wiki of all is Wikipedia (wikipedia.org), the amazing, online, volunteer-built encyclopedia. It seems counter-intuitive that an "editable by anyone" collection of over a million documents hasn't descended into chaos, but a community of professional and amateur scholars have devoted themselves to Wikipedia and fiercely guard the veracity of the information deposited there. Don't rely completely on the information found there—it's always a good idea to find a second, corroborating source—but if you're not already familiar with the site, you should definitely consider it as an online reference source. It's also fun and easy to add new material or correct what's already there. If you're knowledgeable about a particular subject, you can share that knowledge with the world by joining the Wikipedia community and lending a hand. (Make sure to read up on the guidelines for editing and adding content before messing with anything—the "wikipedians" can be real sticklers.)

Wikis have caught on so quickly in part because it's easier and faster to post content with them than by using HTML or other Web publishing tools. A series of simple tags are used to indicate bold text, italics, hyperlinks, or inline graphics. Anybody, not just propellerheads, can learn the basic formatting tags in a few minutes and be off and running. You can make your wiki private, invitation-only, or open for public consumption and modification. Wikis are great for creating a quick collaborative site, managing a work project, or gathering a body of knowledge like Wikipedia does.

You can greatly improve the productivity of a work group by creating a wiki instead of sending emails back and forth and having separate conduits of communication such as calendars, PDF documents, and the like. All of this can be centralized and hyperlinked through a wiki. To get started, try PBWiki (pbwiki.com), a free, easy to use, but reasonably full-featured wiki. The "PB" in the name is for "peanut butter," as in the creator's claim that creating a wiki site with their software is no harder than making a peanut butter sandwich. That might be a slight exaggeration, but not by much. It's probably more like a Reuben sandwich, with two kinds of cheese, on Portuguese bread. But that would have made the name too long.

▶ How Can I Create My Own Wiki?

For a simple, quickie wiki, make yourself a PBWiki

There are a dizzying array of Web-based wiki tools out there, from quick and simple ones such as PBWiki, to slightly more elaborate ones such as wikidot.com, to large, sophisticated ones like centraldesktop.com that charge a monthly fee and are geared towards business collaboration. To see a comparison chart of all the major wikis, search on "Wiki software" on, where else: Wikipedia.

PBWiki allows you to register (for free) and set up your own wiki (or wikis) in minutes. You get an impressive 5 GBs of storage space, the ability to password-protect content, use pre-made design templates, use style sheets, and lots more. You can even set up an RSS feed for your wiki to receive alerts whenever anyone adds or modifies content. PBWiki uses very simple wiki formatting that you (and anyone else who's going to use your wiki) can learn in a few minutes. This is a great way to quickly cobble a Web site together to do anything from plan the family vacation to manage a work project to create a database of knowledge on some obscure subject on which you're an expert (*Finally*, a place to expound on your encyclopedic grasp of Hummel figurines!).

▶ How Do I Get the Most Out of Wikipedia?

A short guide to the world's most popular encyclopedia

Wikipedia's free, online encyclopedia has over 1.5 million user-submitted articles and grows larger by the hour. Even though it is immensely popular, some people say that it can't be trusted for the very reason that anyone can make changes to it. However, the community

DEEPER

Installing a wiki on your server. If you prefer installing a wiki on your server instead of using PBWiki's hosted wiki, try MediaWiki (mediawiki.org) the free wiki software that was created for Wikipedia, the granddaddy of all wikis. Visit mediawiki.org/wiki/Installation to find out about the system requirements for installing and using your own copy of MediaWiki.

of Wikipedia users has proven to be excellent at policing itself. That's why it's important to know the history of Wikipedia and how it is managed before deciding how much trust you should put into it.

In the late 1990s, I wrote an article called "The New Encyclopedia Salesmen" for the now-defunct Internet business magazine *The Industry Standard*. The article was about three online start-ups that were trying to create user-made, Web-based encyclopedias. One of these, Nupedia, had a stated mission "to set a new standard for breadth, depth, timeliness, and lack of bias, and in the fullness of time to become the most comprehensive encyclopedia in the history of humankind." When I asked the editor of Nupedia how many articles were online so far, he said there were two: an article about the Classical era of Western music, and another on atonal music. "The project is only partially off the ground right now," Sanger said. "But we have 115 articles in the hopper right now. Several dozen have been written and are undergoing the review process and another several dozen have been assigned." The editor explained that the great thing about Nupedia was that nothing could be published until it passed a vigorous peer review process. Unfortunately, because of this, very few articles were ever published on Nupedia. It took $250,000 and a year and a half to produce 12 articles. This wasn't because Nupedia required peer review, but because Nupedia prevented publication *before* peer review. It just bogged the process down. But then Nupedia switched the order around. They started publishing articles as they were written, first-draft, and, using a wiki as their platform, invited anyone to edit the articles in real-time. In just one year, they had close to 20,000 articles online. Today, there are over a million articles on the site, which is now known by its more famous name, Wikipedia.

How can you trust an encyclopedia that anyone with Internet access can change to their heart's content? A former *Encyclopedia Britannica* editor said Wikipedia was like a public toilet, because you didn't know who had used it before you got there. But that's an opinion you'd expect from someone at a company threatened by Wikipedia's amazing popularity. In truth, there are thousands of diligent volunteers who comb through Wikipedia around the clock, correcting instances of vandalism and obvious errors. In general, Wikipedia is an excellent reference, especially when used in conjunction with Google to verify the information in articles. Here are a few ways you can use Wikipedia:

Try the Firefox extension. (See page 57.) Googlepedia is a Firefox add-on that integrates Wikipedia with Google. When you do a search on Google, your results are returned side-by-side with the most relevant article from Wikipedia. Download it here: addons.mozilla.org/firefox/2517.

Get the Wikipedia CD. Download a file with a selection of 2,500 educational articles from Wikipedia (including articles on geography, biology, science, and general knowledge) chosen by the orphan charity SOS Children. You can download a copy to burn on a CD or save on a flash memory drive by visiting fixedreference.org/2006Wikipedia-CD-Selection.

Make changes to an existing Wikipedia article. It's surprisingly easy to edit Wikipedia articles. All you have to do is click the "Edit this Page" link at the top of the screen, enter your changes in the text window that appears, and then click "save." But before you do so, read Wikipedia's help section on editing carefully at en.wikipedia .org/wiki/Help:Contents/Editing_Wikipedia. Many articles are tagged to be edited and improved by the first person who has the time to do so, either because the existing article doesn't meet Wikipedia's formatting standards or isn't long enough (a "stub"). Seeking out and tweaking these sub-par articles can be a lot of fun.

Occasionally, articles are locked for editing by moderators when there's a wild debate on a controversial issue. You won't be able to edit those until the flame wars die down.

Many articles also have discussion pages associated with them, where you can read (and write) comments about the edits an article has gone through. Oftentimes, these discussions are more interesting than the articles themselves!

Create a new Wikipedia article. Would you like to create a new entry in Wikipedia? It's simple. First, enter the subject in Wikipedia's

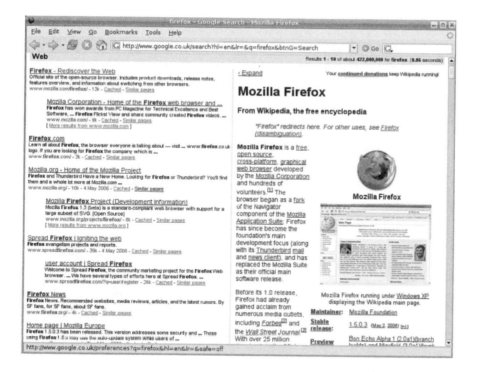

Googlepedia is a Firefox add-on that adds a Wikipedia article to your Google search results.

search field. If Wikipedia returns no results for that subject, you'll have the option to create a page with the name of the subject. You can also visit en.wikipedia.org/wiki/Wikipedia:How_to_start_a_page. Enter the name of your article and click "Create Page." Be sure to read the "Your First Article" tutorial at en.wikipedia.org/wiki/Wikipedia:Your_first_article before getting started. Here you'll find an introduction to editing, a tutorial, a simplified rule set for new editors, and a cheat sheet that shows you how to format the text.

Read a blog of rejected Wikipedia articles. WikiDumper (wikidumper.blogspot.com) is a blog that presents articles that were flagged as inappropriate by Wikipedia users. I am fascinated by these articles that are deemed unfit for Wikihood, which cover subjects such as corporeal reanimation ("the theoretical concept of reanimating a dead organism"), therianthropy ("a generic term for any transformation of a human into another animal form"), and kynoid ("refers to any being whose body structure resembles that of a dog, especially in the context of science fiction and fantasy fiction").

▶▶ SOCIAL NETWORKING

▶ What's All the Fuss About Social Networking?

Social networks, connecting and re-connecting friends and friends of friends, have become part of the connective tissue of the Web

Social networking probably first got its start with Classmates.com, a site designed to reconnect you with long-lost friends from high school and college. Other sites followed, like the networking site SixDegrees (sixdegrees.com) and product review site Epinions (epinions.com). Epinions was the first to meld the user reviews of Amazon with a network of trusted friends—that is, people who have been given the thumbs-up by people you already know and trust ("the friend of my friend is my friend"). Then came Friendster (friendster.com), a site designed to combine the friend-of-a-friend networking of SixDegrees with the social and personal features of a dating site (based on the assumption that people who are both friends with you might want to be friends with each other, and maybe even more than friends).

Friendster become so popular so fast, in fact, that it became a victim of its own success, as traffic on the site frequently ground it to a standstill. This gave other social networking sites, particularly MySpace (myspace.com) and Facebook (facebook.com) time to catch up. Both sites have since eclipsed Friendster in popularity. The friend-of-a-friend concept of social networking also became a key part of the Web 2.0 approach. Web 2.0 is a catch all term for Web sites and technologics that combine user-created content, social networking, and new publishing technologies such as blogging, podcasting, and wikis. Web 2.0 sites such as flickr.com, digg.com, dodgeball.com, and technorati.com make use of user-created content and social networking. If you're looking to expand your circle of friends, find a mate, explore online "taste tribes," or find people clustered around an interest area, then try joining a social network.

▶ Which Social Network Is Best for Me?

Choose your social network based on what you're interested in getting out of it

Most social networking sites are geared towards a particular type of social group. Friendster is designed for establishing new friendships

Retro advice for the lovelorn

Miss Abigail (missabigail.com) collects vintage advice books and recycles the words of wisdom contained therein for modern-day lonely hearts and other personal advice-seekers. For example, "Tammi" emailed her the following question: "How can I tell if a boy likes me?" Miss Abigail turned to a 1956 article entitled "What Boys Say They Like in Girls," a survey of 1,600 teenagers. Some answers:

"I like a friendly smile" (17-year-old boy)

"I like a girl with plenty of good sense at parties and dates" (17-year-old boy)

"I like a girl to be a good dancer, a lot of fun, and to have a good sense of humor at the right time" (17-year-old boy)

"I like a girl to be able to carry on an intelligent conversation" (17-year-old boy)

Some things never change.

and finding dates. It basically started as a dating site, so that's its biggest strength. Meetup (meetup.com) links people together around specific interests and helps them arrange face-to-face meetings. It's a great place to go if you want to, say, start (or join) a book club, gaming group, or dining-out club. LinkedIn (linkedin.com) is mainly a business network, so it's designed to link you up with colleagues, business associates, and potential business contacts based on those in your field with whom you're already associated. This network can be especially helpful if you're self-employed or run a small business and are looking to expand your circle of colleagues, contractors, or potential client base. I'm not a huge fan of MySpace because I think their pages are usually ugly and hard to navigate, but the site is hugely popular. The new trend in social networking is in mobile location-based services such as Dodgeball (dodgeball.com) (see "How Can I Find Nearby Friends When I'm Out on the Town?" on page 209).

PHOTOGRAPHY AND VIDEO

▶ What's the Best Way to Share and Store My Photos Online?

Use Flickr to backup and share your digital photographs

DEEPER

Social networking sites. To see an up-to-date list of social networking services, search on "social networking websites" at Wikipedia.

If you're like me, owning a digital camera means that you take a lot more pictures than you did in the days of film cameras. I have thousands of photos, all of them stored on my computer. When I wanted to share my digital photos with friends and family, I used to do one of two things: resize the photos and send them by email or resize them and upload them to a custom Web page. While these beat taking the negatives to a film processor to make extra prints and sending them by mail, neither option comes close to the ease of use and power offered by Flickr.

Like all good Web services, Flickr is very easy to use, yet it contains many powerful features that stay hidden until you start looking for them. Flickr has an awful lot going for it. In fact, there are entire books dedicated to showing you how to use everything Flickr has to offer. But don't worry: I'm still going to show you how to use Flickr to store and share your digital photos.

To get started, go to flickr.com and register for a new account. In 2005, Flickr was purchased by Yahoo!, so if you already have an account with Yahoo!, you can use that to log in. Otherwise, you'll have to create a new Yahoo! account.

Flickr accounts come in two varieties: standard, which is free, and pro, which costs $25 a year. A free account lets you upload 100 MB worth of photos per month. One picture from my 4-megapixel camera is about 1 MB, so I could upload about 100 photos per month to a standard account. You can only display the most recent 200 photos you've uploaded, and you are limited to three "photosets" (groups of photos sharing the same title, e.g. "My Vacation to Mars"). If you don't take a lot of photos, a standard account might be fine for you. I ponied up the $25 for a pro account, which gives me unlimited monthly uploads, unlimited photo storage, unlimited photosets, and a host of other benefits.

Whichever way you want to go, the methods for storing, organizing, and sharing are the same:

Storing. To copy digital photos (or any image) on your computer to Flickr, you need to be signed in. Click "Upload Photos," from the "You" pull-down menu at the top of the Flickr window, and then click the "Browse" buttons on the subsequent page to navigate to the photos you wish to store on Flickr. Note that you can "tag" the photos you upload. A tag is a label for your images that will come in handy when you (or others) want to search for them later. For example, you could upload your photos with the tags "puffer fish Hawaii." Then, whenever you searched for any of those terms, those tagged photos would show up in the results. You can also tag pictures with phrases in quotes: "Mark Snorkeling."

Before uploading the photos, choose a privacy setting. Private photos can only be seen by you. "Friends and family" photos can

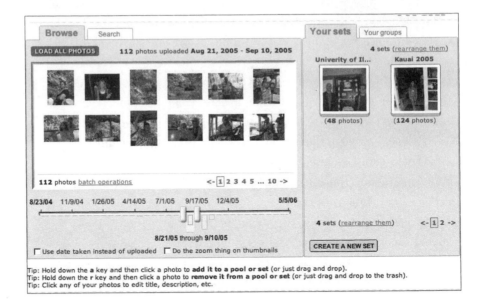

Adding photos to Flickr sets.

only be seen by those Flickr users you have identified as friends and/or family. Public photos can be seen by anyone who comes to the Flickr site. Don't worry if you aren't sure what level of privacy you want for your photos. You can always change the settings later. Now click "Upload." Depending on the size and quantity of your photos and the speed of your Internet connection, this could take anywhere from a few seconds to a few minutes. When the pictures have been uploaded, you'll be presented with the opportunity to give each picture a title, a description, and tags.

Organizing. Flickr offers a number of ways to organize your photos. If you're more likely to keep your paper photos in a shoebox, simply tagging your photos might be enough. But if you would like the equivalent of a photo album, you need to make "sets." Click the "Organize" link to get started. You'll see a window like the one shown here. (See above.) Click the "Your Sets" tab and then click "create a new set." Give your set a name and a description. (See page 64.)

On the bottom of this window there's a row containing all the images you've ever uploaded to Flickr. There are a number of different options for searching, browsing, and filtering through your photos. To add a photo to your set, just drag it into the gray window above the row of photos. To remove a photo from the set you are creating, drag it back into the photo row.

The white rectangle above the set title should be occupied by your favorite photo in the set, because that's the image everyone will see when browsing your collection of sets. Once you've added all the pictures to your set, click save and you're done. You can always come back at a later time to add or remove images from the set.

Sharing. The simplest way to share a set of photos with someone is to email the set's URL to your friends and relatives. You can get the URL by going to your Flickr home page, clicking on the set you want to share and copying the URL from your browser into an email.

My favorite way of sharing photos with my more Net-savvy friends is to give them the RSS feed of my Flickr photos. (RSS stands for Really Simple Syndication and is a basically a way to subscribe to new information—a.k.a. "feeds"—on a Web site. You need to use an RSS reader application to see feeds. See page 27 for more on RSS). You can find your RSS feed address at the bottom of your home page. Mine says "Subscribe for Frauenfelder's Photos." Right-click the "Feed" link and choose "Copy Link Location" from the drop-down menu. Email the address to your friends and, from then on, their RSS reader will display your photos as soon as you upload them to Flickr.

Another fun way to share Flickr photos is by getting them printed in a perfect-bound book. Qoop (qoop.com/photobooks/flickr_user) has partnered with Flickr to create photobooks that you can send as gifts or keep on your coffee table at home. A twenty-page book costs $12.99, and each additional page is 40¢. You can put more than one photo on a page, making it quite economical. You can also make posters and, with Flickr's other business partners, photo DVDs, postcards, business cards, and more.

One of Flickr's most powerful aspects is its API, or application

DEEPER

Batch uploading photos to Flickr. Flickr's Web interface for uploading photos is great for uploading a few photos at once, but what if you want to upload dozens of photos from your computer at the same time? For that, you need an uploading tool, and there are a number of good ones available. If you're a Mac user and you keep your photo library on iPhoto, use FlickrExport (connectedflow.com/flickrexport/), an affordable plug-in that lets you select any number of photos in iPhoto and then export them to Flickr directly. For Windows users and Mac users who don't use iPhoto, try the Flickr Uploadr (flickr.com/tools), a stand-alone application that lets you drag any number of photos into the application window and upload them all at once.

Creating a photo set in Flickr keeps your collection organized.

programming interface, which allows software developers to incorporate the heart of Flickr into their own applications. The Color Fields Experimental Colr Pickr (www.krazydad.com/colrpickr), for instance, displays a beautiful wheel containing various shades of colors. Click on any of the colors, and you'll be treated to Flickr photos that generally match that color. For a directory of interesting applications and services that use the Flickr API, visit Flickrbits (flickrbits.com).

▶ How Can I Download Many Flickr Photos at Once?

Batch-download multiple photos from a Flickr set with a free utility

It's tedious work downloading a bunch of full-resolution photos from a Flickr account to your computer, requiring a lot of back-and-forth mouse clicking. Windows users have it much easier: they can grab a copy of FlickrDown (greggman.com/pages/flickrdown.htm), a

Recover accidentally deleted files from your digital camera

Most people seem to be unaware of the fact that a computer storage device, like a hard drive or a removable memory card, doesn't actually delete files when you trash them. It simply tosses away the address of where to find it. The file space itself just sits there until new data is added which will, eventually, overwrite the previous files. By using a recovery program, you can pull those files out of the trash, hopefully before new stuff gets piled on top of them. In the case of the removable media used on your camera, that's where a photo recovery program comes in. There are a number of recovery utilities available; some are free, most cost money. To see if you're lucky enough to find a free one that works with your camera/card and computer OS, go to download.com and search on "photo recovery." Art Plus Digital Photo Recovery (artplus.hr) is a free recovery utility for Windows operating systems. It works on all types of memory cards used in digital cameras and can even read cards that are so corrupted that Windows can't recognize them. Digital Photo Recovery (photosrecovery.com) is another popular recovery tool. You can try it for free (to see if it at least finds your photos) and then buy it once you're certain it works. It costs $29. For the Mac, there's MediaRECOVER Mac (mediarecover.com) for $39.95. You get one free file recovery with the trial version. It works on all of the major memory card types used in cameras, PDAs, cellphones, etc.

nifty utility that makes it easy to download dozens or even hundreds of photos from Flickr in one fell swoop. After launching FlickrDown, enter the Flickr username you're interested in. After the thumbnails load, you can check the ones you want, or select "All photos" (if the user has lots of photos this could take a lot of time and consume quite a bit of hard disk space, so be careful). Then select a directory to store the files and click "Download."

▶ How Can I Immediately Share Photos Taken with My Cell Phone?

Use a Blogger or Flickr account to email camera phone images to your blog or online photo gallery

Now that the resolution of cell phone cameras is approaching that of full-scale digital cameras, some people are using them as their only point-and-shoot option. One nice thing about cell phone cameras is that you can send the photos to your blog or Flickr gallery directly. (Unless you have a plan that allows unlimited data transfer, you should check to see how expensive it is to email photos.)

To upload photos by email to a Flickr account (see "What's the Best Way to Share and Store My Photos Online?" on page 60 to learn how to use Flickr) visit flickr.com/account/uploadbyemail, where you'll find a special email address you can use. Use the subject line of the email to give the photo a title, and write a description of the photo in the body of the email.

To upload photos to a Blogger blog, see the instructions on page 33 ("How Can I Blog Using My Mobile Phone?")

▶ How Can I Arrange Photos Visually by Where They Were Taken?

Platial combines blogging, tagging, and online maps

Just as every picture tells a story, so does every place. But unless someone has taken the time to mount a brass plaque at the location of a historical event, it's hard to find out just what that story is. Flickr allows you to "geotag" photos so that other people can see where the photos were taken. To use geotagging in Flickr, click the "Organize" tab at the top of your Flickr page, then click the "Map" tab. Your photos will appear in a scrolling horizontal strip below a map of the world. Now you can enter an address into the search field and the map will zoom into that area. You can then drag the photos taken at that address to the corresponding spot on the map.

In addition to leaving written descriptions of a place, you can add photos from your computer or the Web, and even upload videos. You can also create your own maps—of your favorite dance clubs, for instance—and publish them to your personal Web site using Platial's MapKits functionality. Platial is a fun way to document your travels and an excellent way to plan a trip.

DEEPER

Put your photos on a map. A Web site called Platial (platial.com) lets you stick virtual pushpins into a satellite photo map, and then write about the spot in its corresponding "PlaceBlog." The ultimate goal is to give every square inch of the planet its very own PlaceBlog. What kind of places get pinned and blogged on Platial? Restaurants, for one. Many of the restaurants in major cities have multiple reviews, as well as stories about what happened to the bloggers who ate there.

Make a comic book from your vacation photos

If the drug companies could bottle other people's vacation photos, they'd have billion-dollar sleep medication on their hands. If you don't want to put your friends to sleep the next time you come home from a holiday, buy a copy of Comic Life (Mac, $24.95, plasq.com) and turn your photographs into a comic book, complete with speech balloons and whiz-bang sound effects. Comic Life's pre-designed templates make it easy to create action-packed stories that'll make you feel like a superhero.

Snipshot is a Web-based photo-editing utility.

▶ How Can I Edit and Retouch My Photos Online?

Use Snipshot to make quick adjustments to snapshots and other digital images

Photoshop is overkill for people who just want to enhance, resize, and adjust their digital photos. Lately, I've been using a nice little Web-based photo editor called Snipshot (snipshot.com) to upload digital photos and tweak them to my heart's content.

One of the nice features of Snipshot is its ability to import images from Flickr (or any other Web site) using a bookmarklet. Once you drag the bookmarklet into your browser's bookmark bar, you can go to any Web page, click the bookmarklet, then choose the photo you want to edit in Snipshot.

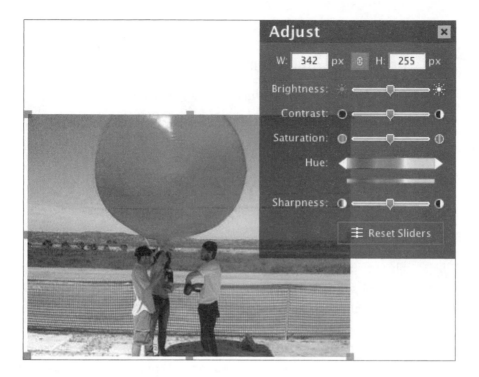

Adjusting a photo with Snipshot.

Here's what you can do in Snipshot:

Resize. Click one of the red squares and drag your mouse. Select a corner square to preserve the size ratio of the original image.

Crop. Drag the crop window around the image, and resize it by clicking and dragging a red square. Once you're happy with the crop, press enter or double-click the image. (See page 68.)

Enhance. Bring out the color of an image with a single click. If you aren't pleased with the result, click "Undo."

Adjust. Change the size, brightness, contrast, saturation, hue, and sharpness of the image. (See above.)

Rotate. Click to rotate the image 90 degrees clockwise.

You can save the photo in a variety of formats, or upload it to your Flickr account with one click.

▶ How Do I Reduce the Size of Several Digital Photos Before Emailing Them?

Use a batch re-sizer to reduce file size before emailing

How do you like it when someone sends you a digital photo that's four times larger than your display? Many kind-hearted folks who send their digital snapshots to friends don't realize that they should scale photos down before emailing them. Not only is a photo from a 5-megapixel camera way too big to fit on a computer display, the file size is large and takes a long time to email (and download). Don't be one of these gargantuan-photo senders. Scale your images first. Most digital photograph management software, such as iPhoto for Mac and Windows Picture Tasks, let you resize images before sending them. Apple's Mail program lets you rescale photos after you attach them to an outgoing message. Use these features and your friends will stay friends.

You can also use the Web-based Snipshot (see page 68) to resize photos. But what if you have a big batch of photos that you need to reduce? This is where a standalone program comes in handy. For Windows, my favorite is Easy Thumbnails (fookes.com/ezthumbs), a free utility that automates the process of creating thumbnails of any size. It includes a number of other useful features, such as a preview mode and the ability to adjust the photos' contrast, brightness, sharpness, and quality, as well as save them in different file formats. Mac users can use the free PhotoTool CM (pixture.com), which lets you highlight any number of photos in the Finder and then right-click the mouse to bring up a contextual menu to resize and rename the photos in a batch process.

▶ What's the Best Way to Share and Store My Videos Online?

There are better ways to share online video than YouTube

YouTube is hugely popular. It's the first place people go when they want to watch a thirty-second video of a mischievous monkey or a fight between parents in the bleachers at a Little League game. It's also a repository for thousands of questionably legal music videos and movie clips. My beef with YouTube is the playback quality of the videos. It's awful. YouTube's bandwidth charges are purported to be $20 million a year, and to keep that number from going up, YouTube compresses the videos so much that they end up blocky and jerky.

For better quality results, sign up for a free blogging account at vox.com and upload your digital videos to your blog. Each video can be up to 50 MB, which is large enough for at least ten minutes of high-quality video, depending on the size of the video. (See page 18 for complete instructions on using vox.com.) Your videos will look much better on Vox than they would on YouTube, but remember— YouTube is the place where everyone goes to be entertained by short videos. Those looking to achieve viral video fame might want to stick with YouTube.

For videos larger than 50 MB, consider using the vast resources of the Internet Archive (archive.org). File size is not a problem here; in fact, people regularly upload entire movies in high-resolution. The Internet Archive is free, but there's a catch, sort of. In order to make use of the service, you can't copyright your video. Instead, you have to either donate it to the public domain or assign it a Creative Commons license, which lets you protect your work without the restrictiveness of a traditional copyright (learn more at creativecommons.org/learnmore/).

To upload videos to the Internet Archive, the Creative Commons has created a handy application called CC Publisher. There are versions for Mac and Windows, and you can learn how to use it here: creativecommons.org/video/publish-internetarchive. Once your video is uploaded, the Internet Archive creates a unique Web page for it that offers the video for download in a variety of formats. You can copy the address and email it to friends or post it on your blog.

If you'd like to add captions and comments to existing YouTube and Google Video videos, try Mojiti (mojiti.com). The site grabs videos from YouTube and Google Video and allows you to annotate them.

DEEPER

Editing video online. Nothing is more boring than a twenty-minute video of your kid's birthday party, unless you happen to be the kid or the kid's parent. But you can edit those twenty minutes down to two or three minutes that your friends will be able to tolerate. An easy way to edit your digital videos online is with Jumpcut (jumpcut.com). Upload videos and cut out the boring parts in your browser. Add titles, effects, and sound effects. You can make your videos public or invitation-only. The final quality of the video is pretty low, but if you don't care about that, Jumpcut is a quick way to edit and share videos online.

▶ Where Can I Get Free Sound Effects for My Videos?

Choose from thousands of copyright-free sound effects at the Freesound Project

Home videos are much better with a soundtrack. It's easy enough to import a song into your video-editing program, but you can further enhance video with some well-placed sound effects. Add a "boing" to a clip of your kitten pouncing on your napping uncle's belly, or spice up footage of your kid riding her bike with the scream of a dragster engine. You can find almost any sound clip you might need at the Freesound Project (freesound.iua.upf.edu), a treasure trove of over 25,000 sound files, from the crunch of walking on gravel to the shake of a can of spray paint. If you use these sounds for a video you plan to upload for public viewing, remember that you need to credit the creator of the sound effects you use from this excellent archive.

SHARING

▶ How Can I Share Large Files with Other People?

Use free Web services to upload and share movies, music, and other large files

Have you ever tried emailing a large file or folder to someone only to have the email rejected because the attachment was too large? Most Internet service providers refuse to transmit email attachments over 10 MB. That's plenty for sending a few photographs or most documents, but if you want to send a 40 MB PowerPoint presentation or a 75 MB video clip of your first skydive, email just won't cut it. That's when you need a file-sending service. My favorite free service is MediaFire (mediafire.com), which allows you to upload "unlimited size" files and notify the recipient that the file is waiting for them. The best thing about it is that you don't need to register to use it. Just go to the Web site, pick the file you want to upload, and click a button. It's ad-supported and includes a progress bar so you can gauge how long you'll have to wait for uploads and downloads. After you upload a file, MediaFire will give you a link to the file to share with your recipients.

How Do I Find Shared Files to Download?

Mine the best sources for user-shared content

The Internet abounds with content waiting for you to read, listen to, play with, and watch. While a good deal of the stuff out there is copyrighted and available without the copyright holder's permission, plenty of it is either in the public domain, licensed as a Creative Commons work (creativecommons.org), or available with the permission of the copyright holder. Here are my favorite treasure troves of free content.

Internet Archive (archive.org): This nonprofit organization was founded in 1996 to preserve the content of the Internet and structure it like a library. It contains text files, audio files, movies, software, and

DEEPER: SHARING A SYNCHRONIZED FOLDER

Microsoft's free FolderShare (foldershare.com) is an excellent way for Windows and Mac users to share files with each other. Start by downloading the right version for your operating system. Then, select a folder or create a new one that you'd like to share with anyone you invite. You can then drag files (up to 2 GB) into the folder. FolderShare also lets you synchronize files between any Mac or Windows machine you have connected to the Net. Or, if you're on the road and want to get a file on your computer at home, go to FolderShare and click "Access My Files."

archived Web pages. There's enough here to keep you occupied for the rest of your life. Fancy a Buster Keaton movie? There are thirty-six of them here. Sherlock Holmes? Download *The Memoirs of Sherlock Holmes* as an audiobook. Or read tens of thousands of books by authors from Isaac Asimov to Emile Zola. There are old radio plays, industrial films, cartoons, computer games, songs, and more. You're only limited by your hard-drive capacity.

Project Gutenberg (Gutenberg.org): Founded in 1971, Project Gutenberg enlists volunteers to scan the pages of out-of-copyright books and convert them to text using optical character recognition. I've read books downloaded from Project Gutenberg by Dickens, Sinclair Lewis, Dumas, Edgar Rice Burroughs, Dreiser, and many others. So far, over 20,000 books have been converted to digital format.

Manybooks.net (manybooks.net): This site offers titles from Project Gutenberg and other sources and makes them available in formats for reading on your PDA, iPod, phone, or eBook reader. They offer quite a few science fiction books from the 1950s and 1960s, as well as more recent books, such as *Blood, Sweat & Tea: Real Life Adventures in an Inner-City Ambulance*, by Tom Reynolds.

Print

Printer: Balthazar

Presets: Standard

Copies & Pages

Copies: 1 ☑ Collated

Pages: ◉ All
○ From: 1 to: 1

? PDF ▼ Preview Supplies... Cancel Print

Save as PDF...
Save PDF as PostScript...
Fax PDF...

Compress PDF
Encrypt PDF
Mail PDF
Save as PDF-X
Save PDF to iPhoto
Save PDF to Web Receipts Folder
Fax with eFax Messenger
Save PDF in Yojimbo
Edit Menu...

Any Mac document can be emailed as a PDF file.

Email a Web page to a friend

It's easy to email a Web site link to a friend using Firefox. Just select "Send Link" from the "File" menu, and Firefox will open your mail browser, inserting the name of the Web page in the subject line and the URL in the body of the email message.

You can also email an actual Web page. On the Mac, select "Print" from the "File" menu, click the PDF button in the lower left corner, and select "Mail PDF," as shown above. (Note: you can use the "Mail PDF" function to email any document. It's very handy.) To convert a Web page (or any other file) to a PDF in Windows, download PDFCreator from pdfforge.org and send the file as an attachment.

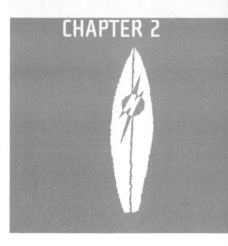

CHAPTER 2

SEARCHING AND BROWSING

Imagine a reference book without an index. It wouldn't be very useful. When the Web was young, you couldn't go to a search engine to look something up. The only way you could find out about a site was by reading about it on someone else's site. Then directories like Yahoo! came along, which hired people to traverse the Web, link-by-link, and build annotated lists of Web sites they deemed noteworthy. Other companies used software agents, not people, to crawl the Web, indexing every single Web page they came across, making a searchable database for the Web.

Today, Google's home page is the first Web page most people load when they fire up their browser. That's because they know Google will find what they're looking for, and fast. In this section, you'll learn to refine your searching skills and turbocharge your browser for the ultimate Web experience.

SEARCHING

▶ How Does Google Really Work?

Understanding the technology behind the world's biggest search engine will make you a better searcher

Google is my launching pad to the Web. When I start up my browser, I have it set to automatically load Google (see page 89 to learn to make a browser home page from any Web address). I use Google at least a dozen times a day; when I'm really busy, I'll query it over a hundred times. To get the most out of Google, it helps to understand how it works.

First of all, when you use Google, you aren't really searching the Web. It would take days for Google to scan the text of every one of the billions of pages on the Web to find what you were looking for. Instead, Google looks for your search terms in an index of the Web created by software called "spiders." It takes several days for the spiders to do a complete crawl of the Web. Why is this important to know? Because it means you won't be able to find a site that was created after the last snapshot of the Web taken by Google's crawlers. (However, Google's spiders aren't dumb; they search "important" Web sites like *The New York Times* and top-rated blogs many times every day in order to keep the database as fresh as possible. But the crawlers don't visit smaller Web sites nearly as often.)

In addition to building a massive index that can be instantly searched for any page in the database, Google also ranks Web sites based on how "important" those sites are, using a special mathematical method called PageRank ("Page" stands for a Web page, as well as for Google cofounder Larry Page, who started Google as a Stanford grad school project with his colleague, Sergey Brin). PageRank is determined by looking at the sites that point to a certain site being ranked. Here's an example: say there's a Web site about investing in gold and platinum. If CNN and *The New York Times* point to that site in articles about gold or platinum investing, it will be considered an authority on the topic and will appear at the top of related search results. If, on the other hand, the only site that links to the investment site is Crazy Seymor's Investment Tips and Knife-Sharpening Store, you can bet its Google rank will be at the bottom of the barrel.

But even a low rank is better than no rank at all—if a page

doesn't have another Web site linking to it, Google's spiders won't be able to find it, because they crawl the Web from link to link. Web sites with no incoming links (that is, no links from other Web sites) are in effect invisible and can't be found on any search engine. Of course, that may be OK if someone sets up a page with photos and text meant for sharing with a family or small group of people. In fact, people who don't want their Web sites to show up on search engines can insert a special note in the code of their Web pages telling spiders they're not welcome. See page 34 to learn how to turn spiders away when they come crawling up to your home page. However, if you have a Web page that you want to add to Google's index, or raise in its rankings, visit Google's Webmaster Central (google.com/webmasters/) for all the tools and tips you'll need.

▶ How Can I Find Someone's Phone Number Even If It's Unlisted?

Use Zabasearch to find almost anyone

As a freelance journalist, I need to hunt around a lot for phone numbers. All of the big search engines offer some kind of people-finder service, but they are little more than online phonebooks. If a person has an unlisted number, you are out of luck. But not if you use Zabasearch (zabasearch.com). The search engine, which gets its information from public databases that aren't directly linked to the Web, has got the goods on almost everyone. Even though many of the addresses and phone numbers in it are outdated, I've used it successfully more than once to track down someone I needed to get in touch with for a story I was writing. One such person, a well-known author, asked me how I got his phone number. When I told him about Zabasearch, he checked out the site himself and emailed me back, thanking me for introducing him to this useful service.

When Zabasearch launched in 2005, several news stories came out about the company, citing privacy concerns. After all, when someone asks the phone company not to list their number, it means that they don't want people to be able to look them up (or worse, drop by for an unexpected visit). Sure, there's potential for abuse. I have to admit, I hesitated about including Zabasearch. But I decided to for three reasons: One, it's useful to honest people. Two, anyone determined to stalk someone can easily go to one of hundreds of information brokers who buy information from public records keepers and get the same information, and much more, for $25 or less. And three, it's important for people to know that this kind of service exists, so they can look up their own name and find out what kind of information is linked to it. I only ask that you use the power of Zabasearch for good, not for evil.

Case sensitivity for URLs

Don't worry about typing an ObNoXiOuSdOmAiN.com exactly as you see it printed in a book or magazine. ObNoXiOuSdOmAiN.com will get you to the right place, as will obnoxiousdomain.com. However, you must type in the correct capitalization for the part of a Web address that follows a domain. For instance, obnoxiousdomain.com/ UnEnDuRaBLE.html is not the same as obnoxious domain.com/unendurable.html and you have to enter the part after the slash (/) exactly as written, or you'll probably end up at a dreaded 404 page, which is what shows up when your browser can't find the page you're looking for.

▶ How Can I See a Web Site That No Longer Exists?

The Internet Archive (archive.org) provides a fossil record of extinct Web sites

The World Wide Web is made of bits, not atoms, and when a Web page is deleted, it's gone forever. This unfortunate reality about on-line media bothered entrepreneur Brewster Kahle, so in 1996 he developed software to "crawl" the Internet, making a copy of every-thing it found. These Web pages are stored on hard drives main-tained by Kahle's foundation, the Internet Archive (archive.org).

The heart of the Archive is called the Wayback Machine (named after the time-traveling vehicle used by Sherman and Peabody in the classic Jay Ward cartoon), a collection of nearly 2 petabytes of Web pages, and which gets fatter by 20 terabytes a month. (A petabyte is 1,024 terabytes. A terabyte is 1,024 gigabytes, or about one trillion bytes.) To use the Wayback Machine, enter the Web address you hope to find and click "Take Me Back." If you're lucky, the Archive will have at least one copy (or more, organized by date).

Note: In addition to being a repository of Web pages from the last decade, the Internet Archive houses a gargantuan and fascinating col-lection of digitized movies, music, electronic books, and other forms of electronic media. They are always looking for donations of digital material to preserve. If you have something that fits the bill and you want to share it with the world, send email to info@archive.org.

Sometimes a Web page will have expired on the original site, but

DEEPER: USING GOOGLE'S CACHE TO FIND AN EXPIRED OR MISSING WEB PAGE

If you click a link only to learn that the Web page has been deleted or changed, you may still have enough time to grab it using Google's cache of the page. Enter the entire URL into the Google search field. Google will return a page with several options, one of which is "Show Google's cache of…" Even simpler, enter `cache:Web siteyouarelookingfor.com` into Google's search field.

will exist as a copy on another site. For example underwatervideos.com/belizecoral.html might have been deleted from underwatervideos.com, but you can enter `inurl:belizecoral.html` to see if there's another copy of that page somewhere else on the Web.

Firefox users can install an extension called Errorzilla (addons.mozilla.org/firefox/3336/) that displays a special error page when you can't reach a Web page. It gives you the option to try loading the page again or checking Google Cache or the Wayback Machine.

▶ What's the Easiest Way to Search for Something on a Particular Web Site?

Add a keyword to search for content on certain Web sites using Firefox's address bar

Here's a neat trick for Firefox users: you can easily search within Web sites without first having to visit the site. For instance, go to *The New York Times* Web site (nytimes.com) and right-click in the search field, right below the paper's logo. In the pop-up menu, select "Add a keyword for this search . . ." Enter "New York Times Search" in the Name field and "nyt" in the Keyword field and click the "Add" button.

The quickest way to get to a Web site without knowing its address

Most people never use Google's "I'm Feeling Lucky" button. They don't even know what it does. It's very useful. When you enter a search query and click the "I'm Feeling Lucky" button instead of the Google "Search" button, Google sends you directly to the Web site of the top search result.

With Firefox, there's an even easier way to use this feature. Just enter your multi-word search term in Firefox's address bar, and press the Enter/Return key. Firefox will automatically load the same page the "I'm Feeling Lucky" button would have sent you to.

Now, in Firefox's address bar you can enter "nyt" followed by any search terms you like. When you press the return key, you'll be sent immediately to *The New York Times*' search page, displaying your results. You can create keywords for any Web site that has a search field in it.

▶ What Are Some Tips for Getting Better Search Results on Google?

Drill down to the information you're looking for

You probably already know that searching using quote marks in a Google search will give you more accurate results. For example, if you enter snow and globe in Google without quote marks, you'll get 30,000,000 results, many of which are pages that contain both the words "snow" and "globe" in them, but which have nothing to do with snow globes. If you enter "snow globe" in quotes, however, your search will be restricted to the 724,000 pages that contain that exact term.

But there are many other ways to make your searches even more effective on Google. It really pays to learn them, because a good searcher is a happy surfer. Here are some ways to get the most out of Google search.

Wildcards. "George * Bush" will return pages containing "George Bush," "George W. Bush," "George H.W. Bush," "George Dubya Bush," and any other page that has something between the words "George" and "Bush." You can also use more than one asterisk, like this: "* million Americans eat *" to learn that 40 million Americans eat peanut butter, 76 million Americans eat beef, and 75 million Americans eat toast on a daily basis.

Excluding words. If you want to search for pages that don't contain a word or phrase, use the minus (−) character directly before the word you want to exclude. For example, turkey −bird will return all pages with "turkey" or "Turkey" (the country), excluding those that also have "bird."

Synonyms. ~auto repair will search for pages with auto, repair, car, automobile, and so forth.

Searching within a site. site:boingboing.net funny

`video` will find pages at boingboing.net that have the words funny and video in them.

Searching for a title. `intitle:"avocado salad"` finds all Web pages with the term "avocado salad" in the title.

Searching for a URL. `inurl:balloons "clown party"` will find pages belonging to any Web address that has "balloons" in it (such as balloonagencies.com.au) as well as the term "clown parties" on the resulting page.

Searching for specific types of documents. Did you know that Google can search for more than Web pages? It can also find Word documents (doc), Excel spreadsheets (xls), Adobe Acrobat documents (pdf), Shockwave Flash (swf) files, and more. All you need is the document type's three-character extension. For instance, `filetype:doc "george orwell"` finds all Microsoft Word documents on the Web that have "George Orwell" in them.

Using Google as a calculator. Just enter numbers and standard arithmetic operators (such as $3 + 9 + 276$, or $(3 + 12) * 18$) into Google to do quick calculations.

Cooliris Previews (addons.mozilla.org/firefox/2207): When you move the mouse cursor over a search result, a preview of that page appears without you having to open a new page.

Google Preview (addons.mozilla.org/firefox/189): Places thumbnail-sized images of Web sites in Google's search results.

Fastest way to get a word definition

Can't remember what **weltschmerz** means? Type `define:weltschmerz` in Google's search field and Google will return as many definitions as it can find.

Clear Fields (addons.mozilla.org/firefox/2408): Adds a small eraser icon next to the search field that you can click to wipe out the contents of the field.

Advanced Dork (addons.mozilla.org/firefox/2144): Highlight any word or group of consecutive words in Firefox and right-click the mouse to bring up a menu of powerful Google search features for the highlighted words. A real time-saver.

Cache View (addons.mozilla.org/firefox/2323): If you try to view a site that too many other people are trying to see at the same time, the site might not load. With Cache View you can right-click and take a look at a cached version of the site.

GDirections (addons.mozilla.org/firefox/1104): Highlight any street address on a Web page, right-click, and GDirections will use Google Maps to tell you how to get there from your home address.

▶ What Can I Do When Google Doesn't Find What I Need?

Ask a human to help you with a tough question

Sometimes, using a search engine doesn't pan out. Either it can't find a site with the answer you're looking for ("Who built the dinosaur and ape models for the original version of King Kong?") or your question isn't really suited for a search engine ("Where can I find biographical information about my great grandfather who moved from Russia to the United States in 1924?"). To answer questions like this, you don't need a search engine—you need a research assistant.

Fortunately, you can use several services to ask real people your tough-to-answer questions.

Ask Metafilter (ask.metafilter.com) is a free, community-based question-answering service. Here, you post a question and anyone who is a member can post their answer for everyone else to see. Other users can tag certain answers as being especially helpful, so that people who have the same question in the future can quickly find them. Be warned: some of the people on Ask Metafilter can be rather snarky, so it helps to have a thick skin.

Amazon has two question-answering sites: Askville (askville
.amazon.com), which, like Ask Metafilter, is free and relies on the
community to answer questions, and NowNow (nownow.com), which
is designed primarily for mobile users. To use NowNow, you must
first sign up using your Amazon.com account. Then, email your
question to (ask@nownow.com). NowNow's human staff will research the question and send you up to three different "best" answers. At the time of this writing, Amazon had not set a fee for using
NowNow, but it's expected to cost less than 25¢ per question.

Microsoft's Free QnA (qna.live.com) is another question-
answering community. Members post questions and the community
answers the questions and votes on the best answer.

Yahoo! Answers (answers.yahoo.com) claims to have 65 million
answers in its community answering site. The questions are arranged
by category, making it easy to browse through previously asked and
answered questions.

▶ How Can I Search Podcasts for Certain Words or Phrases?

Search audio for certain phrases using a specialized search engine

As wonderful as podcasts are, you can't search them like you can
search for text with Google. But Podzinger (podzinger.com) is to
podcasts what Google is to text. This podcast search engine uses
speech recognition technology to maintain a searchable database of
over 250,000 podcasts. Podzinger is smartly designed: enter a search
term and when you click a word in the results, the podcast begins
playing at that point.

One of the cool features of Podzinger is the way it can capture
new podcasts that mention a subject you're interested in. Say, for
example, that you are a fan of author Charles Bukowski.

Here's how to find new podcasts that mention him:

Enter "Charles Bukowski" in the search field and click "Zing It."

On the results page, you'll see an orange RSS button. Right-click
it and select "Copy Link Location" from the contextual menu.

Open iTunes, select "Advanced" → "Subscribe to Podcast," paste in the address, and click OK.

Now, whenever Podzinger comes across a podcast (audio or video) that has your search term, iTunes will automatically download it.

▶ How Can I Search My Computer for Files?

Use Google's lighting-fast search technology to find files on your hard drive

If Google can search billions of Web pages in a fraction of a second, why does it take so long for Windows to find a file on your computer? Google uses powerful technology to create an index of the Web, and Windows' built-in search is no match for it. That's why Google Desktop (desktop.google.com) is a must-have utility for Windows users (If you're on a Mac running OS × 10.4 or later, on the other hand, all you need to do is activate Spotlight, the excellent built-in search application).

The first time you launch Google Desktop, you might be confused, because the program opens in your browser and looks almost exactly like the standard Google home page. But when you enter a search term

Find a word within a Web page

It can be frustrating to search Google for a certain term and then go to one of the Web sites it returns only to discover you can't find the term your searched for. A quick way to find the term is by typing Ctrl-F (Cmd-F on Mac) and entering the word. By typing Ctrl-G (Cmd-G on Mac) you'll be taken to the next occurrence of the term on the page. You can also click the "Highlight All" button at the bottom of Firefox's window to give all occurrences a yellow highlight.

and click the new "Search Desktop" button, Google will search it in the documents on your computer. And because it searches an index instead of the actual files, Google Desktop is lightning fast.

Google Desktop has other features not found in the Web-based version. The "Browse Timeline" link shows you when content on your computer has been added or changed. You can click any item in the timeline to open it. The timeline can be filtered into emails, files, Web history, and chats, making it a great way to find something even if you can't think of a search term that'll dredge it up from the bottom of your hard drive.

You can also customize Google Desktop by adding "Google Gadgets," little widgets that contain weather reports, news, and simple games.

Windows Vista also offers a built-in desktop search, along with customizable small applications, called Gadgets, many of which

Find out what Google thinks of you (or anybody else)

Googlism (googlism.com) is a fun way to use Google to quickly find out what others think of certain people, places, and things. Just type in a name, a product, or a location and click the "Googlism!" button. The service then uses Google to search for descriptions, returning them as a list, like the one here (for Pee-wee Herman):

pee wee herman is an adult who never let go of his childish tendencies

pee wee herman is making a comeback in three new films

pee wee herman is dead

pee wee herman is a legend in at least six countries

pee wee herman is a genius

pee wee herman is an annoying freak

pee wee herman is goth

pee wee herman is his biological father

pee wee herman is not a bad guy

pee wee herman is one sick son of a bitch

pee wee herman is unquestionably gay

pee wee herman is now allowed to vote in florida

pee wee herman is a baseball fan?

perform search functions. See a list of Gadgets here: microsoft-gadgets.com/Gallery.

▶ How Can I Make Google Easier to Use?

Customize Google and improve your searching

This sounds like a dumb question. Google is unquestionably one of the easiest services on the Web. It's blindingly obvious what to do there—you enter some text and click the Google "Search" button. But there are a lot of ways to make Google even better, at the expense of losing some of that elegant simplicity.

If you have a cable modem or DSL service, the first thing to do is click the "Preferences" tab to the right of the Search field. Scroll down to "Number of Results" and select 100 from the pull-down menu. Then click "Save Preferences." From now on, Google will return 100 results on a page. This will save you from having to click to a new page and wait for it to load if you don't find the answer you're looking for on the first page of results.

Google has been likened to a Swiss Army knife. There are lots of cool tools attached to it, but they're folded away. To open these tools, click the "Personalized Home" link. You'll be taken to a page where you can add and move around sections of content, such as movies, weather, driving directions, and news from a wide variety of sources. By entering your Zip code, Google will localize all the information, turning the page into a kind of personalized interactive newspaper. Click the "Add" content link to customize your page.

To have the ability to see your custom page on any computer, you need to create a Google account. You can do this by clicking "Sign In" in the upper-right corner, and then clicking "Create an account now." Now you're all set to use your custom Google page at any computer. A note of caution: as with all password-protected Web sites, if you are using your custom Google page at a public computer, be sure to log off by clicking the "Sign out" link in the upper-right corner when you're done. (See page 90.)

Customize your Google page at google.com/ig.

 BROWSING

How Can I Visit a Web Site That's Been Blocked?

Use special Internet proxies for an untraceable, encrypted connection across the Internet

John Gilmore, one of the co-founders of the Electronic Frontier Foundation (eff.org, an organization committed to protecting your

الموقع محظور

نأسف إن الموقع الذي أردت تصفحه قد أحجب وذلك بسبب إحتوائه على نشاط مخالف للقيم الإجتماعية أو السياسية أو الثقافية أو الدينية لدولة الإمارات العربية المتحدة.

في حالة أردت فتح موقع قد أحجب، الرجاء قم بتعبئة استمارة الملاحظات الموجودة على موقعنا.

We apologize the site you are attempting to visit has been blocked due to its content being inconsistent with the religious, cultural, political and moral values of the United Arab Emirates.

If you think this site should not be blocked, please visit the Feedback Form available on our website.

SITE BLOCKED

Countries with repressive governments censor the Web.

rights online) once famously said, "the Internet interprets censorship as damage and routes around it."

The governments of countries like Saudi Arabia, Qatar, and China control the way their citizens use the Internet. One way they do that is by blocking access to Web sites that contain political criticism or adult material. Most of these countries use "censorware" developed in the United States. Censorware works by comparing all Web site requests against a list of forbidden Web sites. If you are in the United Arab Emirates and try to access a forbidden site, you'll see something like the above image on your screen.

Some hotels, libraries, companies, and other organizations block certain Web sites from Internet users, too. Fortunately, there are ways to get around censorware. This is especially useful for people who live in repressive regimes, but it's also useful for anyone who finds themselves behind a censorware barrier that blocks access to sites they want to access.

One of the most effective ways to defeat censorware is by using Java Anonymous Proxy (JAP, anon.inf.tu-dresden.de/index_en.html), a free service developed by a university in Dresden, Germany. JAP works by creating a bunch of untraceable, encrypted connections across the Internet, making it impossible for anyone to trace the source or the destination of the data going through it.

Because JAP doesn't let censorware know the destination address of the site, the censorware's blacklist of forbidden sites is useless. In addition, your IP address is hidden, making you effectively anonymous. (You can find out what other Web sites know about you by visiting whatsmyip.org/more. You'll see your IP address, type of Web browser you are using, screen resolution, and more. When you use JAP, your IP address will be replaced with something like "proxy1.anon-online.org," instead of your actual IP address.)

Of course, if your cookies are active, then the Web sites can still identify who you are. (To learn about cookies, see "What Are 'Cookies' and What Do I Need to Do About Them?" on page 358.)

It's important to note that while a proxy might let you get past a firewall and access block sites, it doesn't prevent a company (or a country's) system administration staff from finding out that you are using a proxy or monitoring what you're looking at online. Proceed with caution.

▶ How Do I Restart an Interrupted Download?

Save time and aggravation by resuming a failed download

It's annoying to be in the middle of downloading a large file, only to lose the Internet connection right before the download has finished. It means restarting the process all over again and crossing your fingers, hoping it won't happen again.

Instead of relying on luck, get yourself a download manager. These utilities work with your Web browser to automatically resume interrupted downloads at the point where the communication broke down. They are especially useful for downloading files when your Internet connection is flaky. The best download manager also happens to be free: DownThemAll (downthemall.net) is a Firefox extension that not only auto-resumes interrupted downloads, but also speeds up downloads and lets you download every linked file on a page with a single click. DownThemAll is loaded with other useful features, too, such as filtering (so you can download just the image files, music files, or movie files linked on a page), and renaming on-the-fly (so you can give a downloaded batch of photos meaningful names like "HawaiiTrip001" rather than "DSCF1339").

▶ How Can I Prevent Unwanted Pop-up Windows?

Get rid of intrusive ads that appear over Web pages using a pop-up blocker

Why do advertisers think it's a good idea to annoy people with pop-up ads? I hope you'll join me in my boycott against any advertiser that uses pop-ups to tout their products or services. Today, most Web browsers are smart enough to block pop up windows. But if you are getting pop-ups while you use the Web, it probably means that your pop-up preferences have been deactivated for some reason. To kill pop-ups in Firefox, go to Preferences and click the "Content" button. From there, activate the "Block pop-up windows" checkbox. Note the "Exceptions" button next to the pop-ups preferences. Click it to add Web sites that have pop-ups you want to see. For instance, some sites use pop-ups to display large photos or other content that is part of the editorial content and not an advertising come-on.

When you have the pop-up blocker activated, you'll occasionally see a message that says: "Firefox prevented this site from opening a pop-up window," as shown on page 95. Click the "Preferences" button next to the message and you'll see a menu of options. You can choose to allow the site to display pop-ups or take a peek at the pop-up without allowing the site to show them as a matter of course.

▶ How Can I Block Annoying Ads on Web Pages?

Banish obnoxious banner ads from the Web sites with Firefox

I don't have anything against Web sites that make their money displaying ads. Boing Boing, the blog I co-edit, displays ads. But we have a strict policy about the format of ads that appear on our site. We don't allow ads that display endlessly looping animation, ads that change size when you move your mouse cursor over them, ads that have audio tracks, or ads that blink or vibrate. Of course, pop-up ads are out of the question. When I visit a Web site that has an obnoxious, distracting ad in it, I feel no guilt in nuking it on the spot. It's simple to do: in Firefox, just right-click the offending ad and select "Block Images from nameofserver" (where nameofserver is the name of the Web server hosting the ad. Firefox fills in this information for you automatically). After you block it, any image from that server will never appear again on any Web page you visit. This feature alone has doubled my Web surfing pleasure.

▶ How Can I Block Unwanted Flash Animation?

Get rid of distracting Flash animation using Flashblock

Many Web sites use a programming technology called Flash to add animation, games, and interactivity to their pages. Advertisers use Flash for certain effects, too, but sometimes the results are annoying. Some Flash ads can dance all over the screen like a pesky moth, others can change size or emit sounds when you run your mouse cursor over them. Flash ads used to be difficult to block. But a Firefox extension called Flashblock (addons.mozilla.org/firefox/433) lets you decide which Flash elements to keep on a Web page. After installing it, any time Firefox encounters a Flash element on a Web page, it will display an iconic letter "F" in a circle where the Flash element is. If you click it, the Flash element will run one time. If you right-click the icon, you can tell Flashblock to completely hide the Flash element or allow it to run on the page forevermore.

Firefox's pop-up blocker in action.

▶ I Tried Clicking on a Thumbnail Image in Google's Image Search, but the Large Image Is Not Available. Is There a Way to Find It?

How to find photos that appear in a Google Image's thumbnails but are no longer on the source Web page

Google's software crawls across billions of Web pages, indexing not only the text it finds, but also the images. It converts each image into

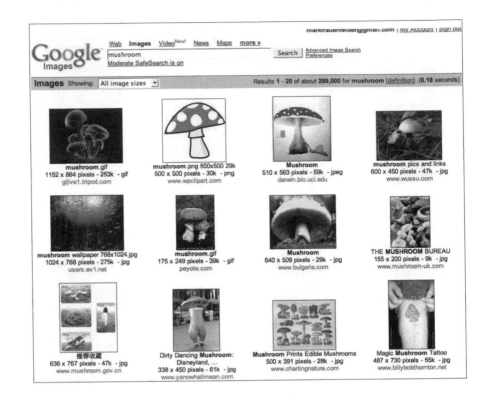

Make the text of a Web page larger (or smaller)

What is it with Web page designers and their inordinate fondness for teensy text? When I have a hard time reading a page, I press Ctrl-plus (Cmd-plus on Mac) as many times as necessary to make the text legible. If you need to make the text smaller, Ctrl-minus (Cmd-minus on Mac) will do the trick. If your mouse has a scroll wheel, hold the Ctrl key (Cmd on Mac) and roll the wheel to adjust the font size up or down. To return the text to its original size, press Ctrl + 0 (Cmd – 0 on Mac).

a small "thumbnail"-sized version. When you do a Google Image search (images.google.com), those thumbnails, which are stored on Google's servers (see page 96), are what you see.

When you click one of these thumbnail images, Google takes you to the Web page where the actual, full-size image resides. But sometimes the image is no longer available because the owner took it down. That doesn't necessarily mean you're out of luck, though. Here's how you might be able to see that full-sized image:

1. Click the thumbnail image you're interested in.

2. Copy the Web address following "Below is the image in its original context on the page:"

3. Paste the address into the Google search bar and click "Google Search."

4. If Google has the full-size image in its cache, you'll see "Show Google's cache of . . ." Click the link. There's a chance the photo you want is on this page.

▶ What Are Browser Extensions and How Do I Use Them?

Improve your browsing experience by using Firefox extensions

If you add up all the time you waste online each year waiting for Web pages to load, waiting for files to download, and dealing with annoying pop-up and pop-under ads, you could have written a novel, learned a new language, and found a cure for poison ivy. I'm (probably) exaggerating, but it's true that your Web browser could stand tuning up. With one big change, and a few simple ones, you can make your online experience faster and more productive.

The big change: start using Firefox (mozilla.com/firefox). Sure, your computer came with Microsoft's Internet Explorer (or, if you're a Mac user, Safari) installed and ready-to-use, but you can do better, much better, with Firefox, a free browser created and maintained by a community of smart and committed volunteers. Firefox is better than Internet Explorer in many ways: installing Firefox is more straightforward; Firefox has hundreds of free third-party plug-ins that allow you to customize the browser to your heart's content; Firefox has better tab and RSS feed management; and it has a much better reputation for security than Internet Explorer, which historically has been plagued by lots of vulnerabilities that criminal hackers can exploit to take control of your computer and pump it full of viruses and spyware. Safari is an excellent browser for the Mac, and it plays nice with other Mac applications, but Firefox's huge library of add-ons give it a decisive edge over Safari.

Think of Firefox like a new car on the dealer showroom, and think of extensions like options such as a turbocharged engine, tinted windows, power seats, and so on. Only, in the case of Firefox, the options—and the car—are free.

To take a look at hundred and hundreds of extensions you can download, go to (mozilla.com/extensions). Click "Firefox Add-ons." From here, you can search or browse for different extensions that will enhance the application. It's very easy to add an extension to Firefox. When you find one you like, click "Install Now." Sometimes, you'll have to restart Firefox to activate the extension.

Here are my favorites:

NoScript (addons.mozilla.org/firefox/722/): Unscrupulous individuals and companies sometimes add malicious small programs, called scripts, that run when you visit their Web sites. Some scripts are useful, but others are annoying and can be a security hazard. When you install NoScript, you can forbid Web sites from running scripts. NoScript places a small icon on the bottom of your Firefox window. When you visit any Web site, NoScript prevents scripts from being run at that site by default. To allow the scripts to be run (either temporarily or permanently), just click the NoScript icon and check the option you want. Better safe than sorry.

VideoDownloader (addons.mozilla.org/firefox/2390): Have you ever wanted to save a video from YouTube on your computer

A Firefox add-on called DownThem All lets you download files from any Web site as a batch.

so you can watch it offline? VideoDownloader puts an icon on the bottom off your Firefox window that lets you download videos, Flash movies, MP3s, and other content from over 60 popular sites. To watch YouTube videos you've downloaded this way, you'll need a Flash Video player. I recommend Proxus FLV Player (flvplayer.com).

Forecastfox (addons.mozilla.org/firefox/398): This handy extension gives you the weather conditions and forecast for any town you specify when you roll your cursor over the icons in Firefox's status bar.

FoxyTunes (addons.mozilla.org/firefox/219): You can control most popular music players, such as iTunes, Winamp, Windows Media Player, and RealPlayer with this extension. It puts a customized set of controls on your status bar or menu bar so you don't have to switch applications to change or replay a song.

▶ How Do I Browse Sites Without Endangering My Computer?

Protect yourself from malicious software and the people who use it to break into your computer

The media likes to focus on the threat of hackers, con artists, cyber-terrorists, viruses, Trojan horses, spyware, adware, and other online dangers that lurk under every hyperlink on the Web. But the threat is overblown. The Web doesn't need to be a scary place if you learn how to defend yourself. With the right software in place, and a little bit of common sense, you can keep your computer system and your personal information safe.

Note: This section is aimed primarily at Windows users. That's because, to date, only four viruses have been found for the current Macintosh operating system, and none of them are a big enough problem to worry about, while there are thousands of viruses designed to attack Windows computers, and some of them are very dangerous indeed.

The first thing you should do to protect your computer from viruses and other malicious programs is make sure you have "Automatic Updates" activated for Windows. Visit microsoft.com/athome/security/update/msupdate_keep_current.mspx to find out how to activate Automatic Updates for your particular version of Windows. If you discover that Automatic Updates was not already active, activate it and then visit Windows Update (windowsupdate.com) to download the latest update to Windows (Microsoft posts a new security patch on the second Tuesday of every month).

Here are some additional measures you can take to be extra safe:

Get anti-virus software. There are a lot of excellent anti-virus programs available, but Grisoft's AVG Anti-Virus (free.grisoft.com) has the added benefit of being free for home (but not business) use. AVG Anti-Virus scans your hard drive at regular intervals, and scrutinizes your incoming email and memory for trouble-making programs.

Dump Internet Explorer and start using Firefox. If you're still using Internet Explorer to browse the Web, you're begging for trouble. Explorer has a lot of features that allow friendly Web sites to make their pages interactive. Unfortunately, people can use these same features to wreak havoc on your computer. Stop using Internet Explorer and download a copy of Firefox, the open source browser, from mozilla.com/firefox. It's much more secure, and you can make it extremely secure by installing a free Firefox add-on called NoScript (see page 98).

Use a firewall to block unauthorized attempts to access your computer. Windows comes with a "firewall" that protects your computer from malicious attempts to access it. That's good, but it's even better to download ZoneAlarm Free from zonelabs.com, a no-cost program (for individual and non-profits) that blocks unauthorized Internet traffic to and from your computer. It might take a little poking around on the Zone Labs site to find the free version but, trust me, it's there. ZoneAlarm Free does two things: it makes your computer invisible to Internet hackers, and actively blocks attempts to hack into your computer. Start using it today.

Use Google to find solutions to problems. A couple of years ago I was visiting my parents and sat down to use their computer. For some reason, their version of Internet Explorer was behaving strangely. It would display pop-up ads every couple of minutes, and there was a banner across the top that wouldn't go away, even when I reinstalled the browser. Somehow, their computer had become infected with adware. So I entered a description of the symptoms in Google's search field, and the top result gave me the instructions to get rid of the adware. When you have a problem like this, Google is your friend.

For more ways to protect your computer, visit the "Protecting and Maintaining" chapter beginning on page 351.

▶ How Do Browser Tabs Work?

Keep your open Web sites organized by using the tabs feature in Firefox

Nothing creates desktop clutter faster than opening new windows for each Web site you visit. It's convenient to keep lots of Web sites open at once, but it quickly becomes a confusing mess. That's what tabs

Managing tabs in Firefox will greatly improve your Web-browsing experience.

were invented for, and it's an essential Web browsing skill to learn. Once you start using tabs, you'll wonder how you ever got along without them. Tabs allow you to have many Web pages loaded at the same time. By clicking on the tabs, which appear at the top of your Web browser's window, you can quickly jump from one page to another.

To create a new tab in Firefox, use the keyboard shortcut Ctrl-T (Cmd-T on Mac). You can then enter a Web address as you normally do. To go back to the first Web page, just click the tab to the immediate left. There's no limit to the number of tabs you can have open.

Tabs are even more useful when you open new pages via a link. Just right-click a link and select "Open Link in New Tab." Even easier: use Ctrl-click (Cmd-click on Mac) to load the link into a new tab.

Before you start using tabs, you should customize the way they work. You can do this by opening the Tabs preference window in Firefox. See my settings above.

>Here are some useful keyboard shortcuts to use with tabs.

(If you're a Mac user, substitute the Cmd key for the Ctrl key.)

Keyboard shortcut	What it does
Ctrl-W	Close active tab
Ctrl-T	Create a new tab
Ctrl-Tab (Opt+Right Arrow on Mac)	Next tab
Alt+Enter (Opt+Return on Mac)	Open address in address field in new tab
Ctrl-(1 to 9)	Select tab 1 to 9

▶When I Start to Enter a Web Site into My Browser, It Autocompletes an Address That I'd Rather It Not Complete. How Can I Fix That?

How not to leave breadcrumbs behind you when you visit Web sites

Firefox and other Web browsers remember the addresses of the sites you visit. This makes it easier for you the next time you revisit a site, because as you start typing the address into the address field, the browser will display a list of addresses that match the characters you've typed in. It's certainly convenient, but if you've visited Web sites on a computer that other people in your home or office use, they'll see those sites when they enter addresses on the browser. Depending on where you go online, you might not want to give people the opportunity to follow your footsteps through cyberspace. To zap previously visited addresses from your Firefox's memory, enter them into the address field, use the down arrow key to select them from the drop-down menu, and then press Shift + Del. No one will be the wiser. (If you revisit one of the sites you zapped, remember to Shift + Del it again.)

This keyboard combination also comes in handy when the autocomplete starts to load a Web site you rarely visit instead of a site you use frequently.

▶ My Browser Keeps Showing an Outdated Version of a Page. How Can I See the Newest Version?

Force your browser to reload the freshest version of a Web page

When you surf the Web, your Web browser makes copies of the pages you visit and stores them. If you return to one of the sites you recently visited, the browser will display the copy stored on your computer, which is much faster than fetching a new copy from the Web server. Your Web browser usually compares the remote copy and the one stored on your computer for signs of differences to determine whether or not to get a fresh copy. This usually works, but once in a while, the differences between the remote Web page and the page on your computer (called the cached page) are unrecognizable to the browser, and it will incorrectly load the cached version. To take care of this in Firefox, you can override the cache and force it to load the remote page by entering Ctrl-R (Cmd-Shift + R on Mac).

▶ What's the Quickest Way to Clear All the Windows on My Desktop?

Clean your screen with a single keyboard command

Your computer's desktop is a lot like your real desktop. Over time, it can become cluttered with documents. Mine does. Often, I'll need to get to an icon on my desktop that's buried under countless open windows. Instead of closing them one at a time, I just press Windows-D, which clears everything from the desktop (if only it were that easy to clean my real desktop!). When I'm done, I just press Windows-D again and the clutter returns. On the Mac, it's even easier—just press the F11 key, which hides all the open windows on your desktop. If you'd rather see all the open windows on your desktop at once, press F9 to make every window shrink to fit your display. Then, click the window you want to use and your desktop will go back to normal.

DEEPER

Dump Private Data. To delete all your private data, including the list of sites you've visited in the past, press Ctrl-Shift-Delete (Cmd-Shift-Delete in Mac). It'll zap everything at once.

How Do I Change the Home Page on My Web Browser?

Choose your favorite Web site as your default home page

When you launch your browser, it automatically loads a home page. Most browsers come with a default address that points to either the Web site of the company that made it, the Internet service provider you use, or the company that built your computer. You can specify another site (or no site at all) to appear when you launch your browser by setting your browser's preferences. In Firefox for Windows, select "Tools" → "Options" → "Main" and on the Mac select "Firefox" → "Preferences" → "Main." Select "Show my home page" from the drop-down menu and enter the address you want; select "Use Blank Page" or select "Use Current Page" to set the home page to the one you already have open. In fact, if you have multiple pages

Use the same browser settings on different computers

I have one computer in my office and another at home. When I go online, I like having my bookmarks, passwords, history, tabs, cookies, and other browser settings the same on both computers. Google Browser Sync (google.com/tools/firefox/browsersync) is a Firefox extension that does just that. It copies the browser settings from one computer to another, and makes sure they stay in sync after that.

Be careful about using Google Browser sync with computers that other people have access to. Unless you trust them, you probably don't want them visiting sensitive, password-protected Web sites, such as online banks or your eBay account.

open in tabs, you can set the entire batch to open when you start
Firefox with this option.

You can also select "Show my windows and tabs from last time"
from the drop-down menu, and Firefox will restore the pages from
your previous session the next time you run it, so you can get right
back to whatever you were doing. My default home page is
google.com/ig, which is a customizable Google page. (See page 2 to
learn about customizing Google.)

▶ What's the Best Way to Bookmark a Site?

Save your favorite Web sites in your Bookmarks Bar

There are certain Web sites you probably visit every day: your blog (if
you have one), Google, your employer's site, your favorite newspaper site, and so on. It makes sense to have these sites one click away.
When you have a favorite Web site loaded, just click the little icon to
the left of the address and drag it to the Bookmarks Toolbar directly
below the address bar. The Bookmarks Toolbar is actually a folder in
your bookmarks list, and anything that's in the Bookmarks Toolbar
folder will appear on the Bookmarks Toolbar. If the name of the site
is too long in the Bookmarks Bar, you can edit it by right-clicking it
and selecting "Properties" from the pull-down menu.

You can even drag an entire folder filled with bookmarks onto
your Bookmarks Toolbar and with one click, open each Web site in
the folder in its own tab at once.

I keep about twenty of my favorite blogs in a folder labeled "best-
blogs" on my toolbar. I load all the pages at once every morning.
Here's how to do this yourself:

1. In Firefox, select "Bookmarks" → "Organize Bookmarks."

2. Click "New Folder" and give it a name (and a description, if you
   wish).

3. Click OK. The folder will appear on the left of the "Bookmarks
   Manager" window. Highlight it and click "Move."

Using Firefox's Bookmarks Manager to organize your list of sites to save.

4. A pop-up window will ask you which folder you want to move it to. Select "Bookmarks Toolbar Folder" and click "OK."

5. Now you either drag Web sites into this folder in the Bookmarks Manager or you can populate the folder by going to sites on the Web and dragging the icons into the folder on the Bookmarks Toolbar.

When you want to open all the sites at once, click the folder in the Bookmarks Toolbar and select "Open in Tabs."

What Are Some Keyboard Shortcuts for Web Browsing?

Learn keyboard shortcuts to browse at lightning speed

As wonderful as computer mice are, they can bog down your flow when you're on the Web. By memorizing a few keystroke combinations, your productivity (or at least the number of sites you visit while procrastinating) will skyrocket.

>Here are some useful keyboard shortcuts for Firefox.

(If you're a Mac user, substitute the Cmd key for the Ctrl key.)

Keyboard shortcut	What it does
Ctrl-L or F6	Select address field
Ctrl-K	Search
Backspace (Delete on Mac)	Previous page
Shift+Backspace (Shift+Delete on Mac)	Forward page
Alt+Home (Option+home on Mac)	Home page
F5	Reload page
Home	Top of page
End	Bottom of page
Ctrl-P	Print page
Ctrl-+	Increase text size
Ctrl-(-)	Decrease text size
Ctrl-0	Normal text size
Ctrl-F or /	Find text on page
F3	Find next instance of text
Shift + F3	Find previous instance of text
'	Find link (press Return → Enter to load page)
Ctrl-W	Close tab or window
Ctrl-D	Bookmark page
Ctrl-H	History

How Do I Find Out How Fast My Internet Connection Is?

Does your broadband Internet connection seem sluggish? You can find out how fast it really is by going to dslreports.com/stest

In thirty seconds or so, you'll find out two things: your download speed (how fast data is arriving from the Internet on your computer) and your upload speed (how fast data travels from your computer to the Internet). These numbers are expressed in kbps (kilobits per second). A kilobit is 1000 bits. A typical phone line modem has a maximum speed of 53 kbps (even though modems are rated at 56.6 kbps, the FCC caps the connection rate). In the real world, you're lucky to get between 40 and 50 kbps with a dial-up modem. If dial-up is too slow for you (and it is for just about everything), you need a broadband connection. Broadband comes in two flavors: DSL, which piggybacks on your phone line, and cable, which travels through your cable TV connection. DSL connections typically range between 256 kbps and 1.5 mbps (that's megabits, or million bits per second). Cable modems have a wider range than DSL, because their speed is dependent on how many other people in your neighborhood are using it. If you're among just a few users in your area, you could get download speeds of up to 3000 kbps or more. But if there are a lot of other subscribers nearby, expect download speeds of 400 kbps and uploads of 200 kbps or so.

A speed test result from dslreports.com

```
dslreports.com speed test result on 2006-03-23 19:13:15
EST:
3493 / 351
Your download speed : 3493 kbps or 436.6 KB/sec.
That is 2.6% worse than an average user on rr.com

Your upload speed : 351 kbps or 43.8 KB/sec.
That is 15.6% worse than an average user on rr.com

PS: Welcome to dslreports.com! Run more tests! see forums
```

When I switched from an unusually slow DSL connection (topping out at around 200 kbps), to cable, the difference was stunning. The figure at the top of this page shows the results of my speediest at DSL Reports. 3493 kpbs is blazingly fast, and even though my upload speed is just 10% of my download speed, it's still plenty fast for sending photos and video clips to friends.

If you run the test and learn that your connection speed is a lot less than your provider advertised, give them a call and tell them you are going to switch providers unless they raise your bandwidth or lower your monthly bill.

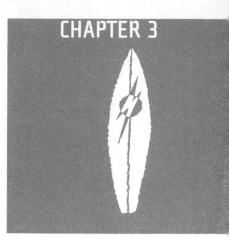

CHAPTER 3

SHOPPING AND SELLING

I made my first online purchase—a pound of coffee beans—almost 20 years ago, on a now-defunct online service called Prodigy. Since then, I've bought tens of thousands of dollars worth of products online, including a new Volkswagen Beetle. The Web is a marvelous place to shop, especially if you know what you're looking for and you stay alert for scammers.

Thanks to search engines that scour the Internet and index information, the Web is great for comparing prices on mass-produced goods and services, as well as for finding one-of-a-kind items and rare collectibles.

This section will teach you how to be a smart buyer (and seller) on eBay, how to get great deals on products, and other tips for making online shopping even better than it already is.

AUCTIONS

▶ What's the Best Way to Win an Auction on eBay Without Overpaying?

Use a sniping service to get the jump on other bidders

When you bid on an eBay item, it's all too easy to get caught up in the thrill of the game. When that happens, the item you want becomes less important than winning the auction, and you end up paying more than you intended.

Because of the way eBay conducts its auctions (see page 113, "What is proxy bidding?"), your most rational bidding strategy is to enter a bid for the maximum amount you would like to pay and then refuse to give in to the temptation of going higher when someone outbids you. But that requires Herculean willpower. Even worse, if you place your bid early on in the auction, you give other bidders an opportunity to run up the price, resulting in an emotionally charged bidding war. This is great for the seller (and for eBay, which collects a percentage of the selling price), but bad for you when you end up paying an inflated price for an iPod or a Kate Spade handbag. But there's a way to take advantage of eBay's method of holding auctions. In a real-life auction, the bidding frenzy for a desirable item doesn't stop until everyone but the highest bidder gives up. However, eBay's auctions end at a precise time, after which no more bids can be placed. Savvy eBay bidders know how to use this built-in time limit to help them win auctions at low prices. They use a bidding strategy called "sniping."

Sniping simply means entering your bid at the very last possible moment before an auction closes, so that other interested bidders don't have a chance to react and outbid you. The truth is, there's no reason to ever place a bid in the first days of an auction—it only encourages others to become interested and bid against you. To avoid competition, always place your bid at the very end of the auction. That's the advice of Harvard Business School professor Alvin E. Roth. After studying different bidding strategies on eBay, he concluded that sniping is a great way to not only win an auction, but to win it at a lower price than you would using any other bidding strategy. In other words, if you're not a sniper, you're a sucker.

There are two ways to become a sniper. The first is the manual sniping method, and it's free: a few minutes before the auction closes, go to the eBay page for the item you're interested in. Enter your bid, and click the "Place Bid" button, but do not click the "Confirm Bid" button that follows. Instead, wait until the last 30 seconds or so before the auction ends, and then press the "Confirm Bid" button. (Use your computer's clock, which you can synchronize to eBay time here: cgil.ebay.com/aw-cgi/eBayISAPI.dll?TimeShow.)

Manual sniping is free and certainly better than simply entering a bid the usual way, but it is inconvenient—especially if the auction is due to end at 3 A.M., or during a meeting at the office—and there's chance you'll hit the "Submit" button too late and miss out.

It's better to use an online sniping service that automatically places a last-second bid for you. To use an online sniping service, enter your maximum bid (as early as the first day of the auction if you wish—the sniping service keeps your bid private until it enters your bid on eBay at the end of the auction), and then forget about it. My favorite sniping service is eSnipe (esnipe.com). After a free fourteen-day trial, eSnipe charges 1 percent of the winning auction price (up to a maximum of $10). You only pay for successful snipes, so it's in eSnipe's best interest to make sure you win.

>What is proxy bidding?

eBay uses something called "proxy bidding" to automatically bid for you each time you're outbid. Say you want a cell phone that has a current high bid of $37. If you're willing to pay $100 for the phone, but would like to get it for less (and who wouldn't?) you can still enter a $100 bid, because eBay will instead place a bid on your behalf that's $1 higher than the current high bid. Of course, the current high bidder might also have entered a higher maximum bid, which means you might have to pay a lot more than $38 to get that phone. In any case, you'll never have to pay more than the $100 maximum bid you authorized eBay to make for you.

DEEPER

Search for misspelled items to find a bargain on eBay.
Bless our educational system for producing so many people who can't spell. Many sellers on eBay accidentally misspell the name of the thing they're selling. Go to eBay and do a search on "plam." You'll find lots of Palm brand handheld computers and cell phones for sale (as well as plenty of "plam" tree art jewelry). A "plam" is often bargain priced, because it doesn't show up when people search for a "palm" Pilot or Treo cell phone. Other words to try: "micorsoft," "snoy," and "dinsey." Even easier: go to the Misspelled Auction Search Engine (misspelledauctions.com) and enter the correct spelling for an item, and it'll search eBay using multiple misspelled variants at once. Used in conjunction with sniping, this is the best bet for getting a great deal on eBay.

▶ How Can I Get the Most Money Selling an Item on eBay?

Follow these tips to increase the bids on your eBay items

The trick to maximizing bids on eBay is providing as much high-quality information as possible. That means you need a keyword-friendly title line, clean photographs, and plenty of information in the description.

The item title. Don't underestimate the importance of crafting an effective title. You have just 55 characters to describe what you're selling. Don't waste them including come-ons like "L@@K!" or "Amazing," because buyers don't search for those terms. It's amazing how many sellers add these useless words to the title line. Stick to the keywords a buyer is likely to use when searching: brand names, model numbers, artist, subject (of an art piece), genre (e.g., "retro"), etc.

For instance, if you were selling a classic comic book, you'd want to include the title, the artist's name, the issue number, and any special characters that appear. "FANTASTIC FOUR #49 JACK KIRBY SILVER SURFER GALACTUS" will show up in searches of people looking for Fantastic Four comics, Jack Kirby comics, and comics in which the Silver Surfer or Galactus have appeared.

Search more than one auction site at once

eBay is the biggest auction site in the world, but it isn't the only one. Yahoo!, Overstock, Amazon, and other online companies also offer auctions; and AuctionSHARK (auctionshark.com) lets you search 30 auction and online shopping sites at once. It also offers automated search tools so you can have results emailed to you whenever AuctionSHARK finds results based on your search.

Take a look at the way other successful sellers on eBay describe items similar to whatever it is you're selling and follow their example. Often, they use a specialized collector's jargon to succinctly convey important information. Find out what the jargon means and use it in your title.

Photographs. eBay allows you to include one photograph on the item description page at no charge. That's usually not enough. Buyers want to see plenty of sharp, well-lighted photographs taken from all sides of the thing they are bidding on. Additional photos cost just 15¢ each. It's money well spent. Don't be afraid to show any damage, scratches, or other defects the item may have—full disclosure only gives potential bidders additional confidence that you aren't trying to swindle them. eBay has a short tutorial for taking good pictures with a digital camera: pages.ebay.com/help/sell/photo_tutorial.html.

Description. The idea here is to present the facts about the item in a clear and straightforward manner. Don't waste bidders' time with flashing red letters and hyperbole. Use a plain white background and list the things that bidders are likely to be interested in. Repeat the information in the title line, and then go deeper: Does it come with all the accessories and the user's manual? Do you still have the original packaging? Are you the original owner? Why are you selling it? Again, study how eBay "Power Sellers" describe their similar items and learn from them.

▶ How Can I Keep from Being Cheated on eBay?

Learn to spot cheaters who inflate their eBay score

If you're a bidder, the easiest way to make sure not to get cheated on eBay is to place bids only with sellers who have high Feedback Scores and a high Positive Feedback rating. (This information can be found in a box on the right-hand side of the listing page.)

In my experience, anyone with a Feedback Score of 100 or more and a Positive Feedback rating of over 97 percent is trustworthy enough to do business with. But before placing a bid, you need to

DEEPER

Best time to start an eBay auction. According to a survey of about 1,000 eBay sellers, the best time to list your auction is on a Sunday evening between 6PM and 9PM Eastern time. (Your auction will end exactly seven days later.) That's the interval during which the greatest number of bidders visit eBay.

make sure the seller's feedback is genuine. Unfortunately, there are unscrupulous people on eBay who use eBay to actually sell positive feedback. Here's how it works: Jerk A lists an item of no value, such as a "digital photograph of my dog" with a "Buy It Now" price of $1. The item description makes it clear that Jerk A will give the buyer—let's call him Jerk B—a positive feedback rating as soon as Jerk B buys the photo. Thanks to jerks like Jerk A, jerks like Jerk B can quickly garner a respectable Feedback Score of 100 for $100. You can spot these jerks by clicking on the "Read feedback comments" link located in the Seller information box on the item description page. From there, click the "From Sellers" tab and then click some of the item numbers to see the things the seller has purchased on eBay. If any of the items are phony feedback rating items, make sure that you never bid on anything this seller offers, because he is a swindling jerk.

Now, what if you're interested in buying an item that's being offered by a seller with a low Feedback Score? Well, you probably don't have to worry. The only thing a low Feedback Score means is that the

What should I do if an eBay seller insists on payment in the form of a wire transfer?

Never use an instant cash wire transfer—it's too easy to get ripped off.

eBay forbids sellers from requiring you to pay them via a wire transfer (the kind offered by Western Union or MoneyGram). If you pay by check and get cheated, eBay will cover your loss up to $200 (minus a $25 processing fee). Your best bet is to use a credit card (the major ones offer "zero liability" for eBay purchases) or PayPal, which offers a $1,000 buyer protection program when you buy something from a qualified seller. The item description page will indicate whether or not the seller is a qualified PayPal merchant.

seller has not sold very many items on eBay. Everyone on eBay has to start out with a Feedback Score of 0. I've bought quite a few low-priced items from people with a Feedback Score of 10 or less and have never been ripped off.

A low Positive Feedback Rating is a different story. The rating is a number from 0 to 100 indicating the percentage of transactions the seller has completed to the satisfaction of the other party. Steer clear of anyone with a Positive Feedback rating of 95 percent or less. If you still want to take a chance, you should at least check out the complaints made against the seller by clicking on the "Read feedback comments" in the Seller information box to see what kind of beef they had with the seller.

▶ What Are Some Common Scams on eBay That I Need to Watch Out For?

Avoid getting ripped off by learning to identify con artists' tricks

Empty box trick. Occasionally, someone will list a "Brand-New Playstation 2 Box." After you pay for the item, you get the cardboard box the Playstation was shipped in, with nothing inside but the stench of the small-time con artist who cashed your bank draft. A variant is to advertise a "Brand-New Xbox 360" and then include fine print at the bottom of the auction listing that reads "You are bidding on the opportunity to buy me a brand-new Xbox 360."

The wholesale list. As I write this, eight poor suckers have bid on an item described as a "NEW 20" FLAT SCREEN LCD COMPUTER MONITOR WHOLESALE LIST," with free shipping. The high bid is $51. "GET THIS GREAT ITEM AT A GREAT PRICE, NOW," reads the description. So far so good—a 20-inch monitor for $51 seems like a great deal, right? However, if you read the entire description closely, you will see that the seller is offering a list of wholesale dealers who sell monitors, not an actual monitor. The winning bidder gets nothing but a text file with contact information for computer equipment wholesalers—something you could find on Google in 20 seconds. For this particular auction, the

DEEPER

Keeping two eBay accounts.
Many eBayers are hesitant to leave negative feedback for a buyer or seller who didn't live up to his end of the bargain because they are afraid the other party will leave negative feedback in retaliation. You can reduce the damage by keeping two separate eBay accounts. Use one account for buying and one for selling.

seller has chosen to keep his or her Feedback Score private. That means you can't read the comments left by the scam artist's customers. Never bid on anything from a seller with a private Feedback Score.

Triangulation. You place the winning bid on a new, still shrink-wrapped digital camcorder. It arrives in the mail a few days later and it is exactly as advertised. So far, so good, right? Unfortunately, in a month or so, the police knock on your door (or more likely, invite themselves in by kicking the door off the hinges) and arrest you for credit card theft and receiving stolen property. Thousands of dollars in legal fees later you figure out what went wrong. The seller used a stolen credit card number to order your camcorder from Amazon or an online camera store. When the true owner of the stolen credit card number saw the charge on his statement, he called the bank to dispute the charge. The bank called Amazon and asked for the address (your address) to which the camcorder was sent. That's when Officer Friendly pays a visit and lets you try on his shiny handcuffs.

To avoid this scam, never make a payment using a wire transfer. And if your item comes shipped in a box from Amazon marked as a gift (which hides the address of the person who paid for the item) you should immediately contact eBay and Amazon to explain the situation.

eBay phishing. If you get an email that looks like it came from eBay, asking you to correct some information in your account, or answer a bidder's question, don't click any of the links in the email. There's a good chance it's a scam known as "pagejacking." If you click the link, you'll be taken to a fake eBay site and asked to fill out a form with your eBay username and password and credit card information, which the pagejacker will use for nefarious purposes.

Here's a simple rule to prevent being pagejacked: never click a link in a message sent by eBay, no matter how official it looks. Instead, open your Web browser and type in "ebay.com," log into your account, and check your messages there.

DEEPER

Call before you bid. The best way to avoid getting scammed is to talk to the seller on the phone before bidding on a high-priced item. If the seller is willing to provide you with a phone number, the odds are in your favor that the transaction will end on a happy note.

Set up eBay searches to be sent to you via email.

How Can I Be Alerted When Something I Want Is Available on eBay?

Instead of going to eBay every day to find out if something you want is available on the auction site, set up a Favorite Search and let eBay alert you by email when the item becomes available

Here's an example: say you want to be alerted every time there's a new auction for an Eberhard-Faber Blackwing 602 pencil (a high-demand pencil that used to cost 50 cents until the company stopped making them in 1998, after which the price for an unused one jumped to $20 on eBay).

Just enter "blackwing 602" in eBay's search field and click "Search."

Here you can see that there's one current auction for a Blackwing 602 pencil. Next to that information is a link that reads "Add to Favorite Searches." Click it.

In the screen that loads, enter a name for the search, such as "Blackwing pencil" and activate the checkbox that reads "Receive a daily email when new items appear for:" You can also choose how long you'd like to continue being sent email about new Blackwing pencil auctions. Now click "Save Search."

You can manage your favorite searches by clicking on "All Favorite: Searches" on your My eBay page.

Note: You can also add sellers and categories to your favorites list.

▶ How Can I Shop Online Without Having to Use My Credit Card Number?

Keep your real credit card number in your wallet by using a single-use or spending-limit virtual credit card number

As more people use the Internet to shop and pay bills, the threat of identity theft becomes more ominous. In June 2005, a hacker broke into a major credit card–processing database and gained access to 40 million credit card numbers. By law, cardholders are responsible for just the first $50 of fraudulent charges made with a stolen credit card, but having to cancel cards, file theft reports, and clear your credit record is a huge hassle.

That doesn't mean you should avoid shopping on the Web again, however. If you're a Citi, Bank of America, or Discover cardholder, you can shop online with abandon and never give out your real credit card number. These three card companies let you use what are called "virtual credit card numbers" or "single use numbers" to make on-line purchases. All three virtual card programs work pretty much the same way. Bank of America cardholders who log in to bankofamerica .com can click the "ShopSafe" link, and enter a spending limit and expiration date into an online form. Bank of America then generates a unique and temporary 16-digit number that looks and works exactly like a regular credit card number, with one important difference: it can only be used for a transaction up to the limit specified. If a hacker steals the number and tries to use it to make a purchase, the card company will reject the transaction.

Here's my ShopSafe credit card number: 5413 4959 7887 7597. Go ahead, criminals, try ordering a dozen laptops using it. But let me warn you, the credit limit is $5, and I've already spent it, so you're out of luck.

▶▶ SHOPPING

▶ How Can I Visualize the Size of a Product I'm Interested in Buying Online?

Get a feel for the size of electronic gadgets with this nifty size-comparison Web site

When I'm shopping online for a new camera or other expensive little box-shaped item, I have trouble visualizing the size of it. For example, the Exilim EX-Z70 digital camera is $95.2 \times 60.6 \times 19.8$ mm. That doesn't mean much to me. Even when I convert that into inches, it's still hard to visualize. A site called sizeasy (sizeasy.com) lets you enter the dimensions of the gadget you're interested in and compare it to other common objects (a deck of cards, a box of matches, a CD case, etc.) so you can see how large or small it really is.

▶ What's the Best Price-Comparison Service?

Use special product search engines and deal sites to find bargain prices on all kinds of products

If you're looking for a bargain on a digital camera, a computer, cosmetics, furniture, or anything else sold online, price-comparison services can help you find the best deal. My two favorites are Shopzilla (shopzilla.com) and Froogle (froogle.com), Google's shopping service.

Shopzilla's search functionality is excellent. For instance, if you enter "Palm," Shopzilla displays a list of categories to narrow your search down to PDAs, home lighting (think palm tree lamps), bedding, outdoor furniture, skin care products, candles, sporting equipment, or gloves and mittens. When you drill down to the product you're interested in, Shopzilla displays the prices from a list of online retailers, highlighting one as the "Smart Choice"—which generally is the lowest priced item from a highly rated merchant.

Best of all, you can see the shipping charges up front. Enter your ZIP code and Shopzilla will include sales tax, shipping, and handling costs in the price comparisons. The reason this is useful is because many so-called discount retailers will sting you with ridiculously high shipping charges.

Froogle is not as easy to use as Shopzilla, but if you're willing to dig around and take your chances with an uncertified online retailer, you can find some great deals. For instance, I was interested in getting a portable DVD player for my kids to watch on plane trips. I used Shopzilla to browse through the portable DVD player category until I found a model I liked. The best deal offered (including tax and shipping) was $112.91.

Then I searched on Froogle for the same make and model. Froogle found a store selling it for $54.99. This seemed like a terrific bargain, so I added it to the shopping cart and proceeded to check out. After filling in my address information and selecting my method of payment, I noticed that they were tacking on a shipping charge of $29.99 for UPS ground. I quickly backed out and looked at what else Froogle had turned up. Best Buy (bestbuy.com) had it for $69.99, and shipping was about $10, making the total five dollars less than the first store.

When looking specifically for consumer electronics, it's worth checking out a few other places before buying. Dealnews (dealnews.com) is a useful site that reports some excellent deals, discounts, and rebates for handhelds, phones, digital cameras and camcorders, notebook and desktop computers, tools, and even clothes and sporting goods. They also offer useful coupons (I found a 10 percent in-store discount coupon for Home Depot) and a "Top Reader Picks" section, where I learned about Amazon's amazing "Outlet" department, which sells electronics for at least 70 percent off.

Another place worth checking is Crutchfield's "Scratch and Dent" section at Crutchfield.com (search "Crutchfield Scratch and Dent" at Google). Everything comes with Crutchfield's standard return policy. Be sure to check out Crutchfield's education sections. Each week, they run informative articles about the latest trends in consumer technology, and also offer useful installation guides, some of which are in video. If you are in the market for a car stereo, I recommend

Crutchfield. The site takes you step-by-step through the process of finding out what equipment fits your car and how to install it.

If you don't have a specific product in mind, but just want to find a great deal on all types of techno-baubles, head over to Woot! (woot.com) Woot! offers just one product every day, and if you don't buy it that day, it's gone forever. Go there early in the morning; the stuff they offer often sells out in a matter of hours. Better yet, subscribe to the RSS feed and the daily deal will be delivered to your reader every day.

How Can I Get Promo Codes When I Shop Online?

Find discount codes and save money on your online purchases

You've probably seen that field marked "Promo code" or "Coupon code" in the checkout section of online shopping sites. Where can you get these code numbers? Usually, you get them in the mail or via email from online retailers who want you to shop at their store. Another way to get them is by going to CurrentCodes.com and searching for the name of the merchant. You can also browse for coupons by product category. A quick look through the site revealed 15 percent off orders at 1-800-flowers.com, $5 off any order over $30 at ThinkGeek (thinkgeek.com), and $10 off any purchase over $49 at Amazon's grocery store.

The fine folks who created BugMeNot (see page 148) have a Web site called RetailMeNot (retailmenot.com), which lets you search for and share coupon codes with other users of the site. It's slick and easy to use.

How Can I Use My Mobile Phone to Check Prices on Stuff When I'm in a Store?

Before buying something in a brick-and-mortar retailer, use your mobile phone to check for a better deal online

Next time you're out shopping and are about to buy a big-ticket item like a TV set or a camcorder, pull out your Web-enabled cellphone

DEEPER

Getting stuff for free.
There's no better price than $0. Freeafterrebate.info has links to software, computer equipment, and other items that costs nothing (except for a few bucks shipping and handling). Some of the deals have strings attached. For instance, a 512 MB USB flash memory drive normally costing $30 at Buy.com is indeed free after rebate (even the shipping is free) but you have to sign up for a one-month "risk-free" subscription to an identity theft protection service. If you forget to cancel, you'll have to pay a monthly service charge that quickly costs more than $30.

and do a little online comparison shopping. Download the Scanbuy Shopper application onto your phone by entering your phone carrier, email, and phone number at scanbuyshopper.com. The application will be sent to your phone. Once you install it, click "Check Price" and enter the barcode number of the product you are thinking of buying. You'll see the best available price (both new and used), links to reviews, and product information. You can send the results to your email address if you want to order the product online, or if you have enough nerve, you can show the results to the salesperson at the store and ask him or her to match the price.

Other mobile shopping sites worth checking out: Overstock Mobile (mobile.overstock.com), Froogle Mobile (wml.froogle.com), PriceGrabber Mobile (atpgw.com), and Yahoo! Shopping (shopping.yahoo.com). Remember, if your phone calling plan does not include unlimited data, you may be charged for accessing the Web.

▶ How Can I Find Out Whether or Not an Online Retailer Is Reputable?

Find out what other customers think of a company before you do business with them

Most price-comparison services have merchant ratings on their site, but it doesn't hurt to also check an online store's report at ResellerRatings (resellerratings.com). Not only will you see the store's scores (from 1 to 10) on prices, shipping and packaging, customer service, and returns, you'll also be able to read first-hand reports from customers who've made purchases from that online merchant. If you look at some of the lowest-rated stores here, you'll see some hair-raising stories about sleazy dealers. One guy wrote about how he bought a Nikon D70 for $650 from an online store, but found out the camera didn't come with standard features like a battery or a lens. He ended up paying over $1,300 for everything, when he could have gotten it from an above-board store like Amazon for less. To add insult to injury, the merchant didn't give him a promised rebate, and Nikon would not guarantee the camera because the merchant was not an authorized dealer. The lesson? Before you buy online, check here first. Other sites you can check include BizRate (bizrate.com), BBBOnline (www.bbbonline.org), and Rip-off Report (ripoffreport.com).

▶ I've Been Cheated by an Online Retailer. What Can I Do About It?

Don't let yourself be victimized by a crooked dealer

Dishonest online merchants are rare, but they exist. Some will send you inferior quality knockoffs or equipment with missing components. The worst ones will take your money and send you nothing at all. If an online retailer has cheated you, and your repeated demands for setting things straight aren't met, then it's time to ratchet up the tactics. Turn the page to see what to do.

Get the latest computer gear before anyone else

Why is it that Japanese technophiles get all the coolest gear first? For one thing, they're much more willing to pay for it than most U.S. customers, who aren't nearly as quick to adopt cutting-edge technology. But if you're one of those people who happens to like powerful sub-notebook computers, mobile phones with a mind-boggling array of features, and exotic tablet and handheld computers— and you're willing to pay dearly for the privilege of cutting to the front of the line—then Dynamism (dynamism.com) is the online store for you. This company imports the latest technology from Japan and configures it for use by English-speaking Americans, which involves installing new software and providing the necessary power adapters. From a Sony sub-notebook that weighs less than 3 lbs ($2,599) to a Hello Kitty USB keychain ($149), Dynamism will scratch your techno-itch.

Complain to the post office. If the U.S. Post Office delivered your package, you can file a mail fraud complaint at usps.com/postalinspectors/fraud/welcome.htm.

File a complaint with the Internet Crime Complaint Center. The FBI and the National White Collar Crime Center have teamed up to crack down on "cybercrime," which includes busting sleazy online merchants who rip off their customers. You can file a complaint here: ic3.gov.

Ask the National Consumers League for help. This organization's National Fraud Information Center (fraud.org) has an online incident report form you can fill out, which will be forwarded to law-enforcement agencies.

Let other people know about your experience. Don't let your fellow online shoppers get ripped off by the same crooked dealer. Go to ResellerRatings and Rip-off Report (see page 124, "How Can I Find Out Whether or Not an Online Retailer Is Reputable?") and warn folks to steer clear of the rip-off artist.

▶ How Can I Get a History Report on a Used Car I'd Like to Buy?

Find out if the used car you're looking at has been in an accident

Before buying a used car, enter its vehicle identification number into Google. You'll see a link for CARFAX (carfax.com), which sells reports that let you know the car's history—accident reports, the number of owners, service records, odometer fraud, etc. A CARFAX report costs $20. I suggest you ask the car owner to pay for the report, which he can use to help him sell the car. In fact, if you are selling a car, it's not a bad idea to buy a CARFAX report and email a copy to any interested buyers. Many people who sell cars on eBay now include links to CARFAX reports, too.

If you're shopping for a used car and plan to look at more than one, you can order unlimited reports for 30 days from CARFAX for $24.99.

▶ I Want to Sell My Old Car and Buy Another. What Should I Do?

Find out how much your old car is worth before you sell it, and find out how much you can expect to pay for a new or used car

Is it time to trade in that wheezing, oil-leaking heap in your garage? If you're like me, the idea of playing mind games with a high-pressure dealer ranks right up there with tax audits and Yanni CDs. Fortunately, the Web is loaded with resources to help you from becoming a sucker in the sales room.

The first place to stop is Kelley Blue Book (kbb.com) to get the trade-in value of your old clunker. The site works pretty much like the print version of the famous Blue Book: you specify the year, make, model, options, and condition of your car; the site crunches the numbers and comes up with a fair trade-in price.

Next, go to Edmunds (edmunds.com) to read a "pros-and-cons" review of the car you're interested in, with full specs, insurance information, and the actual invoice price the dealer pays the manufacturer for the car. Be sure to check out the lengthy section that explains how to negotiate with the enemy, too.

Another place to obtain detailed pricing information is MSN Auto (autos.msn.com), which lets you "build" your dream car by checking off the options you want and observing how it affects the manufacturer's Suggested Retail Price.

Once you've done your homework, you can either walk into your local dealership armed with reams of printouts, or you can avoid the smiling sharks and buy the car through the Web. At Autobytel (autobytel.com), you can fill out a form specifying the make, model, and options you want and in a couple of days, you'll get a call with a no-haggle price. Make sure you use several car-buying services—MSN Autos (autos.msn.com) and Autoweb (autoweb.com) are both good—so you can be sure you're getting a fair quote. The representatives from the services will sometimes imply that your request for a

DEEPER

Send a mechanic to inspect a used car anywhere in the U.S. Sites like eBay and Craigslist are loaded with offers for used cars. Some of the prices are enticing, but buying a car sight unseen is a risky proposition. You really need to check out the car's condition or have someone do it for you. That's where Carchex (carchex.com) comes in. For $100, they'll send a mechanic out to the seller's home to inspect the vehicle and email you a report about any potential problems the car might have. It's a small price to pay for the assurance that you aren't sending your money to a stranger who wants to sell you a giant lemon on wheels.

quote is equivalent to a promise to buy a car from them. Don't let them fool you; tell them to buzz off if you don't like their offer.

If you do like their offer, but don't keep that much money under your mattress, you can apply for a loan online at E-Loan (eloan.com). The site offers two kinds of loans: a traditional installment plan, or a quasi-lease called an "Easy Loan." You can use the site to find out exactly how much your monthly payment will be; and if the loan is approved, you'll have a check in hand to take to the dealer the next day. Before you commit to a loan, though, it makes sense to compare loans from different lenders at LendingTree (lendingtree.com).

The best espresso in the world

When I got my fancy Rancillio Silvia espresso maker, I started hanging out on the espresso nerd sites like Coffee Geek (coffeegeek.com) and Espresso Porn (espressoporn.blogspot.com—*check out those hot photos of tar-thick, creamy coffee oozing out of portafilters!*) to learn how to make the perfect shot of espresso. I learned four things: (1) You need a good espresso maker, (2) you need a burr, not blade, grinder, (3) you need to pack the ground coffee into the portafilter with about 30 pounds of force, and (4) you need great coffee beans. Time and time again the experts pointed me to Black Cate spresso blend, made by Intelligentsia Coffee (intelligentsiacoffee.com/store/coffee/blends/blackcat). This blend of Latin and South American beans is Intelligentsia's "fanatical quest to build the perfect espresso blend." With a paradoxically smooth and bitter flavor, and plenty of delicious *crema* on the top, Black Cat is the stuff that kept me going long into the day while I wrote this book. I am forever in Intelligentsia's debt.

▶ Where Can I Buy One-of-a-Kind Gifts Online?

Shop for high-quality handmade items at Etsy

Online stores typically sell mass-produced goods. But at Etsy (etsy.com) you can buy thousands of wonderful handmade items. It's a fun site to browse. Click the "Sampler" link to see 100 small photos of things for sale; you can also click a color to shop for products that match that color or a map to find products made in a certain part of the world. You can also shop by category (Art, Bags and Purses, Bath and Beauty, Books and Zines, Candles, etc.). From stonewear serving bowls to crocheted robot dolls, Etsy has something for everyone and makes a great alternative for holiday shopping.

▶ How Can I Search for a Book on More Than One Site at Once?

Look beyond Amazon to find a better deal on books, new and used

Just as eBay is the king of online auctions, Amazon rules the world when it comes to online book sales. But there are hundreds of book merchants on the Web and, often, some have better deals on particular books than Amazon does. At BookFinder4U (bookfinder4u.com) you can search 130 bookstores and 60,000 individual booksellers in a single search. Just enter a search term and click "Compare Prices." The site finds the best price for you, including the shipping charges. You can also search the site's used, rare, out-of-print database, which includes over 90 million books.

▶ How Can I Avoid Paying High Fees for Inkjet Cartridges?

Refilling your ink cartridges is fun and saves a lot of money

A nice color inkjet printer typically costs $100 or even less. But the so-called "demo" inkjet cartridges included with the printer contain a fraction of their ink reservoirs' capacity. That's because the printer manufacturer wants them to run out of ink immediately, forcing you to go back to the store and buy new cartridges totaling $70 or more. According to an article in the March 24, 2006, edition of *The Chicago Tribune*, 70 percent of Hewlett-Packard's printer business profits comes from sales of printer supplies.

I'm not one to begrudge anyone from trying to make a profit. But when a company sells ink costing more per ounce than Dom Pérignon champagne, I feel justified in fighting back. For $39, I can buy a "jumbo ink refill kit" at misterinkjet.com for my Hewlett-Packard printer, containing one eight-ounce bottle of black ink and four four-ounce bottles of colored ink (cyan, magenta, and yellow), which is enough for eight black cartridge refills and fifteen color cartridge refills. With black cartridges running $20 each and color ones going for $35, one refill kit can save you a whopping $645!

Of course, the printer companies are onto the fact that refilling is cutting in on their racket, and they are fighting back. They've added special circuitry to their inkjet cartridges to try to make refilled cartridges not work. If you refill an empty cartridge and stick it back into your printer, the printer will inform you that the cartridge is empty (even though it's not, because you just injected it full of ink 30 seconds ago) and will instruct you to put a brand-new cartridge into the printer. Sneaky, eh?

What can you do? If you own an Epson or HP printer, there are a number of workarounds. For Epson printers that have these refill-prevention chips, you can buy a "cartridge chip resetter" for about $10 (do a Google search for "Epson chip resetter"). When you insert a refilled cartridge into the chip resetter, it resets the smart chip back to its original factory specifications so the printer will recognize it as having full ink levels.

HP printers use a different scheme than Epson printers. Their inkjet cartridges have a small contact strip on them that contains a unique serial number. When you plug a new cartridge into your printer, that serial number gets stored into the printer's memory. If you refill the ink cartridge and stick it back into the printer, the printer will recognize the serial number and lie to you that the cartridge is empty. You can correct this problem in one of two ways. The easy way is to keep a couple of extra empty cartridges at hand. That's because the printer only remembers the last two cartridges that have been plugged into it.

Start by refilling the cartridge according to the instructions that came with the refilling kit—it involves the use of syringes and solvents, and is actually quite a bit of fun to use. Then plug it into your printer. Let your printer print out a test page if it wants to. Take out the cartridge and insert one of your extras. If it prints out a test page, let it. Repeat with a second extra cartridge. Finally, re-insert your refilled cartridge and you should be good to go.

If you don't have any extra cartridges lying around, you can still clear the printer's memory by taping over certain contacts on the cartridge. Because there are so many different kinds of cartridges I'll refer you to Mister Ink Jet's page on resetting your HP printer's estimated ink level: misterinkjet.com/hpreset.htm. There's help for dealing with other inkjet brands, too.

I Lost My User's Manual for Something. Where Can I Find It?

Get the online guides for hundreds of products

When I buy a new product, like a coffee maker or a portable heater, the first thing I do is put the user's manual in a plastic bin that I use to store all my user's manuals. But when I buy a used piece of equipment (from eBay, or a garage sale) it usually doesn't come with the manual. If I need to figure out how to do something with my new device, the first thing I do is enter the name of the device along with "instructions" or "manual" in Google. That'll usually get me either the instructions from the manufacturer's Web site or a user-supplied set of instructions (which is often better than the manufacturer's guide). If Google doesn't help, I try UsersManualGuide (usersmanualguide.com), which has digital copies of hundreds of consumer electronic device manuals. Last resort: eBay, where you might be able to buy a manual or a scan of a manual (especially for vintage tech, like old tube radios).

▶ How Can I Track My Packages?

Keep tabs on the delivery status of your online purchases

You can use your RSS reader (see page 27 to learn about RSS readers) to find out where your in-transit packages are. Just add the tracking number to the following Web addresses and subscribe.

Fedex Air: shaftek.org/code/track2rss/track2rss.pl?type=fedex_air&trackingnumber=

Fedex Ground: shaftek.org/code/track2rss/track2rss.pl?type=fedex_ground&trackingnumber=

UPS: shaftek.org/code/track2rss/track2rss.pl?type=ups&trackingnumber=

USPS: shaftek.org/code/track2rss/track2rss.pl?type=usps&trackingnumber=

Another way to track a package is by going to the Web site of the carrier, entering the tracking number at the appropriate page, and dragging the resulting URL into your bookmarks toolbar folder. That way, you can check the URL whenever you want to know where the package is. You can also sign up for email alerts from each of the major carriers.

▶ How Can I Exchange an Unwanted Gift Certificate?

Trade or sell your unwanted gift certificates using an online swapping service

It was so sweet of Aunt Gertrude to send you that gift certificate to Jim's Pickled Pig Knuckles for your birthday. Isn't it a shame that you're deathly allergic to pickled pig knuckles? Don't despair. Go to Swapagift (swapagift.com) and sell your gift certificate or swap it for a gift card for something you really want. Swapagift charges you $3.99 to list your gift card, and costs nothing to buyers. A similar service, CertificateSwap (certificateswap.com) charges 7.5 percent of the sale price of your unwanted gift card. Both sites are also good places to buy gift cards at a discounted rate.

Buyers and sellers shouldn't forget eBay as a source for good discounts on gift cards as well.

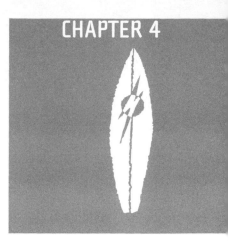

CHAPTER 4

HEALTH, EXERCISE, AND SPORTS

One of the risks of using the Web is turning into a mouse potato. After all, unless you have a computer mounted to a Stairmaster, being online means you're basically dead from the waist down. It's important to balance your life with plenty of physical activity, a healthy diet, and good medical care. This section will point you to sites that'll teach you about the latest in medicine, healing, weight loss, and fitness.

HEALTH AND MEDICINE

Where Can I Get Information About Alternative Medicine?

Learn how to deal with common ailments using natural methods

The Internet is the first place people turn to when they start to feel sick or discover a symptom suggesting illness. It's always a good idea to consult your doctor when something goes wrong. But whenever I'm feeling out of sorts, I visit Dr. Andrew Weil's Web site (drweil.com). Weil is an M.D. who also specializes in natural methods of healing and therapy, including herbs and dietary changes.

His Web site has helped my family and me back to health many times. For instance, my wife and I both suffer from hay fever every year in the late spring. I used to take prescription medicine, but it made me dizzy. I looked up "hay fever" on Dr. Weil's site and he recommended taking capsules of dried stinging nettle plant. During allergy season, I pop a couple of capsules when I wake up, and every couple of hours throughout the day. The stuff works like magic, and I don't feel any side effects. I also suffer from frequent ear infections. Instead of heading over to the doctor to get an antibiotic prescription, I've started dripping garlic oil into my ear whenever I feel an infection coming on. It always nips the infection in the bud, and the only side effect is that I crave Italian food when I smell the garlic.

NOAH, the New York Online Access to Health Web site, has a section dedicated to complementary and alternative medicine at noahhealth.org/en/alternative. When my mother-in-law suggested that I try the Feldenkrais method to help me with my shoulder stiffness, NOAH's site directed me to some good basic information about it. You can also find out about many other forms of alternative medicine, from the Alexander Technique to the Trager Approach. A good

Hay fever alert

Hay fever sufferers can check the four-day allergy forecast for their region at Pollen.com (pollen.com/Pollen.com.asp). You can also sign up for a two-day forecast by email from the same page.

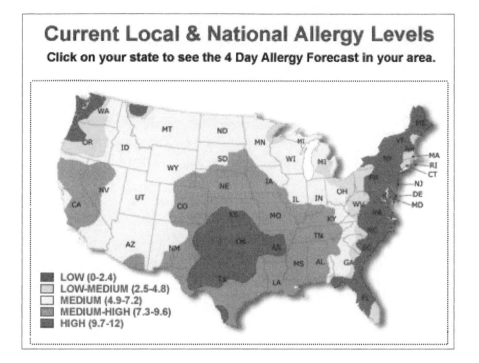

site for finding out about specific herbs and their medicinal qualities is the National Center for Complementary and Alternative Medicine (nccam.nih.gov). You'll learn here, for instance, that studies of echinacea, which was previously touted as a cold and flu reliever, indicate that the herb is pretty much worthless. You'll also learn that taking a combination of glucosamine and chondroitin sulfate has been shown to provide "significant relief" to osteoarthritis patients suffering moderate-to-severe pain. And if you've been tempted to try kava as a way to fall asleep, you should know that the FDA warns that kava use has been linked to severe liver damage risks.

▶ ## How Can I Track My Exercise and Weight Loss?

*Use online tracking tools to chart your course to successful
weight loss*

Traineo (traineo.com) allows you to set a weight loss goal to be
achieved by a certain date. Each day you enter what kind of exercise
you did, and for how long. You also enter your diet and weight for the
day. Traineo generates graphs based on your input and creates a
page to chart your progress.

Healthy Weight Forum (healthyweightforum.org) is an Australian
site that offers a host of valuable resources designed to help you lose
weight and keep it off. If you're trying to decide which diet is best for
you, the site offers descriptions and pro and con reviews of popular
diets, such as Atkins, South Beach, The Zone, Negative Calorie, Cab-
bage Soup, and Mediterranean. Once you select a diet plan, you can
use tools such as the body mass index calculator to determine how
much weight you need to lose to be considered healthy. (Because this
site is Australian, it uses kilograms and meters, instead of pounds
and inches. To convert your weight, use Google's handy conversion
feature. Type "convert 165 lbs to kg" in the search field and click the
"Search" button.) The calorie counter offers a checklist of dozens of
activities—from "Piano" to "Sex (vigorous)"—and when you enter
your weight and how long you plan to engage in the activity, it will return the number of calories you'll burn.

CalorieKing (calorieking.com), costs $45 a year to join, but it of-
fers many more features than the Healthy Weight Forum (and it uses
standard, not metric, measures, so you don't have to convert kilos
into pounds). It offers diaries, a large food database, calculators, personalized meal plans, and online educational programs. Once you
sign up, CalorieKing has you fill out a survey about your height,
weight, age, gender, etc., which it uses to determine how many calories you should eat each day to reach and maintain an optimal weight.
It then creates a meal plan for you, with the proper proportions of fat,
protein, and carbohydrates. It also includes a journal to enter the
food you eat and how active you were during the day. A progress bar

shows you how many calories you have eaten and how many more you are allowed that day.

How Can I Look Up Ratings for Different Hospitals and Doctors?

There are several online databases you can check

If you've used sites like RateMyTeachers (ratemyteachers.com) or RateMyProfessors (ratemyprofessors.com), you should have an idea of what RateMDs (ratemds.com) is about, because it looks like it uses the same database software. You search on your state for a list of rated doctors. You can also sort by city, specialty, number of ratings, and overall quality. Each doctor's record shows you comments from patients, and ratings on punctuality, knowledge, and helpfulness. There's also a Google Maps link for each doctor. Like a lot of these customer-review services, relying on reviews, especially if there are only a few posted, can be a disservice to you and to the provider, as you don't know who the reviewers are. So, take a bad review from one patient with a grain of salt, but pay keen attention to bad reviews from a whole bunch of people. (I was pleased but not surprised to discover that my general practitioner is highly rated here.)

Finding a good, well-run, and safe hospital is becoming increasingly hard in the U.S. The Leapfrog Group (leapfroggroup.org/cp) is a consumer advocacy organization trying to offer the best possible information on hospital quality and safety and to offer incentives to hospitals that maintain high standards. Their Hospital Quality and Control Survey rates hospitals on criteria related to health and safety. Searching the database is free, and the charted results look a lot like quality comparisons in *Consumer Reports*. Unfortunately, not many hospitals participate, so you're likely to find a lot of hospitals listed with a bunch of blank spaces on the chart. Leapfrog's usefulness will increase as more hospitals (hopefully) sign on. To encourage this, they're working with healthcare insurers, employers, and others to offer incentives and rewards to hospitals that participate and meet standards goals.

DEEPER

MD reports. If you're planning on going through a major procedure, suffering from a potentially life-threatening illness, or are suspicious that your doctor may be a few pills short of the prescribed dose (if you know what I mean), you may want to pay to have a search done for any malpractice cases or disciplinary actions your health practitioner has faced, what organizations and hospitals he or she belongs to, etc. Castle Connolly Medical (castleconnolly.com) offers a number of such background searches: some free, some pay. You can search for any disciplinary actions by state for free, and do a "shallow" doctor check with a free registration. Digging deeper costs $22 per year. The site even offers a one-on-one doctor-finding service at $275 for a consultation, which may be worth it if you have a particularly serious or complicated medical condition.

Consumer's CHECKBOOK (checkbook.org) offers excellent rating databases for both doctors and hospitals. The hospitals ratings are especially useful and informative as they show statistics on things such as the overall rating of doctors in the hospital, numbers of deaths during procedures, hospital inspector's accreditation ratings, and more (all compared against a national average). Consumer's CHECKBOOK is an excellent investment and a great way to get sound, real-world-tested advice on all sorts of products and services. It costs $34 for a two-year subscription, which includes access to all of their Web-based products and a quarterly print "bookazine."

▶ Are Online Pharmacies Safe and Legal?

They are if you shop at the right ones but if not, you may end up getting sugar pills, baby laxatives, or worse

Online pharmacies, especially ones operating out of Canada, the U.K., Australia, and Israel, have been a godsend to the elderly, those with lower incomes, and others who can't afford the astronomical cost of many meds in the U.S. They've also become a source of quasi-legit site-prescribed drugs, for things like erectile dysfunction meds, anti-anxiety drugs, and other medicines that users want

Assess your risk of common diseases

Harvard Center for Cancer Prevention's Your Disease Risk (yourdiseaserisk.harvard.edu) offers an extremely useful set of tools for assessing your risk for diseases such as cancer, heart disease, stroke, and diabetes. To discover your risk factors, you fill out a series of questionnaires. At the end, you're presented with a risk assessment along with a list of concrete things you can do to lower your risks. The site also has additional material, such as a list of screening tests you should get and general suggestions for improving your health and reducing your chances of life-threatening illness.

either for a legitimate reason they would like to keep private or for recreational use. We'll look at these two situations separately.

With a doctor's prescription. The first clue that an online pharmacy is legit is if they require that you fax them a doctor's prescription before they dispense your drugs. If you're skittish about buying drugs online, consult the National Association of Boards of Pharmacy's VIPPS list (nabp.net), consisting of online pharmacies that meet NABP's strict policies and guidelines. So strict, in fact, that it had none of the online pharmacies people I've known have used to great satisfaction. The list tends to represent the online arm of established bricks-and-mortar pharmacies such as Walgreens and CVS. You'll likely save little money ordering from these outlets.

Big money can be saved if you get your scripts filled in Canada or overseas. While the drug companies and the U.S. government want you to believe that these drugs might not be of the same quality, that they might ship you the wrong dose, or that they might be outright counterfeit meds, this is largely fear-mongering. The drugs come from the exact same sources, mainly U.S. companies and, if anything, the online pharmacies, the reputable ones anyway, go out of their way to make sure you're getting the right meds.

Given this vigilance (because these non-U.S. pharmacies are under so much scrutiny), you might be even safer getting your drugs from Canada and elsewhere. While that might be an exaggeration, it's no exaggeration that you'll get them more cheaply. You can save as much as 70 percent on some drugs. To see an updated list of the most highly rated online pharmacies, kept by an independent organization, check out PharmacyChecker (pharmacychecker.com).

Without a prescription. Obviously, buying drugs online that your family physician didn't prescribe for you, like Viagra, Ambien, or Propecia, can be dangerous. It is not illegal, though. This type of online pharmacy skirts the potential illegality by employing their own doctor to issue you a script after a long-distance "evaluation" (usually a short online questionnaire). The cost of this doctor's consultation is usually added to the cost of your first order. There are reputable (if that word applies here) online pharmacies that operate this way, but far more disreputable ones, mainly overseas outfits, sell counterfeit drugs at exorbitant prices and sometimes steal your credit card number and/or identity in the process. These drugs may not only be ineffective but outright harmful. If you must use such an online pharmacy, follow these safety tips: unlike legitimate online pharmacies, where you save money by using non-U.S. entities, you want to make sure the company you buy site-prescribed drugs from is based in the U.S. (as most of the counterfeit ops are foreign). Check to be sure they have a U.S. street address, not a P.O. box, and call the phone number to make sure it's legitimate. There should be a real person on the other end, not a recording. Check to see if they sell "generic Viagra," even if that's not what you're buying. If they do, move along, there's no such thing. Amazingly, there is one online pharmacy listed on PharmacyChecker that offers site-prescribed drugs: KwikMed (kwikmed.com). They meet our test of real people, real address, and real drugs. They even got a 5-star rating on PharmacyChecker! So, if you're not able to "stay in the game," or "you're not batting 1000 anymore," or you just can't get the football through the tire swing like you used to (erectile dysfunction ads love their sports analogies), KwikMed may be worth a look.

▶ How Can I Find Recipes Matching the Ingredients I Have in My Fridge?

Make a meal from whatever you have at hand with this neat recipe search engine

Google Base (google.com/base) is a giant, shared database where anyone can submit content and make it searchable on Google. There are already lots of recipes available there and you can search for them by listing the ingredients you'd like them to include. Enter "eggplant" and "cheese" and you'll get almost 1,500 recipes ranging from Pesto Eggplant to Eggplant Cheese Casserole.

For delicious recipes, nothing beats Epicurious.com, where you can search for thousands of recipes. One fun way to find a recipe is by using Epicurious's "Search Spy" to see what recipes other people are searching for. It displays the last ten terms entered into the search box. Click on the "Buzz Box" to see the recipes with the most comments.

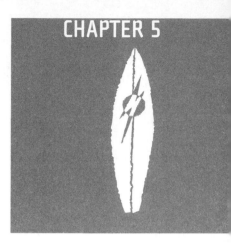

CHAPTER 5

MEDIA AND ENTERTAINMENT

▶▶ ## NEWS AND INFORMATION

▶ ### How Can I Be Alerted by Email About News for Topics I'm Interested In?

Use Google Alerts to stay on top of breaking news on subjects that you care about

Why go searching for news you're interested in when you can have the news emailed to you when it happens? Google Alerts are easy to set up. Here's an example:

Let's say you want to read breaking news stories about monkeys. Go to news.google.com and enter "monkeys" in the search field.

When you click "Search news" you discover that most of the stories are about that yeah-yeah band, The Arctic Monkeys. So, refine your search to "monkeys —arctic" and try again.

This time, all the stories are about bona-fide monkeys. Now, click the "News Alerts" link on the left side of the results page. It will bring up a window that'll let you specify what kind of updates you want (news, Web, Usenet groups, or everything) and how frequently you want to get the updates (as-it-happens, daily, or weekly).

Click "Create Alert" and you're set. If you ever want to edit or delete an alert, visit google.com/alerts.

▶ How Can I Find Out If the Story My Aunt Sent Me Is a Hoax?

Get the real story on questionable stories making the email rounds

I have a relative who likes to forward emails of jokes, inspirational stories, and warnings about dangerous marauding street gangs. One email warned me not to flash my car's highbeams at any car that does it to me first. It's part of a common street gang initiation that will get me killed, warned the anonymous author of the email. Another email contained this dire caution: "Someone is sending out a very cute screensaver of the Budweiser Frogs. If you download it, you will lose everything! Your hard drive will crash and someone from the Internet will get your screen name and password! DO NOT DOWNLOAD IT UNDER ANY CIRCUMSTANCES!"

Whenever I get email like this, I head straight to Snopes (snopes.com), a clearinghouse for urban legends and other forms

Be notified when a Web site changes without having to visit it

Would you like to be alerted whenever a Web site is changed or updated? Instead of visiting (or more likely, forgetting to visit) the Web site regularly, go to changedetection.com/monitor.html and enter the address of the Web site you're in-terested in, along with your email address. Change Detection will automatically visit the site every day, and as soon as it detects a change from the last time it checked, it'll let you know via email.

of Internet bogosity. It turns out that both of the above warnings are totally false. Barbara and David Mikkelson, the people who maintain Snopes (named after a recurring character in William Faulkner's works), field hundreds of emails a day about computer viruses, animals run amok, weird Disney trivia (no, Walt Disney's body was not frozen in a state of suspended animation after he died), outrageous celebrity quotes (yes, Rush Limbaugh once told a difficult-to-understand black caller to "Take that bone out of your nose and call me back"), and popular brands (yes, Coca-Cola once contained cocaine; and no, it's ineffective as a spermicide.) I've even trained my uncle to start using the Web site. The emails he sends around now are prefaced with a note indicating that they've passed the Snopes test.

▶ How Can I Save a Web Site I Know Is Going to Expire Soon?

Use Furl to keep an archive of online newspaper articles that you can read and share

Most newspaper Web sites, like *The New York Times* and the *Los Angeles Times*, allow you to read articles online for about a week past the day they're published. After that, they go into the archives and you have to pay a few dollars to see them. In addition, a lot of regular Web pages vanish because the owners take them down or go out of business.

There are several ways to save Web pages that go up in smoke like the tape in the beginning of the old *Mission Impossible* TV show. The first is to simply save the page as a text file. In Firefox select "Save page as . . ." from the "File" menu and choose "Text" from the "Save as type:" pull-down menu. You can also choose to save it as a "Web page, complete" that will be stored on your hard drive with images and formatting intact. When you save a Web page this way, a folder is created on your hard drive with all the files needed to render the Web page just as it first appeared in your browser.

Mac users have the option of saving a Web page as a standalone PDF file, which can be viewed with Adobe Reader or Apple's Preview utility. For some strange reason, Apple hid this feature in the "File" → "Print" command. In the "Print" window, click the "PDF" button, and select "Save as PDF." There are some other useful options in the PDF button menu, including the ability to email a Web page as a PDF.

All these methods are fine ways to archive Web sites you don't want to lose access to, but if you are serious about saving Web pages, go to Furl (furl.net) and sign up for a free account. Then drag the Furl bookmarklet (the name for a small application that can be saved as a bookmark on your Web browser) into your Bookmarks Toolbar menu (to learn about your Web browser's Bookmarks Toolbar, go to page 219).

Now, when you visit a Web site and find a page that you want to save, click the Furl bookmarklet and fill out as much information as you wish in the pop-up window. You can give the page a rating, a topic of your own choosing, keywords, comments, and a clipping from the text of the site. When you click "Save," the page will be saved to your Furl archive. (See page 147.)

The advantages of using Furl instead of saving Web sites on your hard drive is that you can access them from any computer and you can perform searches to find your Furled pages. You can also search other sites saved by Furl users, provided they weren't marked as private. For collecting shorter text snippets, give Google Notebook (google.com/notebook) a try. Firefox users can download an extension that allows them to highlight text from a page and right-click the mouse to add it to their notebooks automatically.

How Can I Avoid Having to Register at Every Newspaper Web Site I Visit?

Save time and protect your privacy by using BugMeNot

If you try to read an article on *The Washington Post*'s Web site (washingtonpost.com) and have not registered on the site before,

```
○ ○ ○        http://www.furl.net – Furl – Save Page        ⊂⊃

LookSmart
FURL | Your Personal Web File    Find ⊙    Save ⊙    Share ⊙ ™
Where To Look For What You Need.™
Save Page                              Logout ottomatik · Help

        Title  Frontyard Treasure? Just the Shaft - Los Angeles Tin

        URL    http://www.latimes.com/news/local/la-me-digger:

      Rating   4 – Very Good ▾

       Topic   General [24]        ▾   Multi

   New topic   Weird news              (creates a new topic)

  Item status  ☐ private    ☑ mark as read

    Keywords   

    Comments   Man digs a 60-foot hole in his
               front yard, thinks he will
               strike gold.

    Clipping   the crater had shimmied down,  ▣
               a rope tethered to a belt, and  ▲
               was sucking on a garden hose
               for oxygen, neighbors told the ▼

               Save  |  Email  |  Save & Email...
                      Close window



Done
```

Save Web pages before they expire with furl.net.

you may be greeted by a Web page that looks like the one on page 148.

The *Washington Post* isn't the only newspaper that makes you register before you can access it. The *New York Times*, the *Chicago Tribune*,

Already Registered?
Please enter your e-mail address and password to sign in to washingtonpost.com.
Sign In Help   Password Help

E-mail Address:
Password:

☑ Remember me on this computer.   Submit

By submitting your registration, you indicate that you agree to our User Agreement and Privacy Policy.

Many newspaper sites make you register to read them.

the *New York Post*, and hundreds of other newspaper sites require you to submit personal information, including your email address and date of birth, before you can read any articles. Imagine having to enter all this information into a form before being able to open up a newspaper or magazine at a newsstand or library! That's why I wholeheartedly recommend BugMeNot (bugmenot.com), a free service that maintains a database of usernames and passwords you can use to gain instant access to over 100,000 Web sites. The easiest way to use BugMeNot is to go to the Web site and make a bookmark of the "bookmarklet." (The easiest way to do this is right-click the "Bugmenot Bookmarklet" and select "Bookmark this Link" from the pop-up menu; see next page.)

The next time you land on a site that requires a username and password, click the BugMeNot bookmarklet. Another window will pop up with some suggested usernames and email addresses you can try.

Note: Don't try using BugMeNot to access sites that require payment or for banking or auction sites. For one thing, BugMeNot has probably blocked those sites already. For another, if you do happen to get access to a paid site, you'll be breaking the law and could wind up in a world of trouble. Use BugMeNot for its intended purpose and make the Web a better place.

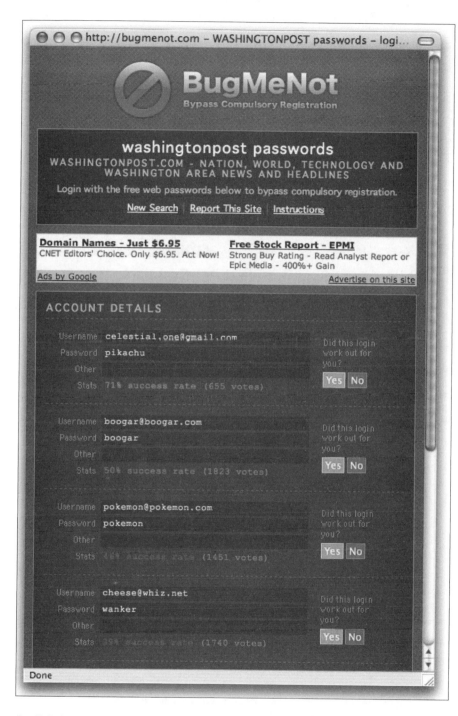

BugMeNot allows you to avoid registering at online news sites.

▶ Where Can I Read Magazine Articles for Free?

Search through a database of free online magazines

LookSmart's Find Articles site (findarticles.com) claims to have 10,000,000 articles from a large number of magazines in its database. And many of the articles are free. To search the free archive, enter your search term and select "free articles only" from the drop-down menu. The "Advanced Search" is also quite useful because it lets you refine your search term, select a date range, and choose the titles of the publications you wish to search.

▶ How Can I Find Out What Political Party My Neighbor Donated Money To?

Use Fundrace to track people's campaign contributions

What's wrong with a little harmless neighborhood snooping? I'm not talking about peering into your neighbors' windows or any other creepy and illegal activity. I mean finding out if and how much your neighbors contributed to political campaigns. Federal law requires

High-density information portal

If you could boil down all the useful business, travel, and news sites onto a single Web page, you'd get something like CEO Express (ceoexpress .com). Thanks to its spartan design, the site loads quickly, and it offers over a hundred links to essential information sites. You'll find pointers to all the business and technology magazines, major newspapers from around the world, and newswires. There are over a dozen links to health sites, as well as links to track express package shipments, get airline schedules, and much more.

that people who contribute to political campaigns provide their personal information. The Federal Election Commission keeps this data, but fec.gov isn't very easy to use. In fact, it's downright confusing. (Imagine that—a bureaucracy that doesn't bend over backwards to help the people it's supposed to serve.) That's where Fundrace (fundrace.org) comes in. Just select "Neighbor Search" and type in an address or a name to be presented with a list of the names and addresses of political contributors from the last presidential election, along with how much they contributed.

The searches aren't limited to your neighborhood, of course. I entered "Barbara Bush" in the search field and learned that she contributed $2,000 to the George W. Bush campaign. I clicked on Mrs. Bush's address (10000 Memorial Drive, Houston, TX 77024), which brought up a list of everyone else in the same area that contributed. Lo and behold, a gentleman named Mr. George H. W. Bush at the same address also donated $2,000 to the George W. Bush campaign.

Beyond satisfying your curiosity about your neighbors' political affiliation, you can use Fundrace to organize a block party (fundrace.org/block_party.php) to raise funds for your party or favorite presidential candidate.

▶ How Can I Translate a Web Site from One Language to Another?

Get a rough idea of what's written on a non-English Web site

Occasionally, I end up on a Web site written in German, Spanish, Japanese, or Chinese. Unfortunately, I don't know any of those languages, but I can use Google's language tools (google.com/language_tools) to give me an approximate translation. You can translate a Web page from several different languages into English by entering the URL and clicking "Translate." Or if you've received an email message in another language, you can copy the text into a box and translate it.

Be warned that machine translation isn't great. At best, you'll get an idea of the subject of the text; at worst, you'll be more confused than you were in the first place.

I translated this section from English to Spanish and back to English again using Google's translate feature. Here's what I ended up with: "From time to time, I finish for above in a Web site written in German, Spanish, Japanese, or Chinese. Unfortunately, I do not know nobodies of those languages, but that can use the tools of the language of Google (google.com/language_tools) to occur a approximate translation. You can translate a Web page of several diverse languages to English surrounds you incorporate the URL and chascando 'to translate.' " And so on. See what I mean?

▶▶ MUSIC

▶ How Can I Get Hard-to-Find Music That's Not on Amazon?

Go beyond the obvious sources for independently produced music

Amazon has an impressive collection of music. In fact, most of the times I've visited Amazon to search for a particular CD, I've found it—even obscure Japanese imports. iTunes, too, has more songs than you could ever hope to listen to in your life. But the online superstores don't have everything. For example, if you're looking for old music that never jumped the digital divide separating LPs from CDs, you're out of luck. Where do you go for a copy of an Enoch Light Singers' LP, or that candy-colored Bozo the Clown record you used to listen to on your Close-and-Play when you were a tot? Amazon can't help you in these circumstances. For true rarities, you'll have to either visit eBay or enter the world of "oddio" (short for "odd audio") fanatics, who take it upon themselves to convert old, out-of-print LPs into MP3s and offer them to the world.

The first stop on the oddio tour of outré musical curiosities is

Basic Hip Digital Oddio (basichip.com), a marvelous site that "collects records from the fifties, sixties, and beyond, focusing on soundtracks, pop instrumentals, and incredibly strange music." Each week, the site's curator selects one album for your listening pleasure. Typical fare includes Phil Moore's "Fantasy for Girl and Orchestra," Richard Hayman's "Genuine Electric Latin Love Machine," Harry Breuer's "The Happy Moog," and Elmer Bernstein's "I Love You, Alice B. Toklas." The amazing album cover art here—mainly from the 1950s and 1960s—is a real treat, and often better than the music itself.

It must be noted that works that are out-of-print are not necessarily in the public domain, and downloading an MP3 of an obscure album which is no longer listed on any music company's catalog might be against the law. Proceed with caution.

To find more oddio, enter "oddio" and/or "sharity" on Google. To get you started, here are a few other favorite oddio sites:

Sabadabada (sabadabada.com): A large collection of Brazilian records from the 1960s and 1970s, with a fantastic gallery of album cover art.

Bellybongo (bellybongo.com): Truly strange and wonderful music, including whistling duos and harmonica trios.

Raymondo's Dance-O-Rama (astroboy.tv/music/): How about a little cha-cha music sung by a couple of Japanese ladies known as "The Peanuts"? I tell you, 1963 was a good year for oddio.

Vegas Vic's Tiki Lounge (vegasvics.com): Get a regular dose of exotica delivered to your MP3 player by subscribing to Vegas Vic's Tiki Lounge Podcast. (For more about podcasts and how to subscribe to them, see page 36.)

The Red Hot Jazz Archive (redhotjazz.com): If you enjoy early jazz music, check out this mind-boggling collection of jazz from before 1930. The site's owner, Scott Alexander, has lovingly compiled hundreds of songs in a cross-referenced database along with biographical sketches of the bands and performers of the era. You can follow Louis Armstrong's career, song by song, starting when he was just a kid listening to his mentor Joe "King" Oliver perform at the

Funky Butt Hall in 1917, and then branch off to explore the other groups he collaborated with, such as Hawaiian greats Andy Iona and His Islanders. Unfortunately, the music on the Red Hot Jazz Archive is presented in RealPlayer streams, so you can't download any of it for later. But you can record it using a utility like Audio Hijack for Mac (rogueamoeba.com/audiohijack) or Real7ime Converter (r7cproj.euro.ru/indexe.htm) for Windows.

Perhaps you want to buy an actual shiny plastic disc instead of downloading a digital music file. Check out CD Baby (cdbaby.com), an independent online music retailer that sells self-produced CDs from unsigned bands. The folks who run the CD Baby warehouse in Portland, Oregon, have listened to and approved every CD for sale in their catalog and, unlike a regular record label, which gives a buck or two to the artist for every CD sold, CD Baby forks over between $6 and $12 for every CD sold, and they cut weekly checks to the artists. If you are interested in supporting the artists who make music you love, see if they sell their work here.

Print out a cover for a CD burned from iTunes

You can produce a nice-looking cover for any CD you burn from iTunes. First, pick the playlist you want to burn onto disk, then select "Print" from the "File" menu. You'll be presented with several different options for printing a cover. For instance, if your playlist includes songs from more than one album, you can print the albums out in a mosaic pattern. Now click "Print," cut out your new cover, and insert it, along with the CD you burned, into a jewel case. (See next page.)

Print "Buck Owens"

Print: ● CD jewel case Insert
○ Song listing
○ Album listing

Theme: Single cover

Prints a single cover from the songs in your
selected playlist or library. Uses the album
artwork from the selected song. The back also
features the album artwork. Prints in full color.

Page Setup...   Cancel   Print...

Is There Anything Like a TiVo for Radio?

*Record your favorite radio programs and listen to them anytime
on your MP3 player or computer*

Ever since I bought a TiVo system, I've stopped watching live television. I say "thank nerds for TiVo" every time I gleefully fast-forward
through TV commercials. I love sitting down on the couch and picking up the remote to choose from a dozen different shows my TiVo
has recorded. It truly is a life-changing device. I've talked all my
friends into getting TiVos, too, telling unbelievers that they won't
"get it until they've got it." And after they've got it and "get it," they
thank me.

Once I learned that I couldn't live without time-shifted TV, I
wanted time-shifted radio, too. The commercial interruptions on
radio are even more frequent and longer than they are on TV. They
are also much more obnoxious. I would rather drive in silence than
listen to some idiot scream about the sale of the century on queen-
sized mattresses or why I'm a fool for not getting in on the ground
floor of the coming boom in gold futures.

I haven't found anything quite as easy as TiVo for my radio, but RadioShark, a $69 shark fin–shaped gizmo, comes close. (The original RadioShark has been discontinued, but can still be found on places like eBay. Griffin announced that it is developing a new version of the RadioShark that offers near CD-quality recording of FM music and near-FM quality of AM music. The RadioSharkHD should be available by the time you read this.) After installing the RadioShark software, you can program it to record any radio station at any time and save it as an MP3 file. I record several different NPR programs every week (they don't have commercials, but it's nice to be able to listen to them on my time), as well as a couple of commercial FM talk shows. From there it's an easy matter to move them onto my iPod, where I can skip and rewind to my heart's content. Like TiVo, the RadioShark also lets you pause live broadcasts and pick them back up from where you left off.

Some radio programs offer podcast versions of their shows. This is the best way to get recorded radio, because someone else has already done the recording for you, and you won't miss a show because you forget to record it. (See "What Are Podcasts and How Do I Listen to Them?" on page 36 to find out how to use podcasts.)

▶ How Can I Discover New Music Based on My Tastes?

Find music you're bound to like, based on your existing preferences

You already know what kind of music you like, but there's undoubtedly lots of music out there that you would love—if you only knew about it. Three services have done a great job of steering me to good music I might have otherwise missed.

The first is Liveplasma (liveplasma.com), a visual music "discovery engine." You enter the name of an artist and it displays related bands. By clicking on any of the bands, Liveplasma generates a map of related bands surrounding it. I thought I'd stump it by entering "Robert Crumb" (the cartoonist, who used to play tenor banjo in

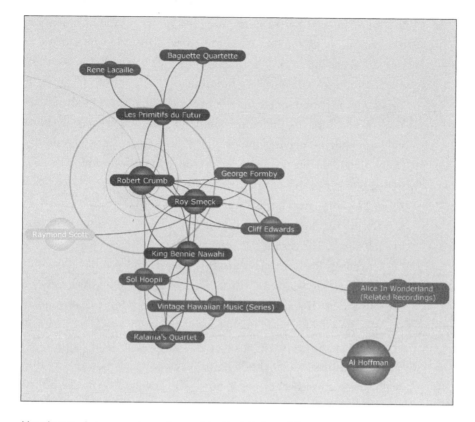

Liveplasma gives you a dynamic graphic of related musicians.

one of my favorite bands, The Cheap Suit Serenaders). I'll be darned if Liveplasma didn't display my very favorite musicians right next to his name, along with some I've never heard of.

How does it work? Liveplasma checks Amazon for people who have purchased music by the artist you enter, and then looks at what else those people have bought. Liveplasma is also terrific at finding movies based on other movies you like.

Last.fm is one of two web-based "radio killers" that do an amazing job of discovering music you like and playing it on your computer. It's free, and you can listen to music on the Web site (last.fm), in a small player or in iTunes or another media player. After you listen to a lot of songs, Last.fm starts to figure out what kind of music you like, and it hooks you up to other users who like the same music as you do (Last.fm calls them neighbors). You can listen to their playlists and start discovering new music.

Pandora (pandora.com) is the other music discovery site I like. You start by entering the name of a band. Pandora creates a "channel" and begins playing music that has similar "music genome" traits. Pandora's magic ju-ju comes from a bunch of employees paid to listen to songs and assign different attributes (or "genes") to each song. The company claims to have cataloged over 10,000 artists so far, classifying the melodies, rhythms, harmonies, lyrics, and so on, of each songs. The results are remarkable.

The songs Pandora plays are full length, and you have a choice of getting a free version (with advertising) or an ad-free version for $36 a year. If a song starts playing that you don't like, you can tell Pandora to never play that song or artist again, and it will remember your preference. Liveplasma, Last.fm, and Pandora let you click a link to buy the song or album, which is one way they make their money—they get a cut of the revenue from the online retailer.

▶ How Can I Automatically Add the Artist, Title, and Album Information to MP3 Files?

Use a free online database to find complete album information for your MP3 collection

When you insert an audio CD into your computer and launch iTunes, it takes a look at certain characteristics of the track (such as song length) and sends this information to GraceNote, an online database. GraceNote processes this data and tries to find a matching audio CD. If it does, iTunes adds the artist, song title, and album information to each song. That way, when you rip the songs to MP3, this information (called metadata) will be included in the song files. But if you've ever inserted a CD that you burned yourself from a bunch of other CDs, GraceNote won't be able to provide any metadata, because it's likely that you are the only person on the planet with that particular mix of songs on a CD.

There are a lot of other reasons why songs in your iTunes directory might show up as generic "Track 01," "Track 02," and so on. It could be that you ripped a CD while your computer wasn't connected to the Net, or maybe you have an obscure CD that GraceNote has never heard about. One way to correct this is to listen to each song and enter the metadata by hand. Depending on how many songs you need to update, that could take a long time. Also, you might not be able to figure out the artist, title, or album by listening to the song.

MusicBrainz (musicbrainz.org) is a user-maintained database that attempts to match metadata to songs by looking at the "audio fingerprint" of a song. Just as every person has a unique set of fingerprints, every song file has qualities that can be expressed as a unique, short string of data. MusicBrainz uses a fingerprinting technique called TRM, and has developed several free applications called "taggers" that can scan your iTunes database and not only fill in missing metadata from your files, but fix incorrect metadata as well. If you're on a PC, try Picard. For Mac, get a copy of iEatBrainz! Both applications are available for download from the MusicBrainz site.

▶ How Can I Easily Trade CDs?

Swap CDs with other people, and automatically compensate the artist

The recorded music industry doesn't care for used CD stores because people buy CDs from these places (without a penny going to the record company or artist), convert them to MP3s, and resell the originals to the same store. The industry may have a point, but there's not a lot they can do about it. Now the record companies have something bigger to worry about: la la (lala.com), a site that lets people trade CDs for $1 plus 75¢ shipping. It works like this: After you sign up with la la, they'll send you a packet of postage-included mailers. List the CDs in your collection that you're willing to trade. When someone wants something in your list, la la notifies you. Put the CD (without the case) in the envelope and send it. When the person who requested your CD informs la la that the CD has arrived and is playable, la la will issue you a credit, good for any CD that other la la members are offering.

It's fair to guess that most CDs in the la la network are quickly ripped to MP3s and re-listed. Does this seem unfair to the poor artist who created the music? Yes, but la la has an answer for that—it says it pays artists 20¢ for each CD traded in the network.

▶ Is There a Cheaper Way to Get Music Than iTunes?

Buy online music at bargain prices

A song on iTunes cost 99¢. That's not a bad price, but I rarely, if ever, buy songs from iTunes. That's because Apple uses copy protection to limit the number of devices you can play your purchased songs on. That's bad for the user. I can't tell you how many times I've lost access to copy-protected songs because a hard drive went bad, or I accidentally deleted them. It's money flushed down the drain. With a CD, I can make as many backups as I want for pennies a disc.

Fortunately, there are a number of great services online that sell unlocked music, so you can enjoy it on any CD player or MP3 player. Here are three popular ones:

eMusic (eMusic.com): For $10 a month, you can download up to 30 songs from eMusic's catalog of over 1.4 million titles. You won't find current Top 40 singles for sale here, but you will find countless back catalog treasures, such as Johnny Cash's *Complete Sun Singles*. Every imaginable genre is included here, and eMusic's on-staff experts do a great job of guiding you to music you might be interested in. At 33¢ per song, it's a fantastic bargain.

Half.com: My favorite place to buy used CDs, games, books, and DVDs online. Great deals abound. For example, last time I checked, a CD of *Let It Bleed* by The Rolling Stones was available for $6. Add $2.69 for media mail shipping to the prices you see when searching for music. I imagine a lot of people buy CDs here, convert them to MP3s, and sell them right back the next day on Half.com, making the total cost $2.69 per CD.

AllofMP3 (allofmp3.com): Charging around 9¢ per song, this Russian Web site containing all the latest and most popular songs seems almost too good to be true. The record industry in the United States has tried in vain to shut down the site, calling the Moscow-based company an "open and notorious" CD pirate, but so far the site remains in operation, complete with a page of legal gobbledygook explaining why the site is not in violation of Russian copyright laws. If the record industry is right, using the site would be illegal. I wouldn't risk it. I haven't tried AllofMP3 myself, but I know of several people who have and say that they've had an excellent experience with it. The MP3s are high quality and, best of all, have no copy protection. Most of the people I know who shop at AllofMP3 use a "single-use credit card number" (see page 120 on how to use these for online purchases), which frees them from the worry of anyone stealing their regular credit card number. In late 2006, Visa announced that it would no longer accept transactions with AllofMP3.

VIDEO AND MOVIES

▶ What Are the Differences Between the iTunes and Amazon Video Download Stores?

Buying and watching videos online is easy, but the choices are limited

First there were video rental stores, which gave you the freedom to choose what you wanted to watch and when. Then came Netflix (netflix.com), which allowed you to rent movies without leaving your house and is one of my favorite ways to spend $20 a month (Mac users should check out the $15 Netflix Freak application, which lets you manage your Netflix queue and do other nifty stuff to improve your experience: thelittleappfactory.com). Recently, Apple and Amazon have taken things to the next level by offering

TV shows and movies you can order and start watching within minutes. (Google briefly flirted with selling videos, but backed out in late 2006.) Both services are slick, and the inventory of material is sure to grow with time.

The problem with these services is the way they encode the videos to prevent you from copying them. Millions of people are already accustomed to the idea of downloading movies using BitTorrent (for more about using BitTorrent to download large files, go to page 169). The selection of movies available on BitTorrent sites is vast and, while it is illegal to download these unauthorized copies, the format is convenient to the user because they can be viewed on computers and iPods, or burned to DVD for TV viewing. On the other hand, the movies and TV shows sold via Apple's iTunes Store and Amazon's Unbox service are expensive (even compared to Blockbuster and Netflix) and the Digital Rights Management embedded in the files makes them impossible to watch on different kinds of players without the express permission of the service you bought them from. With that in mind, here's how the services work:

Amazon's Unbox offers a fair variety of contemporary and classic TV shows, as well as recent movies. It's easy to use, and the ordering process is straightforward, once you register and download the software.

The service requires a PC (it's not available for the Mac). To download and watch a DVD-quality movie or TV show, you first need to download and install Amazon's Unbox video player.

How to buy and watch Unbox videos:

1. When the Unbox player launches on your computer, click the "Shop" link at the top of the window. That will launch a Web browser for the Unbox video store.

2. Search or browse for a program that interests you. To help you choose, you can watch a trailer or preview before paying. TV shows are $1.99, but movies are much more, ranging from $9.77 (*Spiderman 2*) to $19.62 (*V for Vendetta*). The older the movie, the less expensive it seems to be. You can also "rent" a

movie for between $1.99 and $3.99. When you rent a movie, you have 30 days to view the movie, but once you start watching it, you have just 24 hours before it self-destructs.

3. Once you find a movie you like, click the "Buy now with 1-Click." A little box will pop up letting you know that your purchased program has started to download. You will be able to start watching before the download is complete.

Unbox allows you to watch programs you purchased on two computers. If you want to watch it on a third computer, you must buy another copy.

The iTunes Store, as you might expect, has the slickest interface for ordering movies and television shows. Because of Apple's close ties with the Walt Disney Company, it offers plenty of content from ABC, Pixar, and Disney. Movies cost between $9.99 and $14.99. At those prices, I'm willing to wait a couple of days for Netflix to deliver a DVD or, if I'm really in a hurry, drive to the local video store. However, I would definitely consider using the "Gift this Movie" option, which lets you buy a movie for someone else to download.

How to buy and watch iTunes videos:

1. Launch the iTunes application and click the "iTunes Store" link on the left.

2. Click "Movies" or "TV Shows" and browse the offerings.

3. You can watch a short preview or trailer by clicking the "View Trailer" button for movies, or by double-clicking the name of the television program in the episode list.

4. When you find a video you want to buy, click the "Buy Episode" or "Buy Movie" button. The file will download to your hard drive. You can then watch the video on your computer or your iPod. You can also watch it on your television set by getting a miniplug-to-RCA cable to connect the computer's headphone jack to the TV set's audio input and an S-video, VGA, or DVI cable to connect between your computer's video output and TV set's video input. One other option is to get Apple's iPod AV cable to connect your

iPod to your TV set and watch the programs stored on your iPod. Finally, you can watch the programs you buy via Apple's $299 wireless content streaming device called Apple TV.

▶What Are Some Other Ways to Download Videos on My Computer?

iTunes, Amazon, and Google aren't the only ways to get videos on your computer

In recent years, computers have become powerful enough, and Internet connections have become fast enough, to make downloading and watching videos on your computer a relatively hassle-free experience. There's enough free and pay video online to keep your computer busy all day and night downloading it. Where are some good places to find it? Let me count the ways:

Video podcasts. The best way to check out the dozens of free video podcasts is by using the iTunes Podcast directory (see page 36 for more about podcasts). They're all free, and some of them, like Rocketboom—a daily look at the best of the Web—have excellent production values. I also like Vintage ToonCast, which runs old cartoons

Free Mac media player with full-screen mode

NicePlayer (niceplayer.sourceforge.com) is a freeware alternative to the Apple QuickTime player. NicePlayer has some great features, such as a fully resizable viewing window, a really sweet user interface, and support for the Mac's FrontRow remote control. It also supports a number of plug-ins, such as the XinePlayer Plug-In, which allows it to open many popular video formats and supports DVD playback and DVD menus. It also adds a very useful "Save to Disk" feature.

that have fallen out of copyright, and Rolling R's, a Spanish-language tutorial.

Once you download a video podcast episode, you can watch it using the built-in video viewer or copy it over to your iPod.

Democracy (getdemocracy.com). This free "Internet TV platform" is a beautifully designed application that, like iTunes, lets you subscribe to different video "channels." It's available for Windows, Mac, and Linux, and saves shows on your computer so you can watch them at your leisure—kind of like TiVo for Internet video. There are plenty of great, independently produced videos available online and, as more people start making and distributing their videos over the Internet, applications like Democracy are going to become quite popular.

You can use Democracy to automatically grab new shows as they appear online. Here's how (see also page 166):

Once you've installed Democracy, go to tvRSS (tvrss.net/search). It's a search engine that provides RSS feeds of TV shows available online as BitTorrent files (for more about RSS, see page 27, and for more about BitTorrent, see page 169). When you do a search for *The Daily Show* on tvRSS, individual episodes available for download are listed along with the familiar RSS subscribe icon. Right-click the RSS icon to copy the feed URL (Cmd-click on the Mac) and go to Feedburner (feedburner.com). If you're not a member, register. On the front page, paste in the show URL, check the "I am a podcaster!" button, and burn the feed. You'll now have the feed address in a form you can use.

Back in Democracy, choose "Add Channel" from the "Channels" menu. Paste in your Feedburner feed and you're done. Now, whenever a new episode of *The Daily Show* gets posted to a BitTorrent site, your Democracy player will automatically record it (assuming you have the player running on your computer).

Be mindful of the fact that, while large numbers of TV shows are showing up online legitimately (their networks are posting them), others are there illegally. So, you may be breaking the law in downloading certain programs. Just because you find it online doesn't mean that its owners intended it to be there.

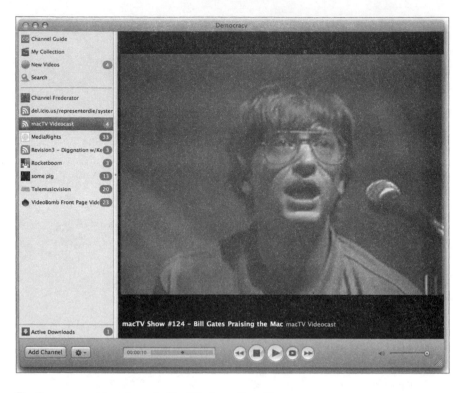

The Democracy video player is like TiVo for online video.

Like any DVR (Digital Video Recorder), Democracy deletes "expired" shows after a certain number of days. The default is six days. To change it (from three hours to "Never") go to the "Disk Space" tab under "Preferences."

Vongo (vongo.com). For $10 a month, this online video subscription service has about 1,000 movies that you can save to your computer and watch using Microsoft's Windows Media Player on your computer or portable video player (but not the iPod, because Apple has thus far refused to let other media companies sell content that uses Apple's copyright protection technology). It's important to note that Vongo is a subscription service—you are free to download and watch as many movies as you want, but if you stop paying the $10 monthly fee, all the content you've downloaded will lock up until you pay the $10 monthly ransom—er, subscription fee—to unlock it again.

AOL In2TV (aol.com/in2tv). Like Vongo, AOL's In2TV is for Windows users only. Unlike with Vongo, all the shows on In2TV are free. In the mood for watching old episodes of *Welcome Back, Kotter, Wonder Woman, Babylon 5,* or *La Femme Nikita?* You've come to the right place. In2TV does not allow you to download movies to your computer. Instead, they are "streamed" to your computer in an unsaveable format. You can choose from six different channels, including comedy, drama, vintage, and action.

Torrent Episode Downloader. Ted, the Torrent Episode Downloader (ted.nu), was created by two guys from Europe who couldn't stand the six-month lag between the time that shows are released in the U.S. and when they appear on TV in Europe. It's basically like an Internet-based TiVo. This free program lets you enter the RSS addresses of your favorite TV series (get them here: ted.nu/wiki/index.php/Supported_torrent_sites) and will automatically tell your BitTorrent application to download them for you. Make sure to use this to download only those TV shows you are legally entitled to.

The Internet Archive (archive.org). The Internet Archive is a nonprofit foundation with a vast collection of historical digital content that's either in the public domain or licensed as a Creative Commons work. Its movies section (archive.org/details/moviesandfilms) contains hundreds of feature films, propaganda films, industrial films, documentaries, and cartoons. The most popular movie on the archive is George Romero's 1968 classic horror film *Night of the Living Dead*, a personal favorite. Unsurprisingly, *Sex Madness*, a 1938 exploitation film "complete with wild parties, sex out of wedlock, lesbianism, etc." is one of the other top downloads. Other can't-miss picks: Charlie Chaplin and other Silent era gems, and the wonderful Prelinger Archives (archive.org/details/prelinger), which include 2,000 educational, corporate, and amateur films from the 1920s through 1987.

▶ What's the Best Movie Review Site?

Metacritic tells you what all the top critics are saying about a movie

When I'm in the mood to see a movie, my first stop is Metacritic (metacritic.com). Launched in 2001 by a trio of lawyer friends, Metacritic gives movies ratings between 1 and 100, based on the average of reviews from thirty well-respected national newspaper and magazine critics.

One excellent aspect of Metacritic's scores is that they are weighted—reviews by critics who have a habit of giving a thumbs-up to every movie they see don't get counted as heavily in the average score as critics who, on the whole, give a more balanced range of reviews. The editors of Metacritic don't reveal exactly what their weighting algorithm is, but its results are spot-on. The interface is easy to use, and you can sort movies by score or name. There's also a

Easy online media format conversions

We all know what a magnificent hassle it can be to download a video, audio, or other data file, and then not have the right (or right version) player/reader you need to open it. The solution couldn't be simpler: get thee to Media Convert (media-convert.com/convert/index.php). This Web-based file conversion service will accept uploaded files from your computer or you can point it to a file online. Then you choose the output type you desire, and the site chitty-chitty bang-bangs away, magically converting the ones and zeros, until out pops the file in a format you can handle. Works with everything from typical office document types (Wordpro, Database, Presentation) to dozens of music and video formats, to file archiving types, even to special formats used in mobile phone media files. This is one of those tools you wonder how you ever lived without.

box with the current and all-time high (and low) scores. (The all-time low score at this writing is *Bio-Dome*, starring Pauly Shore, which earned a score of 1, and the all-time high score is *The Godfather*, the only movie listed on Metacritic with a perfect score of 100).

In recent years, Metacritic has successfully applied its secret sauce to DVDs, music, games, books, and TV.

▶ How Can I Use BitTorrent to Download Large Files?

This file-trading technology shares the load of data transfer among all the participants to speed up the process

In the olden days, rural villages kept communal pastures where sheep belonging to the villagers were allowed to graze. It seemed like a good idea, but the pastures were often depleted because the individual interests of the sheep owners ran counter to the common good. Each farmer tried to fatten his sheep on the grass before the other sheep (owned by farmers operating under the same logic) ate all of it. The end result: a barren commons that couldn't support anyone's sheep.

This phenomenon, known as "The Tragedy of the Commons," occurs in many different forms, including the Internet. Here's an example: some guy videotapes his skateboard-riding dog and uploads it to his Web site. It's funny, so people who download it first email their friends to let them know about it. Very soon, the computer that hosts the file is overloaded with requests, and downloads slow to a crawl. What used to take a couple of minutes to download now takes half an hour. If the downloads increase even more, the computer's connection can become completely clogged, preventing anyone from seeing the video.

BitTorrent was designed to beat "The Tragedy of the Commons." It's a method of sharing files that actually makes the files more, not less, accessible, in proportion to the number of people downloading them. How does it work? It makes everyone's computer pitch in on the job of sharing the files. While your BitTorrent application is downloading the skateboarding dog video, it is simultaneously uploading the part you've downloaded so far to other users. It's as if the sheep on the commons were able to make grass as fast as they can eat it. More sheep, more grass = more users, more bandwidth.

BitTorrent is simple to use. First, download a BitTorrent client, which will allow you to download content in the BitTorrent format. My favorite client for Mac is Transmission (transmission.mok.org), and my favorite for Windows is μTorrent (utorrent.com). Next, visit bittorrent.com and use the search function at the site to find content to download. There are plenty of other Torrent search sites online as well, and many of them point to files of copyrighted movies, music, and software. It's not a good idea to use BitTorrent to download copyrighted material. Aside from the ethical issues, using BitTorrent is not anonymous, and rights holders to movies have successfully subpoenaed Internet service providers into revealing the names of people suspected of sharing movies using BitTorrent. In 2005, a 38-year-old Hong Kong man was thrown in the slammer for distributing three movies—*Daredevil*, *Red Planet*, and *Miss Congeniality*—using BitTorrent.

Watch Windows Media videos on a Mac

In 2006, Microsoft announced that it would no longer support a Windows Media Player for Macs. That would be bad news for Mac users, because a large percentage of online videos are WMVs (the filename extension for a Windows Media Video).

Luckily, there's a free QuickTime component made by Flip4Mac that lets you play WMV files right in your QuickTime Player.

Download it here: flip4mac.com/jump_microsoft.htm.

Instant Handbrake converts DVDs you've purchased into iPod- and PSP-compatible videos.

How Can I Watch Videos on My iPod or PSP?

Use free and inexpensive applications to convert DVDs and online videos for handheld viewing

My video iPod has made me a much healthier person. That's because having one makes it more bearable to use the exercise equipment at the gym. I would feel much too guilty sitting on the couch at home watching a movie in the middle of the day, but watching a movie on my iPod while I climb the Stairmaster takes no toll on my conscience.

>How to get a DVD onto your iPod

1. (See above.) On a Macintosh, converting DVDs to a format compatible with the iPod is easy. You need to get a program called Instant Handbrake, which you can download for free from handbrake.mok.org/?page_id=26. To use it, insert a DVD into your computer's DVD drive and start Instant Handbrake.

Select the videos with long du-ration times using Instant Handbrake.

Select DVD Features

	Title	Duration	Size (Converted)
☑	Title 1	1 hour 23 mins	
☐	Title 6	41 seconds	
☐	Title 9	2 mins 56 secs	
☐	Title 10	38 mins 55 secs	

Instant HandBrake

Settings

Save converted files to: Movies

File format: iPod 5G (H.264)

Picture format: Fullscreen

Preferred audio: English

Preferred subtitles: None

Open another DVD...   Convert

When the application opens, click the "DVD Drive" radio button and then click "Continue."

2. (See above.) It might take a minute or so for Instant Handbrake to scan all the files on the DVD, but when it's finished, you can take a look at the available files from the "Title" pull-down menu. Check the files you want to convert. What I do is look for the file with the longest running length, because it is probably the file that contains the feature presentation.

ImTOO DVD to iPod Converter creates iPod-ready videos from your DVDs.

Modify the settings in the "Settings" portion, if needed, and click "Convert."

You can see how long it is going to take for Instant HandBrake to rip your file by looking at the information line at the bottom of the application window. When it's finished, all you have to do is drag the file from the folder you selected into iTunes. From there, you can copy the file to your iPod.

On a Windows computer, the best way to convert DVDs to iPod is with a $29 program called ImTOO DVD to iPod Converter (imtoo .com).

1. (See above.) To use the application, insert your DVD into the drive, then click the "DVD" button in the bottom left corner to select the drive.

2. (See page 174.) ImToo DVD to iPod Converter has many more options than Instant HandBrake, but you don't have to worry

Right-click the file you want to convert and choose "Rip Selected" from the menu.

about them. Once you've selected the drive and the DVD file or folder you want to convert, right-click the filename and choose "Rip Selected" from the drop-down menu. When the file has been converted, drag it into iTunes.

>Here's how to move a downloaded video to your iPod

I also download a lot of videos in different file formats (mpg, mov, avi, etc.) for watching on my iPod. On the Macintosh, my utility of choice is iSquint (isquint.org), a free program that quickly converts videos in almost any file format into the iPod format. To use it, all you have to do is open the program, drag as many video files into the application window as you'd like to covert, and click the "Start" button.

There are a number of options available on iSquint. You can tweak the quality of the converted video using the slider bar in the

Free iPod Video Converter for Windows does just what its name suggests.

top right corner of iSquint's window. I've found that "Standard" quality does a fine job. When I experimented by saving a file at "High" and "Go Nuts" quality, the resulting file was many times larger than a file converted at standard quality. (The resulting video looked a bit better, but I'll stick with the "Standard" setting.)

"Optimize for TV" is good if you plan to watch the videos on a large screen. But if you plan on watching them on your iPod, stick with the "Optimize for iPod" setting. If you want the file size to be as small as possible, then select "H.264 Encoding." (The downside is that it will take much longer to convert the files.)

If you select "Add to iTunes," iSquint will copy the file to iTunes

*Adjust video and audio quality
in the Settings box.*

automatically, so you don't have to drag the converted file into the iTunes application.

The "Advanced" button gives you access to a number of features that let you crop the window size, change the video bit rate and the frame rate, deinterlace the video, and adjust the audio settings. Again, I think iSquint's default settings are fine for most purposes. You can play the resulting file on an iPod.

For Windows users, a good free converter program is Free iPod Video Converter (ipod-video-converter.org). Based on the "wizard" format of task accomplishment, the application holds your hand and takes you step-by-step through the process of converting a down-loaded video to watch on your iPod (see page 175).

As you step through the procedure, you can change to settings or accept the default values (see above).

After your files have been converted, you can copy them into iTunes and onto your iPod.

>Download a video to your PSP

Mac: PSPWare (nullriver.com/index/products/pspware) is an elegant Mac utility for the PSP. It syncs music, movies, and photos between your Mac and your PSP. Just drag a movie file (it accepts mov, mpg, avi, wmv, vob, flc, dv, and QuickTime plug-ins) from your Mac into the PSPWare's window and it will convert the file and load it on your PSP. The trial version limits the number of files you can sync, but the $15 version unlocks that limitation. For windows, try the free Movkit PSP Video Converter (movkit.com).

▶ How Can I Watch YouTube Videos on My iPod?

Liberate YouTube videos from the browser

YouTube's bottomless barrel of videos are fun to watch, but you can't save them to your hard drive for offline viewing. That's a shame, because I like to save the funny animal ones to show my kids. A nifty $5 program called PodTube, available at Djodjodesign (djodjodesign.free.fr) solves the problem for Mac users. Use Safari to open YouTube.com and go to the video you want to watch. Launch PodTube and click "get video." It will convert the video from the Flash format to an MP4 file, copy it to your desktop and, if you have the "Add to iTunes" box checked, add it to iTunes (see sidebar, right).

Firefox users can install the VideoDownloader extension (addons.mozilla.org/firefox/2390/), which adds an icon on the browser's status bar that lets them download videos from over sixty different video sites.

If you're willing to spend $10 for a more powerful application, get a copy of TubeSock (stinkbot.com/Tubesock), which lets you save YouTube videos in a variety of formats including Sony's PSP. You can also extract the audio portion only, and save it as an MP3 file (this is

TubeSock: Rip. Mix. Copy to iPod.

http://www.youtube.com/watch?v=70wOzCkWN5g   Preview

Save   Video for PSP (MP4) ↕   Add to Movies... ↕

TubeSock lets you save YouTube videos to your Mac or iPod.

great for extracting songs from music videos). Unlike PodTube, Tube-Sock doesn't require the use of Safari, or any browser for that matter. To download and convert a video with TubeSock, you enter the URL of the YouTube video into the TubeSock application and click "Save" (see above).

▶▶ GAMES

▶ How Can I Play Classic Text Adventures on My Computer?

Go "old skool" with these retro-game sites

Most computer games don't age well. Even five-year-old games, which may still be fun to play, look quaint. But there's an exception: text adventure games, which are stories where you decide what happens next.

Text adventure games lack graphics or sound, but because they rely on your imagination and puzzle-solving ability, they remain as fun and as challenging as they were on the day they were released.

The first text adventure games were written by mainframe computer programmers in the early 1970s. When I worked as a Silicon Valley engineer at Memorex in the mid-1980s, so many people in the office were playing a game called Colossal Cave Adventure (written in 1976 by Willie Crowther) that the system administrator had to put a lock on the game so people couldn't play it until after 5 PM. (As a result, many spouses started complaining to the managers that they were keeping their employees at work too late into the evening.)

Colossal Cave Adventure was a Dungeons and Dragons like fantasy game filled with monsters, magic, and wizards. You can download a freeware version for the Mac at lobotomo.com/products/Adventure/, and a Windows version at rickadams.org/adventure/e_downloads.html.

When personal computers started taking off in the mid-80s, a company called Infocom started publishing text adventures. One of its most popular titles was The Hitchhiker's Guide to the Galaxy, a text adventure that followed Douglas Adam's novels of the same name. It was a smash hit, selling 350,000 copies.

Today, you can play many of the Infocom games for free, either by downloading the games or playing them online. The Zork trilogy (based on Colossal Cave Adventure) is available for Mac or Windows at infocom-if.org/downloads/downloads.html. (See page 180.)

The BBC has an excellent Web-based version of the original Hitchhiker's Guide to the Galaxy (bbc.co.uk/radio4/hitchhikers/game.shtml) that has some nice features, such as a compass you can click to move in a certain direction, and a graphical inventory list. You can enter an action and click an inventory item to complete a command.

In the 1990s, Activision, which acquired Infocom, released a CD with 30 popular Infocom text adventures, called *Masterpieces of Infocom*. The CD is out of print, but you can often find used copies for sale online. Try searching AuctionSHARK (auctionshark.com) for a copy. Most Mac users don't realize that their computers come with a free text adventure, hidden on the hard drive, called Dunnet

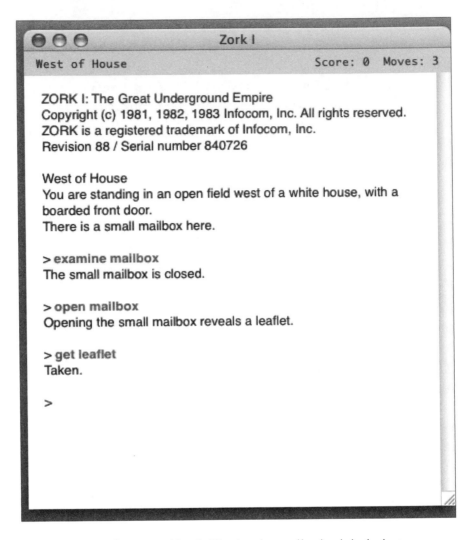

More than twenty-five years old and still going strong—the classic text adventure Zork is still fun to play.

on my Mac. To run it, open a terminal window (it's in the "Applications" → "Utilities" folder) and enter emacs -batch -l dunnet.

The best thing about text adventure games is that they live on. Today, the more common term for the genre is "interactive fiction," and you can download and play plenty of excellent games written by dedicated amateurs. A good place to start is Microheaven (microheaven.com), which has links to award-winning interactive fiction titles and the software you need to play them. I highly recommend The Edifice, a text adventure in which you get to play a prehistoric man who encounters a giant stone monolith. (Sound familiar?) The Edifice won first place in the rec.arts.int-fiction Usenet group competition in 1997, as well as taking home the "Best Puzzles" and "Best Individual Puzzle" prize at the Xyzzy Awards that year.

>A short primer on playing text adventures

The delight of text adventures, compared with so many of today's games, is that you can play them without being skilled at manipulating all the buttons on a controller or having to learn jargon and complicated rules. To play a text adventure, you simply type in commands, such as "climb stairs," "pick up key," "eat apple," and so on. Learning certain conventions and shortcuts will make playing text adventures even more enjoyable. The text adventure's parser (the part of the program that analyzes the sentences you enter) is designed to look for verbs followed by nouns, so your sentences should take the form of "kick door" or "open window." (Think of the way the Incredible Hulk would speak, and enter your text like he would, e.g., "Smash puny elf.") If you want to travel in a particular direction, you can just enter "n," "s," "e," "w," "u," or "d" without having to enter the entire word. To find out what is in the location you happen to be in, enter "look." To get a closer look at an object, enter "look at sword" (or whatever item you are interested in). To take something, enter "pick up sword." To grab everything, enter "take all."

▶**How Can I Play Old DOS Games on My Computer?**

Play classic shareware games from the old days on your Windows computer

I'll admit it—I'm old school, especially when it comes to computer games. I'm more interested in great gameplay than I am in fancy 3-D graphics and realistic sound effects. That's why I keep going back to DOS Games (dosgames.com), a collection of over 400 computer games made for DOS, the predecessor to Microsoft Windows. I've kept myself busy for hours slaying trolls and other beasts in Dark Woods 2, a game that uses ASCII characters like smiley faces, exclamation points, and asterisks to represent monsters and treasures. Another fun challenge is Heavy Water Jogger, a game from 1992 that puts you in the role of owner of the "Three-Miles-Inland" nuclear power plant. To your horror, you discover that your lead

Play retro arcade games, like Space Invaders, on your computer

When I need to take a short break from work, I like to save the planet by picking off a few aliens. I'm talking about Space Invaders, that classic arcade game that ate my high school summer job paycheck, one quarter at a time, in 1979. I'm just as bad at the game now as I was over 25 years ago, which is probably why it's still fun to play—I'm able to fool myself into thinking I'll get better with more practice. Today, I don't have to spend any quarters to play Space Invaders. It just takes a $3,000 computer and a $39-a-month high-speed internet connection to play this and many other retro arcade games, including Pac Man, Asteroids, Frogger, and Q-Bert at classicgaming.cc/classics. Over at 80smusiclyrics.com/games.shtml you can play Donkey Kong, Simon, Tetris, Moon Patrol, Duck Hunt, and even Pong, if you want to get really old school about it.

technician has gone crazy and has pushed the self-destruct button. You have just thirty minutes to get into the control room and prevent a deadly meltdown. Of course, the power plant's hallways are populated by menacing robots that have been reprogrammed to hunt you down and kill you, which makes your job all the more difficult.

Like all the other games here, the graphics are crude and the sound effects and music are laughably primitive. But don't let that dissuade you from browsing the archives. There are some gems here.

If you're on a Mac, grab a copy of DOSBox (dosbox .sourceforge.net), a swell program that lets you emulate an old-timey DOS computer inside a Macintosh window. (DOSBox also comes in versions that run on Windows and Linux.) To use DOSBox, create a folder in your Home folder (the one that has your name and has the icon of a little house) called "dosgames." Then launch DOSBox and enter `mount c ~/dosgames`. Then enter `C:`

You can then use the `dir` command to list the games in the "dosgames" folder. To navigate into a subfolder, enter `cd foldername` where `foldername` is the name of the folder you want to look at. To move back up a directory, enter `cd\`. (Aren't you glad graphical user interfaces are standard today?) To play a game, just enter the name (it'll have the filetype ".exe") and press "Return."

MacMAME is another wildly popular Macintosh-based emulator that plays all kinds of classic arcade games (MAME stands for Multi-Arcade Machine Emulator). To get started, download a copy of MacMAME from macmame.org and read the guide at macmame.org/help.html. The challenge is finding the game file to play on MacMAME. They're called ROM files, and the sites that host the questionably legal files (they are often copyrighted) come and go. Search Google for "macmame roms" for the latest sites that host ROM files.

DEEPER

Sending your Windows computer back in time. Most people complain that their computer isn't fast enough, but for people who play DOS games, today's PCs are often too fast. When you try to play one of these old games in Window's DOS emulator, the action whizzes by in a blur. A $15 utility called Mo'Slo (hpaa.com/moslo/) will let you run DOS games at the speeds they were intended to be played. You can download a free evaluation copy, too.

▶ What Are Massive Multiplayer Online Role-Playing Games (MMORPGS) and How Can I Play?

Try a free version of this exciting new kind of online role-playing game to see if you enjoy it

It's a mouthful of marbles, but "MMORPGs," short for "Massively Multiplayer Online Role-Playing Games," are some of the fastest-growing and most fascinating types of computer-based gaming. As the name implies, these are games where you control an on-line character that interacts with other players' characters and computer-generated characters, either cooperating or competing (or some devilish combination of the two) to meet stated game goals. The world in which your character and others play is usually sword and sorcery, fantasy-based (think: Dungeons & Dragons) or galaxy-spanning space operas (think *Star Wars*), though there are others (think *The Matrix* and Marvel comics). Two of the most popular MMORPGs (or sometimes MMOs for short) are the venerable World of Warcraft (worldofwarcraft.com) and EverQuest (everquest.com). (The addictive nature of MMORPGs—and some mental health professionals argue that it's an actual addiction—has even spawned the pejorative term EverCrack.) To play these and other commercial titles, you have to purchase special game software and pay a monthly subscription fee (paying with your mortal soul is optional). To download and play some free MMORPGs to get you started (you know what they say about the first one), search on "List of free MMORPGs" at wikipedia.org. Cut "free" from your search string to see a list of the most popular commercial MMORPGs.

>House of Uster's Beginner's Guide to Azeroth, by Coriakin

Hail! I'm Coriakin, Warlock extraordinaire and Officer of the House of Uster. My guild master, Bluster, and I were hiking through Westfall the other night, hoping to catch some Horde sneaking into Darkshire. We had just finished running some clueless lowbies through the Deadmines, and were laughing about the difficulties we'd encountered as newbies to Azeroth. "Fluster," cackled Bluster,

DEEPER

Expert advice for WoW newbies. Joining MMORPG can be a daunting task for a newbie. It helps if you can find a friendly local to give you the lay of the land and explain the customs and etiquette you'll need to succeed in a strange new world. I asked a seasoned World of Warcraft veteran, "Coriakin," to offer some tips for World of Warcraft beginners. The information he generously shares will save you countless hours of newbie anguish.

"thought you could tame Murlocks with First Aid!" "Uster," I cried, "didn't realize he had to train his pet bat until he was level 22!"

When we had calmed down enough to talk normally, Bluster suggested I put together some notes to help new guildmates take their first steps. I present them here for the edification of all brave new adventurers in the World of Warcraft. (See art above.)

1. **Take all the quests in the newbie zone.** Talk to everyone with a yellow exclamation point above their heads. These Non-Player Characters (NPCs) send you on short quests that teach game basics and will reward you with armor and weapons to help get you started.

   You can take more than one quest at a time, so do it! Two nearby quest-givers will often send you to the same place, so if you take both quests, you can optimize your travel time.

2. **Quest with other newbies.** I hope you didn't think that collecting those five wolf hides was tough, 'cause that's Murlock's play compared with what's ahead. You're gonna need some help to make your way in Azeroth, so start making friends early. Ask another newbie if they'd like to group. Quests go faster this way, and you're less likely to wind up in the graveyard. Stay in touch

with people you meet by adding them to your "Friends" list. A huge part of MMOs is interacting with other players, and newbie grouping is a great way to meet people. There's something about fighting through those first ten levels together that makes for strong bonding.

3. **Find your nearest city.** Everyone begins near one of the four "starter cities." Your questing will take you there before long, but there's nothing to stop a wide-eyed newbie like you from checking out the urban action. These big towns are where players congregate to hawk their wares, queue for Player-versus-Player (PvP) combat, and work the Auction House. . . .

4. **Love the auction house.** The main attraction of the starter cities is the Auction House. Players buy and sell all sorts of goods here. You'll find better gear at better prices than what you can buy from NPC vendors. And you can sell your loot for much more than you'd get from those same stingy vendors. The Auction House is your new best friend. It's the best way to make money, and you're gonna need every copper you can scrounge up. Did your first ten silver pieces seem like an accomplishment? Well, it takes one hundred of those to make one gold piece, and you'll need around one hundred of those to get your first mount. So start saving now and work that Auction House. Buy low and sell high. There are even mods (game-enhancing modifications, created by players) that can automatically scan the AH, track sales, and suggest pricing.

5. **Don't beg.** Nothing gets you put on someone's "Ignore" list faster than spamming the general chat channel with pleas for money and gear.

6. **Find a guild.** Guilds are groups of players who band together for camaraderie and support. They're essential for tackling the elaborate dungeons that await you at the higher levels, and can be a key component of PvP.

Your guild will have a major influence on your experience with the game, so take the time to find one you like. There are generally two types of guilds: Family-style and Über. Family-style guilds are smaller groups of closely knit players, most of whom may know each other in real life. Über guilds are large and less personal, but highly organized and very effective at PvP and dungeon-raiding. You'll likely find a friendly, casual attitude with the former, while the latter may be less personal and may require a commitment to a certain amount of play-time with the guild. Either way, be friendly and contribute what you can. Remember, it's a two-way street. A good guild will help out needy newbs like you with donations of weapons, bags, and maybe even cash.

To find a guild, talk to people in-game and check your server's forum on the official World of Warcraft message board. It won't take long to get a sense of a guild's reputation. Another way to find a guild is to ask your real-life friends. Millions of people play WoW, and there's a good chance you know someone who does. If you're a businessperson, WoW can even be a valuable networking tool. Warcraft is the new golf.

7. **Tame the gryphons and bats.** Azeroth is huge, so you'll need to learn the shortcuts for getting around. The Deeprun Tram and the Goblin Zeppelin are cheap options at low levels, but to really see the world, you'll need to learn the flight path network of gryphons, bats, hippogryphs, and wyverns.

Ask your guild leaders to take you on a flight path run. Scattered throughout the world are flight masters who control flying beasts that shuttle you to flight nodes in other parts of the world. But you can't fly to a new node until you've spoken in-person with the flight master there. You're far too low in level to get to those flight masters on your own. With a flight path run, the guild gets together and escorts the newbies to a bunch of nodes at a time. It's a fun ritual for guilds to get to know their new members.

There's a lot to learn, and many ways to get help, so don't hesitate to ask around. Remember to keep your chin up and your sword clean. Bail!

Coriakin is played by Jamey C. Shafer on the Firetree server. His blog is located at grandmassoupsack.wordpress.com.

One more excellent resource for newbies is WoWWiki (wowwiki.com), a wiki loaded with essential, hard-fought knowledge about the wonderful world of Azeroth. (See page 52 for more about wikis.)

▶ How Can I Play Parlor Games like Chess and Poker with Other People Online?

Get thee to games.yahoo.com, a popular online gaming portal and an excellent place for budding card sharks and Kasparovs

Yahoo! Games (games.yahoo.com) offers a one-stop shop for all sorts of online board, card, and arcade games. You have to register to play, but if you already have a Yahoo! account, you can log in using that. Besides the breadth of offerings, Yahoo! Games is a good place to look for opponents because it's so popular. At any given time, there can be hundreds of thousands of players on the site, so it's easy to log on, pull up a virtual chair, push back the brim of your ten-gallon hat, and join a rough-and-tumble game of Texas Hold'em. The Yahoo! site and other game portals usually have several different levels of game offerings. In-browser games (ones that load right into your browser, no download required) are usually free but are limited in terms of visuals, abilities to communicate with other players, game variants, etc. Pay versions of games usually involve a one-time charge and a download. You access the Net and the player pool from within the game software. Free trials of these pay games are almost always offered. One nice feature of Yahoo's service is that the Web page for each game includes ratings and user-reviews, so you can see the strengths and weaknesses of each offering. Besides chess and several flavors of poker, Yahoo! offers solitaire, spades, pinochle, backgammon, checkers, Battleshi . . . er . . . naval command, even Monopoly and other well-known board games. If, after playing dominoes with your new best friend Akbar from Jalalabad (and you do make fast friends at these gaming tables), you want to venture farther afield, the Open Directory Project maintains a good list of online cardtables and game boards at: dmoz.org/Games/.

▶ Is There a Netflix for Video Games?

Join one of the many Internet-based game rental services

Based on the success of Netflix (netflix.com), the online video rental service, a number of similar services have popped up to deliver DVD-based video games using the same model. There are slight differences in the features and fees, but they're all basically the same: you sign up, pay a monthly (or per rental) fee, get the game in a flat CD/DVD mailer, and return it in that mailer when you're done. Most of them have no return due date, but you can't get new games until you return the ones you've already got. One of the most popular services is GameFly

DEEPER

Online game rental. There are a number of other rental services that offer more variations on the same theme. For an updated list, go to FAD-MINE (fadmine.com) and click on their "Guide to Renting Video Games Online."

(gamefly.com). For $21.95 per month you can choose two games at a time from their very large selection of games for PlayStation 2, PS3, PSP, Xbox, Xbox 360, Wii and other platforms (but no PC or Mac games). When you return the two you have checked out, you can choose another two. They also offer a one-game-at-a-time membership for $14.95. GottaPlay (gottaplay.com) works the same way as GameFly. Their one-game service is $12.95, with a two-game membership for $20.95, and three games for $28.95. They carry games on all the popular console and portable game systems, and they also carry PSP movies. GameznFlix (gameznflix.com) offers the best deals, with a one-game $8.99 option and a three-game membership for $17.25 per month. They also rent DVDs, HD-DVDs, Blu-Ray DVDs, PSP movies, and audio books.

BOOKS

▶ How Can I Keep Track of All My Books and Other Media?

Maintain an online library catalog and never lose another book

I have thousands of books in my house. Some are on shelves, others are in boxes. I have a hard time keeping track of them. I can't remember which ones I've loaned to friends, or which ones I have duplicate copies of. I'd like to catalog them, but the idea of entering each one into a spreadsheet seems tedious.

The Web offers more than one way to create and maintain an online catalog of your book collection. The great thing about keeping an online library is that you can compare your lists of books with other people who share similar tastes, and learn about books, music, and movies you're sure to like. Here's a rundown of the best online book-cataloging tools:

LibraryThing (librarything.com). This service is very easy to use. To sign up, just enter a username and a password, and you're ready to go. To start adding books to your LibraryThing list, enter the ISBN number, or search for them by the title or author. Library-Thing automatically adds cover images, publication dates, and other data to your list, relieving you of the mind-numbing task of data entry. (If you've got a notebook computer and a wireless Internet connection, you can just walk over to your bookshelf and start entering titles. You'll build up your catalog surprisingly quickly that way.) The service is free for catalogs of less than 200 books. If you want to add more books that that, a yearly subscription costs $10, and a lifetime subscription costs $25 (If you think you've got more than two years to live, go for the lifetime option). If all LibraryThing did was maintain a list of your books online, it would be a waste of money. The cool part about it is that it's social software—by that I mean that it harnesses the power of other people's lists to make it worth your while to list your own books. For instance, you can find other people who have similar book collections to your own, and pore over their lists to see if they've got books you might want to buy.

Listal (listal.com). Similar to LibraryThing, but you can also add DVDs, music, and games collections to the database. It's easy to build up your catalog, especially if you do it by feeding it ISBN numbers. Like LibraryThing, you can tag books with any label you desire, then click on tags to see other books with those tags. When you join, you're asked to create a list of your interests so you can find other members who share your taste in media. Listal has groups you can join to discuss favorite authors, actors, or bands, and you can rate the things you own or mark them as "wanted" if you don't own them yet.

Delicious Library (delicious-monster.com) is a Mac-only standalone application that costs $40 (see page 192). While it's not as "social" as LibraryThing or Listal, it's got two things going for it. One, it's very easy to add books to the database—you can connect a video camera or Web camera to your computer and point it at the bar codes on your books, CDs, DVDs, and video games. The software will

Delicious Library helps you keep track of all your offline media.

pull all the information about the item from the Internet and add it to the database without you having to touch your keyboard. If you're really serious about it, you can buy Delicious Library's Bluetooth scanning device ($174.95) and start scanning your stuff all over the house. If the scanner is in range of the computer (Bluetooth's range is about 30 feet) it'll instantly add the item to the library. If not, it'll save up to 500 ISBNs and dump them onto your computer when you do get close enough to your computer.

The second great thing about Delicious Library is the gorgeous interface. It mimics the look of a real wood bookcase, with color images of your stuff all lined up neatly on the shelves. (If only your real bookshelves were this organized). As you'd expect from an application that costs $40, Delicious Monster comes with lots of nifty features. You can download your catalog to your iPod, for instance, or keep track of who has your copy of Bully for Playstation 2.

The first time you launch Delicious Library, it automatically scans your address book to find people who share your last name, adding them to your borrowers list (you can, of course, change the list of borrowers whenever you want). When you loan out a book or other item, drag the image of it onto the name of the borrower. Items you've checked out are marked with a diagonal yellow "Out" tag. It syncs with iCal to let you know when items are due. When they return the item, you can check the item in just as easily. Delicious Library also provides detailed reviews, recommendations for similar items, and one-click Amazon purchases.

How Can I Read Free eBooks on My Computer and Handheld Device?

Discover the joy of reading digital books with a handheld computer or compatible mobile phone

My Palm handheld computer is an insurance policy against boredom. Anytime I find myself standing in a long line, or sitting in the doctor's waiting room, I pull it out, select one of the 200 novels stored on it, and start reading.

Shutterbug Follies

Bee is a young woman who works at a one-hour photo-processing store called Mulberry Photos. She enjoys sneaking peeks at the photos that the people bring in, but her curiosity leads to big trouble in this excellent comic-noir thriller written and illustrated by Jason Little (beecomix.com).

You can buy a used handheld computer with the Palm operating system on eBay for under $50. Look for one with a color screen, with at least 320×320 pixels. Make sure to get a model with at least 16 MB of memory, too. (That's enough for at least a dozen novels. If you want to store a library's worth of books in your pocket, you'll need to get a handheld that accepts memory cards. A 512 MB card, which will hold hundreds of books, is cheap these days.)

I bought a Sony Clie T615C (which uses the Palm operating system) with a color 320×320 screen for about $75, used. They're going for less than $50 on eBay now. That's a great deal for a 16 MB device. The screen is about 2.5×2.5 inches and it's at least as legible as a computer screen, if not more. The characters are very sharp. This high resolution is key for reading—the kind of screen that comes with the Treo 600, for example, is no good for long texts (if you have a Treo 650 or later, you can use that as an ebook reader).

Once you get your Palm device, you'll need to download a reader. Go to eReader.com and download the free version of the eReader program.

The best place to buy ebooks is eReader.com, which sells ebooks for Palm and Windows handhelds. The selection is quite good, with most of the current and past bestsellers available. The prices are quite a bit less than what you'd pay for a print version. Best of all, there's no waiting for the book to show up in the mail—you get it the instant you pay for it. I've read a couple of dozen books this way, and have come to resent having to read paper books, which now seem too heavy to have to prop up in bed.

I also like to read free books: ones that have either fallen out of copyright or are being offered for free by authors and publishers. By far the best place to get free, public domain ebooks for your Palm and Windows handheld is Manybooks.net, with over 13,000 ebooks available for download in a variety of formats. The site does a wonderful job of presenting "Books of the Month," such as *The Trial*, by Franz Kafka, and *Typee*, by Herman Melville.

Science fiction readers can find plenty of excellent contemporary novels for Palm devices at the Baen Free Library (baen.com/library). You can download any of the novels here without fear of breaking the law because Baen Books, the publisher, is the one making them available. They have learned that giving away science fiction novels as ebooks is a great way to increase sales of the print versions.

My fellow Boing Boing editor, Cory Doctorow, is an award-winning science fiction novelist who has published three novels and a short story collection. You can buy all his books in stores and on-line, but Cory also makes the works available as free digital down-loads to read on your computer or handheld device or print out on your computer. Cory told me he receives a lot of email from U.S. sol-diers aboard ships en route to Iraq and Afghanistan. They can't bring many books with them, but they have Internet connections, so they've been downloading his books and sharing them with their ship-mates. For a list of Cory's works, visit his Web site, craphound.com. Cory also creates audio podcasts of his work, which you can subscribe to here: craphound.com/podcast.php.

Convert any text into an ebook for your iPod

If you don't mind reading on your iPod's small screen, you can easily turn your personal media player into an ebook reader with the iPod Book Creator (ambience.sk/ipod-ebook-creator). All you have to do is upload your would-be ebook as a text file into the site's free conversion program. It converts the material into the iPod-readable Notes format, even automatically dividing it into the appropriately sized files and linking them together in order so you only have to click to get to the next file in the sequence. Once the site has created your files, it offers them in a zipped archive, which you download, unzip, and toss into the "Notes" folder on your iPod. If you don't have enough reading material to keep you busy, they even provide a link to Project Guttenberg, where you can find thousands of free ebooks to convert.

▶ Where Can I Get Free Audiobooks?

Download spoken word audio to your MP3 player

Audiobooks are a nice way to pass the time while exercising, commuting, flying in a plane, or waiting to fall asleep. I enjoy getting audiobooks from Audible.com, but it's an expensive habit. An unabridged audiobook can cost upwards of $30.

Fortunately, there are lots of free and low-cost alternatives. Of course, the downside is that free audiobooks are based on public-domain books, so that means you won't be able to listen to books published after 1923 or so (there are a few exceptions). Most of the free audiobook sites use human narrators. I avoid the sites that use computer-synthesized voices to tell the stories—they sound awful. Here are some of my favorite sources for free spoken word content:

AudioBooksForFree (audiobooksforfree.com). This site has a large number of audiobooks, read by good narrators. Longer stories are broken into many files—for example, Jules Verne's *20,000 Leagues Under the Sea* requires you to download forty-five separate MP3 files—and the sound quality for the free version is OK but not great. If you are willing to spend a few dollars more, you can buy higher-quality files and download them all at once. If you really feel like going for broke, you can buy all 1000+ books burned onto nine DVDs (in MP3 or iPod's m4b format) for $120.

LibriVox (librivox.org). This site offers volunteer-produced, public-domain audiobooks. Like AudioBooksForFree, LibriVox breaks up stories into many files, but they are encoded at a higher sampling rate, which provides higher sound quality. Since LibriVox relies on volunteers to read the books, the performance quality varies (some of the readers are excellent, most are tolerable, a few are awful). In some instances, several readers switch off reading a book, and the effect of hearing a new reader narrate a book can be a little jarring until you get used to it.

Literal Systems (literalsystems.org). Literal Systems offers a handful of titles by classic authors such as Mark Twain and the

Brothers Grimm. The narrators are quite good. If you enjoy their audiobooks, they ask that you support them by making a donation.

Author podcasts. Many savvy authors are now podcasting their novels and short stories as a way to get people interested in their work. My friend and Boing Boing co-blogger Cory Doctorow reads from his excellent science fiction short stories and novellas at craphound.com, and novelist Scott Sigler reads his entire novels as podcasts at scottsigler.net. An excellent source of podcast novels is Podiobooks.com.

How Can I Participate in an Online Reading Group?

Discuss your favorite books online with like-minded readers

One of the joys of reading a book is in discussing the characters, plot, and theme with other people who've read it. This is especially helpful when reading a difficult work that's confusing or might be open to interpretation. My wife has belonged to a reading group for years, meeting at the same coffee shop every month to share their thoughts about novels they selected to read as a group.

If you're interested in starting or joining a reading group but don't know how to begin, visit Reader's Circle (readerscircle.org), a directory of reading groups across the country. You can enter your zip code to search for clubs in your area, and if a club description looks interesting, you can email the head of the club to request more information. Even if you can't find an active club that interests you, you can use Reader's Circle to start your own club and publicize it. For tips on how to effectively run a book group, visit BookMuse's resources page (bookmuse.com/pages/resources/resources.asp) to read tips on starting and maintaining a great book group. The Barnes & Noble Book Club Center (bookclubs.barnesandnoble.com) offers a number of excellent resources for book groups, including printable reading guides for hundreds of book titles, and reading group guides to jumpstart discussions. Penguin Group (USA) also offers reading guides and reading group tips at us.penguingroup.com/static/html/readingguides/startareadinggroup.html.

Sometimes it's not convenient to join a reading group where you have to meet at a particular place on a regular schedule. You can still discuss your favorite books by joining an online discussion group. The Book Clique Café (readinggroupsonline.com) has a directory of reading groups where people meet in online chat rooms to talk about their favorite authors or genres. You can also create your own group and add it to the directory here.

The New York Times (nytimes.com/ref/readersopinions/readinggroup-picks.html) has an online book discussion group but, unlike traditional reading groups, there's no limit to the number of people who can participate, and the discussion is in the form of message posts, not chat room discussions.

I haven't heard of anyone using the audio conference features of Skype or iChat to conduct reading group discussions, but there's no reason you couldn't use it for this purpose. Be one of the first to do it! (See page 272 for more about Skype and Internet telephony.)

How Can I Collaborate on a Book with Another Author?

Write a story with a friend using a Web-based word processor

Google Docs features (docs.google.com) and Spreadsheets a free Web-based word processor that's compatible with Microsoft Word, and is an easy and fun way to co-write a story, article, or other document with one or more people. (To use it, you need a Google account.) You can either start a new document or upload an existing text file or Word document from your computer.

Because Docs is a Web-based application, it comes with special features you won't find in Microsoft Word. For instance, you can use the menu to invite other people to access the document, or even "publish" it to the Web for all to see. If you have a blog, you can post your document as a blog entry. It's especially easy to post to a Blogger account, because Google owns Blogger.

The service also allows you to export to a variety of formats, including Word, and you can open Word documents you find in Google

DEEPER

Attend an author signing in cyberspace. Unless you live in a major metropolis, it's not likely that your favorite author is going to make a stop in your town while on a book tour. A few savvy authors, however, are showing up in the virtual world known as Second Life (secondlife.com) to tout their new books. In Second Life, members control customized cartoon versions of themselves (called avatars) to interact with other members in a 3-D environment. Authors such as Cory Doctorow and Julian Dibbell have donned avatars and entered the world of Second Life to discuss their books with large groups of devoted fans.

Second Life offers events, such as author signings, in cyberspace.

Search for text in a book

When I was writing a book about the history of computers a few years ago, I spent hundreds of dollars in books to help me research the subject. I easily could have spent thousands, but I started using A9 (a9.com) instead. This search engine, owned by Amazon, searches the full text of books scanned by Amazon, taking you straight to the scanned pages containing your search terms. You can also try Google Book Search (books.google.com). Either one is cheaper than buying the books and more convenient than driving to the library.

without downloading them first. You can also compare two versions and review the revision history, and if another person happens to be editing the document at the same time as you, it will let you know. Another bonus: Google Docs are probably a lot safer on Google's servers than on your own hard drive. See page 217 for more about Web-based office applications.

▶ How Can I Find a Book Title I've Forgotten?

Let others help you find the title and author of a dimly remembered childhood book

It appears I'm not the only person who has struggled to remember the author or title of a book read many years ago. I learned that when I posted a question to my blog asking readers if they could help me recall the name of a book series I enjoyed when I was around twelve years old. The only things I clearly remembered about the stories were that they involved a boy whose name started with the letter "H," and that his adventures were whimsical and impossible. One involved a singing mouse, the other involved a garden hose attachment that dyed his skin a bright color (blue?).

Many readers told me the boy was named Homer Price and that the author of the books was Robert McCloskey. Homer, they said, was always getting involved in silly situations, like the time he ran a donut-making machine that he couldn't shut off. I thought Homer was the answer at first, but I woke up in the middle of the night with the realization that it wasn't Homer. Other people suggested Harold (of the Purple Crayon), and Henry Huggins (from Beverly Cleary's delightful books), but I knew right away that neither boy was the one I was looking for. Then somebody emailed me and said that he had read the same books that I had read, and that the boy's name was Hubert. That rang a bell in my head. But not a very loud bell. It just wasn't quite right.

Later, I received another email from someone suggesting I look for the books at Loganberry Books "Stump the Bookseller" site (loganberrybooks.com/stump.html). This used bookstore, located in Shaker Heights, Ohio, has a nifty service that helps you find forgotten children's books. It costs $2 (via PayPal) to ask a question, but you can search through the extensive archives to see if your question has already been answered.

I searched on Hubert, and learned that there was a book called *Hubert's Hair-Raising Adventure*, but it was about a lion, not a boy. On a lark, I decided to try a search on "Herbert," on the hunch that the guy who emailed me was wrong about the name. Bingo! I found a question someone had asked about a boy who "lands on a planet much like Earth, except dogs rule instead of people." Another involves " 'Harold's' adventures with a magic pencil, which does his homework for him." I knew right away this was the kid I was looking for. And my dream came true when I saw that someone had an answer. "Maybe Hazel Wilson's Herbert series? Titles include *Herbert's Homework* (1960) and *Herbert's Space Trip* (1965)."

I went to Google and ordered the books (used, because they were out of print). When I got them and started reading them, I knew for certain that these were the books I had been looking for. I've been reading them to my daughter, and they are as good as I remember them. If "Stump the Bookseller" doesn't give you any joy, you can also try Abe Books' BookSleuth (forums.abebooks.com/abesleuthcom) and the "Lost Childhood Books" page at CBC Radio's Web site (cbc.ca/nxnw/lostbooks.html).

▶ How Can I Share My Books with Other People?

Join Internet communities where you can exchange unwanted books for wanted ones

Each book-sharing service works a little differently. Let's look at three of the popular ones:

BookMooch (bookmooch.com) is an online community book exchange. Membership is free of charge, as are the book exchanges.

The only cost involves shipping your books to other members. To join, you list at least ten books you're willing to send to other members. Once you've entered your titles in the database, you can search for books you want and request them from the listing members. They then send out the book(s), paying for the shipping. For every five books you receive, you have to send out at least one (so it pays to list desirable titles). The handsome, easy-to-use Web site even has a wish list feature where you can see the books that other members want (and list your own). You get an email notification when books on your wish list are added to the database.

PaperBackSwap (paperbackswap.com) works much the same way as BookMooch. As the name implies, their focus is on paperbacks, but members also trade hardbacks and even CDs. You have to list nine books to get started. For those, you get three credits to request three titles. After that, you have to mail out a book (receiving one credit) to be able to request one (1 book equals 1 credit). Like BookMooch, you pay for postage, which for paperbacks is only about $1.60. They also have a convenient mailer you can print out that has the recipient's address and your return address on it. Right now, joining is free, but PaperBackSwap plans on eventually charging a membership fee (likely between $10 and $20 per year).

BookCrossing (bookcrossing.com) is not so much about getting books as it is about gifting them to others, leaving them in public for others to find. The result is a unique blend of sociological experiment, international treasure hunt (or more accurately "treasure find"), and a random act of kindness. To "play" all you do is sign up on the site and register a book you want to release "into the wild." The book is assigned a unique ID and a downloaded card is placed inside the book describing BookCrossing's mission and what the finder is encouraged to do with it, which is basically: read it (if so inclined), go to the book's ID page on the site (the book's "journal"), and describe the circumstances of finding it, what you thought of it, etc. Then the recipient is asked to re-release it, so that its story can grow as it's passed from finder to finder. So far, nearly 3,500 books have been read and released into the wilds of coffee shops, park benches, bus seats, and airport lounges the world over. So far, the

DEEPER

BookMooch search. BookMooch has a browser add-on, called the MoochBar, which allows you to search the BookMooch database while you're on Amazon, Barnes & Noble, or any other online catalog that uses ISBN numbers. From a pop-up window, you can request books the MoochBar finds or add them to your BookMooch Wish List.

most traveled book is the German-language version of *Hoffnung's Constant Readers*. It's passed through 225 hands to date.

▶▶ SPORTS

▶ How Do I Play Fantasy Sports Online?

There are several good fantasy sports portals you can visit, starting with Yahoo! Sports

Fantasy sports have been described as Dungeons & Dragons for jocks. Fantasy baseball was the first such game, but the hobby has expanded to include football, basketball, hockey, even NASCAR. The idea is simple. To play, you assemble a team based on real-world players (using players from any team) and then you use the performance of your team's real-world players to determine your fantasy team's performance. For instance, if the players in your fantasy team scored 8 points in real-world play and the fantasy team you were "playing against" scored 6 points in real-world play, your fantasy team wins. Players of fantasy sports claims that it gets them much deeper into the games, as they closely follow teams and players across the league(s), not just their hometown team. Fantasy sports have gotten so big that there are now dozens of Web sites, blogs, magazines, TV shows, even sports writers that deal with them. Yahoo! Sports (fantasysports.yahoo.com) is a great place to start if you're new to fantasy sports. It offers basic tools for getting your team set up, plenty of opponents to challenge, advice from experts, player profiles, and more. And it's all free.

To delve a little deeper, try SportingNews' Fantasy Games and Research (fantasygames.sportingnews.com). Just as Sporting News has a reputation for taking its sports very seriously, its fantasy site is deeply dedicated to the fantasy sports hobby. The site offers tons of gaming and team management tools, background material, and expert advice.

You can even download a fantasy gaming application for your mobile phone that'll keep you abreast of your players' stats (for baseball and football only). Fanball.com is another popular and full-featured fantasy sports portal worth checking out.

How Do I Get Sports Scores and Other Information with My Mobile Phone?

Try signing up for Sportsline (CBS Sports) or Fox Sports for good mobile sports packages

If you just can't go an inning or a down without being wired into the game, I feel your pain, or at least, the programmers of these services do. CBS Sportsline Mobile (sportsline.com/mobile) offers a full suite of sports-related content to mobile subscribers on most major carriers and most model phones. For $4.99 a month, you get game news and scores, game alerts, real-time scoreboards of games, and fantasy sports info. Fox Sports (foxsports.com/mobile) offers all of that, plus real-time animations of games in progress, audio sports news updates, and the ability to customize your content for the teams you follow. Fox's service is also $4.99 per month, and works with most phones.

DEEPER

Sports Blogs. (sportsblogs .org) is another portal of (mostly) amateur sports blogs and Web sites covering baseball, basketball, football, hockey, tennis, and golf. They too have a "meta-blog" with links to the best content on the network.

How Can I Find the Best Sports Blogs Out There?

One of the best places to start is SportsBlog Nation

If you're a regular denizen of the blogosphere, you may already know the name of Markos Moulitsas Zúniga. Remembering a name like that is a statement about its owner's popularity. But Markos, aka Daily Kos, is probably the most famous political blogger of them all. His powerful and influential Daily Kos blog (dailykos.com) has made (Howard Dean) and derailed (Joe Lieberman) campaigns. But what you may not know is that Kos is as passionate about sports, especially baseball (and especially the Chicago Cubs), as he is about politics. His SportsBlogs Nation (sbnation.com) serves as a one-stop shop for the best amateur sports writing online. Here you'll find dozens of blogs, assembled into a network by Kos and his business partner Tyler Bleszinski, covering baseball, football, college sports, fantasy sports, boxing, and soccer. There's also a "meta-blog" which excerpts from them all, a great way to scan the field without having to run onto each one of them to see if there's anything interesting going on.

CHAPTER 6

TRAVEL AND SIGHTSEEING

The Web may not have single-handedly killed the travel agent business, but it sure didn't help. Today, taking virtual tours of bungalows in Bangkok, hales in Hawaii, or tents in Tanzania, is instantaneous and addictively fun. The Web is not only the world's best vacation-planning tool, it's also the best way to document and share your travel experiences. In this section you'll learn how to coordinate group vacations, broadcast your location to friends, get the best seats on an airplane, find the lowest ticket prices, score a bargain-priced hotel room, and safely surf the Web when away from home.

▶ How Can I Plan a Vacation with My Friends?

Try using one of the many trip-planning tools available online, such as Yahoo! Travel's Trip Planner

Planning a trip and what you want to do on it can be an incomparable thrill. Planning a trip with others, though, can either be a pleasure or a pain, depending on the group and the planning tools you use. Luckily, the latter part of that equation can bc solved through the powerful, free Web resources that are available. One of the easiest and most popular is Yahoo's Trip Planner (travel.yahoo.com/trip). It allows you to set up a page for each trip, invite others to join it (they all must have Yahoo! accounts), and tailor-make your page with hotel recommendations, restaurants, sites to see, a trip schedule, and more. Each member of the trip page can add suggestions, make comments, etc.

One cool feature is that, after you set up the page, Yahoo! Travel will start feeding it with suggestions of things to see and do and places to stay at that location. There are also links to other Yahoo! members who have made similar trips public so you can learn from their experiences. And while you're traveling, you can post blog entries and photos on Yahoo! Maps so your friends and family can follow your progress.

RealTravel (realtravel.com) has a very handsome, feature-rich, and free travel-planning site. It has all of the tools that Yahoo! Travel does, plus a much nicer travel blog and a better interactive map that's keyed into your blog entries and trip photos. RealTravel is not expressly designed for collaborative trip planning, but there's no reason you can't create a single account for your travel group and then give everyone the name and password. You can invite anyone you want to see your travel pages, but without the password, they can't add content.

Another travel site worth checking out is Gusto! (gusto.com). It's set up like a social network site with a profile of you, a friend network you build, a blog area, photo sharing, etc. Like RealTravel, it's not specifically designed for a group, but you can create a private page and invite your group onto it. One of the nicer features of Gusto! is a toolbar applet that lets you add content from elsewhere on the Web to your Gusto! page. For instance, if you see a restaurant review you like, you can hit the Gusto! button on your browser toolbar and add it to your travel page.

One thing that's great about a socially networked travel site like Gusto! is that, unlike travel guides, you're getting a bunch of stories, photos, and travel tips from fellow travelers in addition to editorial content. There's nothing like hearing about some great out-of-the-way eatery or an exceptionally low-priced hotel and then going to that place, having your own experience with it, and passing along your experiences to the next traveler.

How Can I Find Nearby Friends When I'm Out on the Town?

You can use one of the new mobile social networking services

Social networking software, with its ability to show you linkages between friends, friends of friends, business associates, and other clusters of connected people, has become the bedrock of the modern Web. Now this type of social networking is spilling onto mobile devices and putting the "social" back into social networking. One of the most popular services is Google's Dodgeball (dodgeball.com). The site works like Friendster and other social networks: you sign up, link yourself to friends already on the service, and invite others to join. But unlike other friend networks, this one is grounded in the real world, so there are local venues to check out (ones visited by and reviewed by other Dodgeball members) and the location feature, the heart of Dodgeball. All you do is send a text message to let Dodgeball know where you are. It then broadcasts that message to all of the people in your network. If any of them are within a ten-block radius, Dodgeball will alert you. You can switch the service on and off, so you only get these messages when you're out on the town or otherwise want people to know where you are (and what haunts your friends are floating through). Dodgeball can also alert you to the location of interesting venues in the area and to "crushes," people in your friends-of-friends network that you've indicated you're attracted to.

How Can I Find Restaurants and Businesses When I'm Traveling?

Use Google Earth to find restaurants near your hotel

Of all the ways to find places to eat, shop, or do business when you're in an unfamiliar city (or even in your own neck of the woods), Google Earth, a virtual globe constructed from satellite photography and loaded with yellow pages data and other useful geographic information, is my favorite. Start by downloading the free version of

DEEPER

What Is Twitter? Another service similar to Dodgeball is called Twitter (twitter.com). It works in much the same way, but is not as focused on the dating and bar-hopping scene as Dodgeball. One cool thing about Twitter is that they've made the API (that's the Application Programming Interface, the programming tools that allow others to create applications that utilize Twitter's data) available to others. It's the Google Maps API that's allowed people to do so many amazing things with online maps. Already people are creating cute little programs that use Twitter data. One of the first was Celly (twitter.com/celly), a little animated phone that holds up phonecam images of Twitter members who are "on" and "speaks" their typed messages in a cartoon word balloon. To see the latest Twitter-based apps, check out their blog: twitter.com/blog.

Google Earth (earth.google.com) for Mac or Windows. (You'll need an Internet connection when you use the application.) When you launch it, you'll be greeted by a familiar blue planet—that would be Earth. Click the "Fly to" tab in the upper left corner, enter the name of a city, country, or street address and click the magnifying glass. For example, enter "New York, NY." The globe will rotate and you'll descend on the Big Apple.

Now click the "Find Businesses" tab. Say you have a hankering for Cuban food. Enter your cuisine preference into the search field. The map will show all the Cuban restaurants in the area. (To zoom in or out, use your mouse's scroll wheel or the navigation controls in the upper-right corner.) Click any of the restaurants to see more information, including reviews and directions on how to get there. (See page 211.)

If you know the name of the hotel you are staying in, you can enter it into the "Find Businesses" field and easily get turn-by-turn directions to the restaurant of your choice printed on top of the map. You can click the "Play" button and watch Google "drive" along the route. (You'll feel like a TV news helicopter pilot following a high-speed car chase.)

You can also highlight checkboxes to find things like ATMs, railway lines, and crime statistics. The more you play with Google Earth, the more impressive it becomes. For business travelers and vacationers, Google Earth is an essential tool.

Google Maps (maps.google.com) has much of the same functionality as Google Earth and doesn't require a download. I prefer to use Google Earth when I can, though, because I find the interface easier to use.

How Can I Find Out About the Best Seats on a Particular Plane?

Check out the seating plans of different passenger jets before you request a seat assignment

Many airlines let you select your seat at the time you travel. But with so many different seating arrangements, it can be hard to figure out

DEEPER

Google Earth tours. A huge community of Google Earth fanatics has developed and they share interesting finds (military bases, experimental aircraft, unusual landmarks, and other places of interest) and neat Google Earth tricks at bbs.keyhole.com.

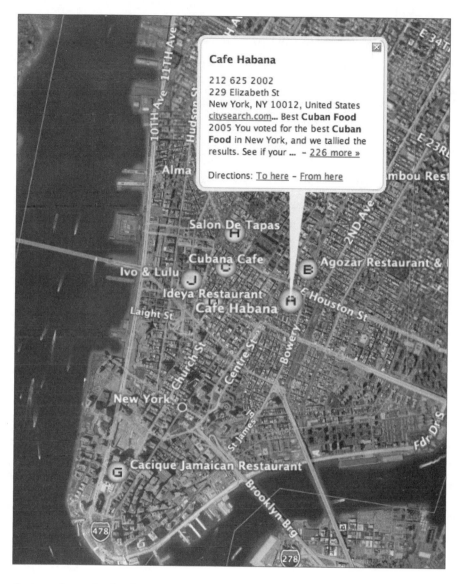

Find a restaurant using Google Earth.

which seats will be the most comfortable. SeatGuru (seatguru.com) takes the guesswork out of seat selection by providing color-coded maps of seating plans for different kinds of planes. Green seats are good, yellow seats have certain problems, and red seats are rated "poor." You can move your mouse cursor over any seat and read a description of that seat's pros and cons. For example, on the Jet-Blue Airbus A320, your best bet is a seat in row 12. It's an exit row with plenty of legroom. SeatGuru warns that exit row seats are colder than other seats, however. Row 11 is also an exit row seat with even more legroom than row 12, but the seats don't recline as far back as the seats in row 12.

SeatGuru has a section explaining how to request seating assignment, and for travelers who need to book a flight when they're on the go, SeatGuru has a fast-loading mobile version of the seating arrangements for handheld Internet devices (mobile.seatguru.com).

In addition to seating information, SeatGuru also has the lowdown on check-in and baggage requirements for each airline, along with Web site and phone numbers.

▶ What's the Best Way to Search for Ticket Prices?

Save money by consulting powerful airfare databases

When planning a trip that requires flying, it's usually best to buy the tickets as far in advance as possible. But that's not always true. Sometimes prices drop as the departure date approaches.

Farecast (farecast.com) uses historical airfare data to try to predict when you should buy tickets. Enter your departure and arrival

Flight delay information

The Federal Aviation Administration page (fly.faa.gov/flyfaa/usmap.jsp) gives you a constantly updated map of the major airports in the continental U.S., with color-coded arrival/departure delay information.

airports along with your dates of travel, and Farecast will examine the pricing trends for tickets and give you its best guess as to whether the airfare will rise or drop. You can also use the "grid" view, which shows you how much you can expect to pay for tickets leaving at certain times throughout the day.

Flyspy (flyspy.com) is somewhat similar, but it provides a graph showing the best prices available for various departure and return dates. If you can be flexible about when you travel, Flyspy's graph will be quite useful.

▶ How Can I Use the Internet Safely When I'm on the Road?

Use a virtual private network to connect safely to a wireless hotspot

The problem with connecting to a wireless hotspot at a café, hotel, or airport is that you never know who is monitoring your signal. It's not

Tell what time it is anywhere in the world

The Internet has a done a job shrinking the planet. I converse with people from all over the world via email, Skype, and instant messaging. But I'm always confused as to what time it is in other countries. I don't want to ring someone up in Tokyo at 3 AM their time, and I shouldn't expect to receive an instant message or email reply from someone in Australia in the wee hours of the morning.

I use the World Clock (timeanddate.com/worldclock) to tell me the time in faraway places. Click the "Personal World Clock" link to create a custom page of times in various cities (see page 214).

Another way to find out what time it is in another city is by going to Google and entering: What time is it in Sydney?

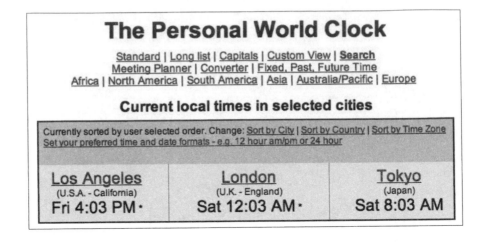

only possible that your communications are being tapped, but a criminal might be tricking you using the "Evil Twin" scam (see page 374), which leaves you wide open to eavesdropping. The best way to prevent criminals from tapping your signal at a public hotspot is by using a VPN (virtual private network) to encrypt all the data sent and received by your computer.

HotSpotVPN (hotspotvpn.com) is an inexpensive service that you can pay for by the month ($8.88), by the week ($6.88) or by the day ($3.88). It works by encrypting all your data as it is sent back and forth between HotSpotVPN's network, creating a "tunnel" of private communications that even the most diligent hacker can't penetrate.

If you only go online at public hotspots to read Web sites, you don't need VPN. And virtually every Web site that handles financial transactions uses encryption, so it's safe to do online banking, use eBay, or shop online at a public hotspot. (You can tell a site is encrypted by looking at the URL in the address bar. If it starts with "https:" it's secure. If it starts with "http:" it's not.)

▶ How Can I Find a Cheap Hotel Room?

Use QuikBook to sleep cheap

Of all the many ways to book hotel reservations online, Quikbook (quikbook.com) is the best. Why? For one thing, its rates are guaranteed to be the lowest (and they'll make up the difference if you come across a lower rate within twenty-four hours of booking). For another, its selection of hotels is excellent, and includes many boutique hotels you won't find on other hotel booking services. And, often, Quikbook has rooms available in hotels when Expedia or Travelocity have run out. Best of all, Quikbook offers a "Book Now, Pay Later" policy, which allows you to cancel or change a reservation without paying a fee.

Quikbook's pre-pay option is excellent. The fee quoted includes the room charges, plus any taxes or fees the hotel charges, so you won't be surprised when you pay the bill at checkout time. And if you need to cancel your reservation, Quikbook will refund your money, less a paltry $10 charge, provided you give four days' notice. (If you cancel or change the pre-paid reservation within four days of your original check-in date, QuikBook charges $35.)

Before booking a hotel room with Quikbook, however, visit TripAdvisor (tripadvisor.com) and enter the name of the hotel in the search field. Check out the reviews written by past guests of the hotel, and click in the "Check Rates" button, which lets you easily find out how much other booking services, such as Travelocity (travelocity .com), Expedia (expedia.com), Orbitz (orbitz.com), Hotels.com, Venere (venere.com), and CheapTickets (cheaptickets.com) charge. You might find a better rate, or learn something from a review that will make you change your mind about the place.

CHAPTER 7

WORK, ORGANIZATION, AND PRODUCTIVITY

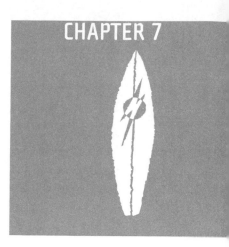

The original purpose for computers and the Internet was business, not pleasure. When the Web came along, using a computer got a lot more fun, and even work- and productivity-related Web sites became enjoyable to use. The Web connects people to each other, and it's always more interesting to work with people than machines. In this section, you'll learn how to use Web-based office applications that replace Microsoft Office, how to use wikis to form virtual offices, how to manage projects with people in different locations, how to deal with credit and finance matters, and even how to create the most efficient grocery list.

PERSONAL PRODUCTIVITY

▶How Can I Work with Documents, Spreadsheets, and Presentations from Any Web Browser?

You can use free online office applications that are compatible with Microsoft Office

In addition to Google Docs and Spreadsheets (see page 198) there are several other Web sites that let you work with Microsoft applications.

Microsoft Office Professional retails for $499. Do you really need it? Maybe not. You might be able to avoid spending that money by using either a Web-based office application or by using OpenOffice, a free downloadable Office alternative. Both let you create, view, and edit most Office-compatible files.

My favorite Web-based word processor is Zoho Writer (writer.zoho.com). Not only does it accept almost any Microsoft Word document you throw at it, it also lets you email your documents to yourself and others in a variety of formats, including Word's doc format and Adobe's PDF format. For similar functionality with Excel spreadsheets, try Zoho Sheet (sheet.zoho.com). Zoho also offers wikis, databases, presentations, project-management software, and more at zoho.com.

Merging multiple PDF files

There are times when you'll want to combine several PDF documents into one. You can do this with Adobe Acrobat Standard, but why spend $300 when you can use a free utility that gets the job done just as well? Mac users can download Combine PDFs (monkeybreadsoftware.de/Freeware/CombinePDFs .shtml). It couldn't be simpler to use: drag PDFs into the application's window, change the order of the pages by clicking and dragging them, and then click "Merge PDF." You can also remove pages from a multi-page PDF using this utility. If you have a bunch of pages to merge, you can set Combine PDFs to beep when it has finished its task.

Windows users can download a free copy of PDFill PDF Tools (pdfill.com), which not only lets you merge documents, but also lets you split pages, encrypt PDFs, reformat multiple pages onto a single page, and other handy tasks.

As the name implies, ThinkFree (thinkfree.com) is a free-of-charge Web-based program that offers a suite of tools that will be familiar to anyone who uses Office. "Write" is a word-processing program that feels just like Word, "Calc" smells a lot like Excel, and "Show" looks like PowerPoint. They fully integrate with these programs too, so docs that you create in ThinkFree will work with the desktop versions of their Microsoft brethren. Subscribers to the free service get 1 GB of online storage and can collaborate with others on documents. The latest version of ThinkFree also integrates with the Flickr (flickr.com) photo service, so you can use Flickr photos in your Word and PowerPoint . . . er, I mean Write and Show documents (see page 60 for more about Flickr). Another nice feature of ThinkFree is that it has the built-in ability to create PDF documents from your files without the need for additional software. AjaxWrite (ajax13.com) is an online word processor that works much the same way as ThinkFree's Write. It looks very similar to Word, so if you know that program, you'll know your way around ajaxWrite. The ajax13 site also offers ajaxSketch, an online drawing, charting, and diagramming tool, ajaxXLS, a spreadsheet program, and ajaxPresents, online presentation software.

The downside to online programs like Zoho, ThinkFree, and ajaxWrite is that you have to be online to use them. If you want a full-featured word processor available anytime, get yourself a copy of OpenOffice (openoffice.org), which offers an integrated suite of applications for word processing, spreadsheets, and presentations, which are all compatible with Microsoft Office. I won't lie to you—OpenOffice's user interface isn't very attractive, but if you're familiar with Microsoft Office, you'll have no problem getting up to speed.

▶ How Can I Access My Bookmarks Anywhere?

You can use one of the many personal online bookmarking tools, or join a social bookmarking site to share your favorite finds with others

As our technology becomes more mobile, we become more mobile with it. Whether you want to work in a different room of the house or need to access files from a different point on the globe, you know that the need to centralize your digital work tools and files is becoming an increasing necessity. And one of the resources we want access to everywhere is our bookmarks.

Maintaining your bookmarks in a centralized location is easy, thanks to features offered by major Internet portals like Yahoo! and Google. To use one of these, go to Yahoo! Bookmarks Beta (beta.bookmarks.yahoo.com) or Google Bookmarks (google.com/bookmarks). Yahoo! lets you import your existing bookmarks; Google doesn't.

Ultimate productivity Web site

For much of my working life, my days were "interrupt-driven." By that, I mean I would start work on something, get interrupted by a phone call, email, or co-worker, and then veer off in the direction the interruption pointed me towards, until the next phone call, email, or visitor to my cubicle sent me off in a new direction. Merlin Mann's 43folders.com is designed to help you manage your time and be more productive than ever before. Mann describes his blog as a "site about personal productivity, life hacks, and simple ways to make your life a little better." You'll learn how to organize your office, deal with email overload, plan a project, and take power naps at this informative and witty blog. His clever essays are filled with excellent ideas that can literally turn your life around. For example, Merlin suggests that you start your day without looking at email for an hour. Don't even launch your email application, he warns. Instead, accomplish a task, or several tasks. Starting the day by checking off things on your to-do list (Merlin calls it a list of "next-actions," based on David Allen's bestselling and highly recommended book, *Getting Things Done*) feels a lot better than getting bogged down in email.

Things get more interesting with so-called "social bookmarking" sites where you can not only centrally store your own bookmarks, but also share them with others and see what other users are bookmarking. The more a particular site gets bookmarked, the higher it rises on the collective lists organized by categories (tech, media, news, health, etc.). The grande dame of social bookmarking sites is del.icio.us (yes, that's the URL). It continues to be one of the more popular. It allows you to import your existing bookmarks, keep bookmarks private, and even subscribe to "tags" (think: keywords) or a particular user's bookmark lists. You can subscribe to "music," for instance, and see every new bookmark tagged "music" that appears on the site. I also subscribe to the Web pages of interesting del.icio.us users I know. The results appear in my RSS reader and it's very useful.

This kind of community sharing of favorite places online has become a whole new form of Net communication and a great way to make new friends, network with business associates, learn about new music, share great travel tips, discover a local restaurant you didn't know about before, find news that's off the mainstream radar, and lots more. Another very popular social bookmarking site is Digg (digg.com). It takes social bookmarking to the next level by combining it with blogging, content syndication, and the ability for users to vote (or "digg") and comment on links they like (or don't).

▶ How Can I Manage a Project with People Scattered All Over the World?

Try creating a wiki for your project team, or if you need more sophisticated features, try using one of the other online collaboration tools—a few of them are even free

For basic project communications and document sharing, a wiki tool, such as PBwiki (pbwiki.com), may be all that you need (see page 52 to learn about using wikis as a productivity tool). For more complex project management, where you want to have a group share a single calendar, task lists, spreadsheets, and other typical desktop

DEEPER

More social bookmarking.
At this point, there is a profusion of online bookmarking tools, many of them for social bookmarking. They all have different looks and feels, and slightly different features. Before committing yourself to one service, it's worthwhile to look at and play around with several. You can find an up-to-date list of bookmarking sites at Wikipedia (wikipedia.org) if you search on "list of social software."

project management tools, you probably want to use an online collaboration suite. A free product called ThinkFree (thinkfree.com) allows you to set up an online workspace where you can create Microsoft Office–compatible word processing, spreadsheet, and presentation files. You can then invite others to review, add to, and edit those files. A more feature-rich and popular collaboration tool is Basecamp (basecamp.com). A free version allows you to track one project at a time. For $12 a month, you can track 3 projects. For $25 per month you can track 15 projects. The Basecamp software offers group messaging, a group calendar, a project milestone tracker, file sharing, to-do lists, whiteboards, and more. You can even tailor the look of your online "office" to make it compatible with your corporate image (with templates, colors, logos, etc.). WebEx's WebOffice (weboffice.com) offers everything that Basecamp does and a lot more. This is a serious business-management tool with added features such as database creation and management, online meeting software, expense reporting, and the like. They offer a 30-day trial, so if you have a short-term project, you could use WebOffice for free. Otherwise, it's not cheap. The five-person group rate is $60 a month, and it goes up from there, all the way to $2,500 for a 500-person workgroup. For non-profits, they have a 10-person rate of $50/month.

Zoho.com, makers of Microsoft-compatible Web-based applications, also offers a project management and collaboration service that costs as little as $5 a month. With Zoho Projects, you can assign tasks to team members, give them deadlines, set milestones, access a calendar with all the activities posted on it, create reports, share files, and keep track of the time everyone spends working on different aspects of a project.

▶How Do I Keep My Data Safe Online?

Use a free online storage drive to keep backups of critical data

I've experienced enough catastrophic hard-drive failures to know how important it is to make regular backups. I backup my entire hard drive onto an external drive every single day when I'm at home. But what if a small meteor crashes through the roof and destroys my computer and the backup? That's why I keep off-site backups of my most important files.

One way to do this is to burn the data to a CD or DVD and give it to a friend for safekeeping, but that could get cumbersome after a while, so I prefer using an online storage service. AOL's Xdrive (xdrive.com) is my favorite, because it's easy to use and works on Macs and Windows machines. And the 5 GB limit gives you plenty of storage.

Unlike most other online storage services, Xdrive lets you upload entire folders, not just individual files, which makes it much easier to backup certain kinds of data, like an email database, which could contain thousands of files.

Windows users should download the Xdrive Desktop software. Your Xdrive will show up on your desktop like another hard drive. You can drag files and folders onto it and save files to it from open applications. It also has built-in backup software so you can program it to back up your files at a certain time every day. Mac users can upload files through their browser.

A handy program for Mac users is Gdisk (gdisk.sourceforge.net), which lets you access your Gmail account as a hard drive for file storage.

Leave a message for yourself

Call a toll-free number at Braincast (braincast .viatalk.com) and leave a voice message that you can retrieve later. Braincast emails you a reminder to check your messages.

▶How Can I Get Email and Cell Phone Reminders of Important Events?

Use Google Calendar to tap your shoulder when it's time to do something.

I'm good at writing down all my appointments into my PDA and cal-endar app, but I'm not so good at checking the calendar every day to see what's on my plate. That's why I'm grateful for the reminder alarms these calendars have—I need something that flashes and beeps obnoxiously to get my attention. For example, fifteen minutes before it's time to call my editor and beg for a deadline extension my computer chimes and a window pops up to alert me.

One of the most feature-rich calendar apps is Google Calendar, (google.com/calendar), an online scheduler that can alert you to ap-pointments via email, SMS, or pop-up window. Here's how to use Google Calendar's notifications.

1. You need a Google account. (If you already use Gmail, Blogger, or any other Google service, you can use the same log-in infor-mation.)

2. Activate the notification settings by clicking the "Settings" link at the top of the page, and then click the "Notifications" tab.

3. To set up cell phone notification, enter your phone number, carrier, and country and click "Send Verification Code."

4. When the code shows up on your cell phone, go back to your Web browser and enter it into the verification code field, then click "Finish setup."

▶How Can I Share To-Do Lists with Other People?

Create a task list that you can share with others online.

Making a to-do list is easy: all you need is a pencil and paper. But mak-ing a to-do list that you can share with other people online normally requires setting up a Web page, which entails a lot more work. Ta-da List (tadalist.com) is a very simple way to set up task lists that you can invite others to view.

Once you set up an account, you start a list by giving it a title and then entering action items. Then you can invite other people to add, edit, and check items off this list. In addition, you can make the list public, so anyone can look at the list (but not change it). If you've invited a lot of people to join the list, the best way to keep track of the changes made to the list is by subscribing to the list's RSS feed.

Another useful site is Remember the Milk (rememberthemilk .com), which lets you manage tasks, set reminders, and send and receive tasks to other users. Some of the cool features include pinpointing the location of your tasks on a map, setting up reminders via email, SMS, or instant message, and adding new tasks to your list via email.

DEEPER

Keep tabs on your pals.
(30boxes.com) has social networking features so you can see your friends' and colleagues' schedules and events. It's an excellent way to coordinate events and make sure you don't miss important events like birthdays, meetings, and parties.

Quick and dirty meeting scheduler

By its name, you might think that Doodle (doodle.ch) is an online drawing program, but it's actually a little app designed to help you schedule a meeting or other gathering with a group of people that don't share a common calendar, groupware program, or means of online event planning.

To use Doodle, you simply create a "poll" with the date range and details of your gathering (time, location). The associates you're trying to wrangle get an email with a link to the poll/calendar. They vote on the days that they're available and the date(s) with the most votes gets scheduled.

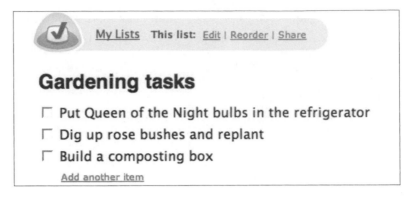

Ta-da list.

How Can I Quickly Fill Out an Online Form?

Save time at online checkout forms by automatically entering your name and address

I do most of my shopping online, and having to enter my name, address, phone number, email address, and other information into a form at checkout time is tedious. With Google Toolbar, you can fill out a master form once, and use the information in it to automatically fill out the fields in any online form. Here's how to set it up:

1. Download Google Toolbar (toolbar.google.com) and install it. When you re-launch your browser, it will appear at the top.

2. Click the "Options" button in Google Toolbar.

3. Check the AutoFill Box, and click "Autofill Settings."

4. In the form, fill out as many of the fields as you'd like. You don't have to fill in every one.

5. Click the "Highlight fields on Web pages that Autofill can update in yellow" box.

6. Click "OK."

That's it. The next time you have to fill out a form with your contact information, just click the "AutoFill" button on the toolbar and watch the magic happen.

▶ How Can I Shorten a Web Address?

Turn a long URL into a short one with an address–shortening service

Have you ever tried sending a very long Web site address to a friend or co-worker, only to have them write back and tell you that the link was broken? Frequently, email applications will add invisible line-break characters into a long address, and when you click the clink, or copy and paste it into the browser, you'll be greeted by the dreaded "404—Page Not Found" message. To solve this problem, several people have come up with free URL-shortening services. My favorite is Metamark (metamark.net). Go to the site and paste in any Web address you want to shrink. For example, when I ran en.wikipedia.org/wiki/Santiago_de_Cuba#Personalities through Metamark, it created xrl.us/koye—a much shorter address. You can also make the addresses more memorable by suggesting a nickname.

The downside to URL-shortening services? If the service goes offline, either temporarily or permanently, the shortened URLs stop working. Metamark also has a policy of expiring URLs after five years (or two years after the last time they were used, whichever comes later). In most cases that's OK, but if you want to make sure the URL lasts as long as the Web page it points to, don't use a shortening service.

For an interesting side-by-side comparison of different shortening services, visit notlong.com/links. But don't be fooled by any site's claims that their shortened links have an infinite lifetime. There's no guarantee that the organization or individual providing the service won't pull the plug one day.

▶ How Can I Speed Up My Typing?

Use abbreviations to enter frequently-used chunks of text

I never learned to touch-type, and now I'm too busy writing every day to take the time to learn. It's a shame, because in the course of a day's work, I tap out a couple of thousand words in the form of emails, blog entries, articles, and book chapters.

Fortunately, I've found a couple of programs that have helped a great deal in making up for my lack of typing skills. These programs convert a few keystrokes into entire words, sentences, even paragraphs. On the Mac, I use a program called TextExpander ($29.95, smileonmymac.com/textexpander). The program runs in the background, watching all your keystrokes. When it recognizes one of the special series of keystrokes you've added to its list, it will swap in the text you've assigned to those keystrokes. For instance, whenever I enter "km," TextExpander replaces those two letters with "Kind Regards, Mark." Whenever I enter "wg" TextExpander replaces it with a multi-page block of text representing the writer's guidelines for a magazine I edit. (by the way, I typed "mg" for magazine, just now). I use "u" for you, "pl" for please, "adr" for my home address, "biz" for business, "baord" for board and "beacause" for because (because I'm constantly misspelling both), and "hdir" for directions on how to get to my house.

TextExpander also works with graphics. You can type in a few characters and the program will paste in a photo, digitized signature, or anything else you assign to it.

For Windows, you can use a free similar program called Auto-Hotkey (autohotkey.com/download).

▶ How Can I Create the Perfect Grocery List?

Generate a shopping list sorted by aisle

I'm one of those meandering shoppers, the kind that rolls down aisle seven for spaghetti sauce, heads over to aisle fourteen for Band-Aids, then hits the produce section for bananas before wandering back to aisle fourteen for shampoo. I probably go up and down each aisle two or more times before I'm finished.

A fellow named Dave Cheong had the same problem. But unlike me, he did something about it. He created a Web-based application

DEEPER

The Grocery List Generator (addons.mozilla.org/firefox/13 27) is a Firefox extension that generates a shopping list based on your saved recipes.

that generates shopping lists based on aisle number, so you can start at aisle 1 and go up and down each aisle, picking up what you need, until you reach the last aisle and go to the checkout counter.

To use Cheong's Grocery Shopping Helper, you need to do a little work upfront. First, make a list of all the stuff you commonly buy at the grocery store. Then, go to the store and write down the aisle number next to each product on your list. When you get home, enter the information in the form at davecheong.com/wp-content/simpletools/groceries/index.jsp. From there, it's easy to generate shopping reports that list the products you need, and how to pick them up in the most efficient way.

▶▶ MONEY AND FINANCE

▶ How Can I Check My Credit Record?

The major credit reporting agencies are required to give you a free credit report if you ask them

You've probably seen ads trying to convince you to fork over money to look at your credit report. It's a good idea to regularly review your credit report because it's important to know if any sleazy identity thieves have opened a credit account using your name and Social Security number. But you don't need to pay for a credit report. That's because Federal law says you're entitled to see your credit report from the big three credit-reporting agencies—Experian, Equifax, and TransUnion—every twelve months without cost.

Go to AnnualCreditReport (annualcreditreport.com). To verify your identity, you'll be asked to answer several multiple choice questions involving your mortgage lender, the street you live on, and the amount of your monthly mortgage payment, if you have one.

This quiz will verify your identity. (Along the way, you'll be asked if you want to sign up for a subscription to your credit report, or pay to see your FICO score, and so on. Just ignore those and move on. What you're looking for is signs of identity theft or negative marks on your credit record.)

Your reports will be presented to you instantly. You can find out how many loan accounts you have (both opened and closed), how good you have been about making payments on time, what your current and past address is, who has requested your credit report in recent months, if you have any potentially negative items in your report, and what to do if you want to dispute a black mark on your report.

Many people are curious about their FICO score, which you can't get for free. Your FICO score is what lenders use to determine whether or not to give you a loan and what rate of interest they'll charge you if they do decide to give you a loan. Each credit-reporting agency calculates your FICO score independently. You can purchase the right to see your FICO scores for $14.95 each from myfico.com, but you can also get a decent estimate of your score by going to bankrate.com/brm/fico/calc.asp and anonymously answering a few questions.

▶ How Can I Stop Getting Credit Card Offers?

Lighten your junk snail mail load by filling out an online form

Cockeyed.com is a wonderful Web site of pranks, cooked up by a fellow named Rob. He once made realistic-looking fake menus for the TGIF restaurant chain and altered the descriptions ("Buffalo wings with bleu cheese dressing and celery sticks. So delicious, you'll want to throw up and eat it again"), then sent copies to people all over the country to plant in restaurants. One of his more educational pranks had to do with a pre-approved Chase MasterCard application he received in the mail (cockeyed.com/citizen/creditcard/application.shtml). He tore the application into tiny pieces, then taped it back together. He then scratched out his pre-printed address on the application, and wrote in his parent's address. Now, most credit card companies tell you to tear up applications for credit cards you don't want (Chase.com says, "If you receive financial solicitations that you're not interested in, tear them up before throwing them away, so thieves can't use them to assume your identity.").

A few weeks after sending the torn-up and taped-together application, Rob got a call from his father letting him know his Chase credit card had arrived. He used his cell phone to activate the card right then and there. The lesson? Tear up your credit card applications into *really tiny* little pieces before throwing them away.

Better yet, visit OptOutPrescreen (optoutprescreen.com), a site sponsored by the major consumer credit reporting agencies, and put a stop to unsolicited credit card offers. You can elect to opt out of receiving credit card and insurance offers for five years by filling out an online form. Or, if you want to opt out for the rest of your life, print and mail the "Permanent Opt-Out Election Form," available at the site.

Want to get rid of junk mail and help the planet? Sign up for a membership to Greendimes (greendimes.com). According to the site, 100 million trees are chopped down yearly to make junk mail in the United States. For $36 a year (about a dime a day, hence the name) Greendimes will delete your family members' names from major mailing lists and plant trees in farmland to stop erosion.

▶ How Can I Figure Out How Much My House Is Worth?

*Get an estimate of the value of your house (or anyone else's)
along with sale history and other information from Zillow*

Would you like to find out how much your house is worth? More important, would you like to find out how much your neighbor's or boss's house is worth? Zip over to Zillow (zillow.com), a treasure trove of residential real estate information. Thankfully, you don't need to fill out any personal information to gain access to the site. Just enter an address or zip code in the search field, and Zillow will return a satellite map with house values superimposed over the

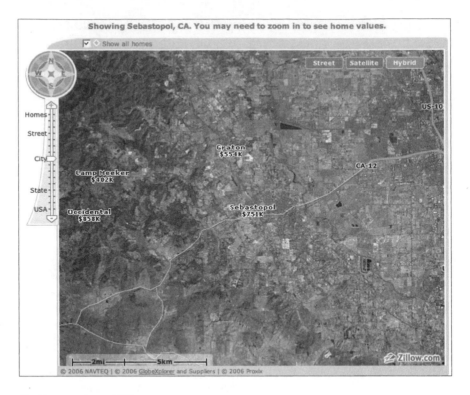

Find home values at Zillow.com.

houses. If you are interested in the average home price for a town or
zip code, enter it in the search field, and Zillow will produce a map
with superimposed values like the one shown above.

Zillow calls its house value estimates "zestimates." To come up
with a zestimate for a particular piece of property, Zillow uses a "secret formula" that takes into account the size of the house, sales data
for comparable properties in the area, and "hundreds of home details." Zillow claims that its zestimates are accurate to within 10 percent of the properties' true values. If you believe the value for a
particular property is off, you can go to "My Zestimator"
(zillow.com/howto/MyZestimator.htm) and edit the known facts
about the home (such as recent remodels).

In addition to the satellite photo views, Zillow offers higher
resolution bird's-eye views of houses in major urban locales.

Check out the bird's-eye views of famous houses (zillow.com/howto/FamousBirdsEye.htm) such as the Playboy Mansion (zestimated value: $6,186,112), the house that was featured in "The Beverly Hillbillies" ($24,871,932), and the *Brady Bunch* house (a relative bargain at $1,022,856).

Zillow is always adding useful features, and it's worthwhile to spend some time exploring them. For instance, its "heat maps" show you color-coded per-square-foot values of areas on a map for major metropolitan areas.

▶ How Can I Find Out If the Government, a Bank, an Insurance Company, or Someone Else Owes Me Money?

You might have money waiting for you to claim online

There's a fair chance that this tip could pay for this book, and then some: go to missingmoney.com/Main/StateSites.cfm, click the state you live in (or have previously lived in) and enter your name in the search form. If you're lucky, you'll discover that someone is trying to pay you money that's owed to you from an insurance settlement, a bill overpayment, or some other matter. My wife checked this and discovered that an insurance company owed her over $200. She filled out a form and several weeks later received a check. She also looked up the names of all her friends and family members and then excitedly called them, letting them know that they had money waiting for them. One friend got a check for over $500. (Her sister didn't bother claiming the $7.14 she had coming to her.)

▶ What's the Easiest Way to Pay Off Small Debts Between Friends?

A cashless way to split restaurant tabs

When you're out for a night on the town with a friend—movie, dinner, drinks at a bar—it's often inconvenient to split the bill. And who wants to break up the fun with a trip to the ATM? That was the thinking behind TextPayMe (textpayme.com), a service that lets you pay and receive money via cell phone text messages.

The beauty of TextPayMe is that you don't need to install anything on your mobile phone to use it. You just need to sign up, specify which credit card you'd like to link to the account, and choose a PIN number.

Say you owe $26.50 to your friend for lunch. Launch your phone's text messenger, enter `pay 26.50 5554340509` (where 5554340509 is your friend's phone number), and send it to sms@textpayme.com. A moment later, your phone will ring and a recorded voice will ask you to enter your PIN number. (That way, if you lose your phone, no one else can use TextPayMe.) Also, if you have a PayPal (paypal.com) account, you can use it to send money with your mobile phone. Enter `send 26.50 to 5554340509` and text it to PayPal 729725.

▶ How Can I Keep Track of Loans Between My Roommates and Me?

Make sure everyone pays their share with BillMonk

DEEPER

Pay via SMS. You can also use TextPayMe to mail a check or wire funds to a bank account. But if your PayPal account is linked to a credit card (instead of your checking account), and you don't have sufficient funds in your PayPal account to cover the transfer, you could incur fees and steep interest for these cash advances.

When I was in college, I shared an apartment with three other students. We taped a sheet of paper to the refrigerator, and whenever one of us bought dishwashing soap, or toilet paper, or some other shared commodity, we'd make a note of it on the piece of paper. If we went out for beer and one of us paid for the tab, we'd make a note of that, too. And when the bills for the phone and electricity arrived, we'd write down how much was owed. Needless to say, the piece of paper got messy rather quickly, and nobody was really sure if the accounts were being settled fairly. Of course, each of us thought that the others were freeloading, but since our system was imperfect, we never knew for sure who was getting the free ride.

If we'd had BillMonk (billmonk.com) back in those days, we'd know for sure if things were square between us. This free Web service keeps track of loans between groups of friends, providing easy-to-read reports that show you exactly how much is owed to whom. To make sure you don't forget to include a transaction, you can text expenses to b@bmonk.com, and then log onto the Web site and add the details. BillMonk also keeps track of books and videos you have loaned out to your group of friends.

How Do I Find the Best Charitable Cause to Support?

Donate money to a good cause and get the money back

Twenty-five dollars probably doesn't mean a lot to you, but to a small-business person in an impoverished nation, it can be immensely valuable. The idea of "microfinance" (lending very small sums of money to individuals in poor countries) has become popular because it helps the recipient, and it makes the person kicking in the money feel like they are really helping someone out, as opposed to funding a large charitable organization with lots of overhead. An excellent microfinance group called Kiva (kiva.org) makes it easy, and even fun, to help individuals around the planet. (Dr. Muhammad Yunus of Bangladesh came up with the concept of microcredits and was awarded a Nobel Prize for it in 2006.)

To get started, visit Kiva, and click the "Businesses" button. There, you'll see photos of the people requesting loans and a description of what they intend to do with the funds. Business plans include the selling of cooked eggs (Samoa), a general store (Bulgaria), an office-supply stand (Ecuador), and steers (Kenya). All loans are under $1,000, and you can contribute between $25 and $375 using your credit card (Kiva passes 100 percent of the funds to the local partners). After you make the loan, you'll get updates about the status of the business and, in time, your loan will be repaid (if the business is a success) without interest. You can then ask to have your money returned, or you can re-invest it in a new business.

▶ What's the Smartest Way to Pay Off My Credit Cards?

A Web site can help you figure out the most efficient way to pay off your debt

More than once I've read that the best way to get out of debt when you have multiple loans is to pay off the smallest debt first. That never really made sense to me though, because this simplistic method doesn't take the interest rates of your loans into account.

The author of the Snowball Calculator (us.whatsthecost .com/snowball.aspx) agrees, and has created an online calculator that figures out the least expensive way for you to get out of debt. You start by entering the number, type, size, and interest rate of loans you have (car, credit, home equity, etc.). Then, you tell the calculator how much money you can spend each month servicing these debts, and click "Calculate." You'll be presented with detailed instructions on how much money to send each lender every month until the debt is paid off. It will also tell you how many months it will take you to become debt-free.

The report also shows you why it's almost always a terrible idea to consolidate your debt into a mortgage, which many people do under the mistaken assumption they'll save money this way (because your home mortgage payoff time is much longer than your credit card's, so even if the interest rate is lower, the total amount you spend to pay off the debt will be a lot more).

▶ What's the Best Way to Get Rich Quick from Investing in the Market?

Now really—if I had discovered a way to get rich from investing in the stock market, do you think I would be taking time away from sculpting on my villa's balcony overlooking the Italian Riviera to write this book? Believe me, I've tried different schemes, but here I am, tapping away at my keyboard in my office in a Los Angeles suburb, accompanied not by the sounds of the surf and Vespas buzzing along cobblestone roads, but by the *chukka-chukka* of helicopters and traffic from the Hollywood freeway rattling my windows. But that hasn't stopped me from trying any number of the get-rich-quick and get-rich-slow schemes that abound online.

I may not be getting rich from investing, but I'm not getting poorer, either. Because I'm not a professional financial advisor, I can't tell you where to put your money. But I will point you to a few online resources that could help you make better decisions about investing.

Dollar cost averaging made easy. If your investment capital is limited to the amount you'd spend on dinner and movie, you can still get in the game. ShareBuilder (sharebuilder.com) allows you to set up an account that automatically invests a certain sum of money at regular intervals into stocks of your choosing. The money is drawn from your bank account automatically. This type of investment is called "dollar cost averaging" because you invest a set amount each month. The nice thing about dollar cost averaging is that when the share price is low, you get more shares at the bargain price, and when the share price is high, you buy fewer shares at the higher price. In other words, this method helps you get the most shares for your money in a volatile market. Another nice thing about ShareBuilder's program is that you can buy fractional shares of high-priced stocks. If you are interested in investing in Google, but don't have enough to buy one share, at $500, you can still invest $25 a month to buy 1/20 of a share at a time. ShareBuilder offers several different plans, with different price structures for each.

Dogs of the Dow. There are hundreds of surefire stock-picking methods, and most of them work no better than a chimp throwing darts at the financial section of the newspaper. But many people swear by a method called Dogs of the Dow. They may be onto something. Since 1973, the method has had an average annual return of 17.7 percent and has consistently outperformed the major market indices. The basic idea (and there are many variations) behind Dogs of the Dow is to buy the same dollar amount of the ten highest-yielding stocks from the 30 stocks in the Dow Jones Industrial Average, hold them for a year, and then sell the ones that rise out of the "dog house," using the proceeds to buy new "dogs." You can get a list of the current ten dogs and detailed how-to instructions at dogsofthedow.com.

Magic Formula Investing. This method is based on Joel Greenblatt's bestseller, *The Little Book That Beats the Market*. The Magic Formula uses a stock's earning yield (basically, how much the stock costs) and its return on capital (basically, how much the stock makes) to rank its value with other companies. Those stocks that make a lot of money but don't cost a lot of money are ripe for buying. Greenblatt, a fund manager with a fund that has grown an average of 40 percent a year for over 20 years, tested his method using historical stock price data and claims that people who stick with the program for the long haul will significantly outperform the market indices. He said his method has a stunning 30.8 percent return over the last 17 years. You can generate lists of high-ranking Magic Formula stocks at Greenblatt's site, Magic Formula Investing (magicformulainvesting.com).

Once you come up with a plan, the best way to track your portfolio is by setting up an account at Yahoo! Finance (finance.yahoo.com) or Google Finance (finance.google.com). They both offer excellent portfolio management and research tools to keep up with your investments.

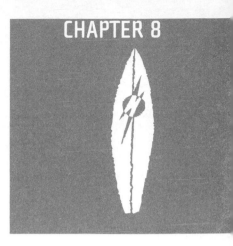

CHAPTER 8

COMMUNICATION

The Web was designed to make it easier for people to communicate with each other. And the wireless Web makes it easy for people to communicate wherever they happen to be. This section will show you how to create a wireless network at home, how to use a wireless network when you're away from home, and how to use great new services that greatly enhance your telephone communication. You might even be able to reduce your phone bill.

 ## WIRELESS COMPUTING

▶ What Is Wi-Fi?

An introduction to wireless computing, and why it's so darn cool

When I opened the box containing my first AirPort Wi-Fi base station in 1999, I had no idea how much the technology behind this flying saucer–shaped object would change the way I, and everyone else, used the Internet. Before Wi-Fi came on the scene, there was no inexpensive or convenient way to access the Internet outside the home or office. In hotels, I'd have to connect my computer to the phone line in my room and dial-up my Internet service provider, which resulted in astonishingly high phone bills at check-out time.

Today, wireless Internet connections abound in urban locations. Most hotels, coffee houses, fast-food restaurants, universities, airports, and businesses have Wi-Fi networks. Many are "open," meaning you can use them without a password (see page 252 for the ethical question of accessing open wireless networks), and places like Starbucks let you use their network for a fee (which you can pay by the day or the month). With my cell phone and my laptop, I can work almost anywhere (which is both a good and a bad thing).

The term Wi-Fi was coined as a snappy substitute for IEEE 802.11x (its geeky technical name) and, contrary to popular belief, it isn't short for "Wireless Fidelity" or anything else—"Wi-Fi" is what it is. Functionally speaking, it's a set of instructions for configuring radios that allow computers to talk to each other without wires.

Think of Wi-Fi as a way to replace data cables. If Wi-Fi didn't exist, all those people at Starbucks would have to plug a cable into their computers that snaked along the floor to the high-speed modem in the back room. Instead, the radios in their laptops talk to a single base station that is wired to the Internet.

Today, Wi-Fi is so prevalent that most computers come equipped with a built in Wi-Fi transmitter. One of the reasons Wi-Fi spread so quickly in just a few short years, besides being so convenient, is that the particular frequencies they use to transmit are unlicensed, meaning anyone can use them without having to obtain a license from the government. Unlike starting a radio station or using a ham radio, you don't need permission to set up a Wi-Fi network in your house or office, which greatly simplifies things.

Of course, the fact that Wi-Fi uses unlicensed spectra (the 2.4-GHz and 5-GHz bands to be specific) means that other uses can interfere with a Wi-Fi signal. Wireless phone handsets are notorious for causing Wi-Fi disruption, as are microwave ovens and baby monitors. Most Wi-Fi equipment can counteract some of these competing signals with so-called "interference robustness," but sometimes your only option is getting a new phone or accepting the fact that you won't be able to surf the Web when you're nuking a meal in the microwave.

▶ How Can I Set Up a Home Wireless Network?

Bathe your home in the warm glow of wireless Internet

So you're ready to go wireless. How do you get started? First, you need an Internet connection—DSL, cable, and even dial-up will do. Next, you need two or more pieces of Wi-Fi equipment: a Wi-Fi card for each computer you want to connect to the network, and a Wi-Fi router to communicate with all of the computers.

Let's take a look at a typical home wireless network. It's got a DSL or cable modem, which is directly connected to the phone company or cable company's network. Then there's the wireless router, which has a Wi-Fi transmitter and an Ethernet jack to connect it to the modem. (The wireless router usually includes other Ethernet jacks in it so that you can connect the router to non-Wi-Fi printers and computers in the network). Finally, there are Wi-Fi equipped computers, PDAs, and peripherals (such as Wi-Fi printers) that communicate with the router using radio signals.

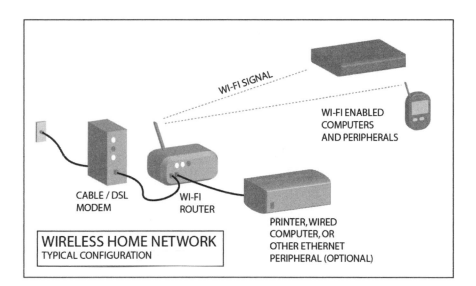

WI-FI SIGNAL

WI-FI ENABLED
COMPUTERS
AND PERIPHERALS

CABLE / DSL
MODEM

WI-FI
ROUTER

PRINTER, WIRED
COMPUTER, OR
OTHER ETHERNET
PERIPHERAL (OPTIONAL)

WIRELESS HOME NETWORK
TYPICAL CONFIGURATION

The Wi-Fi router is the heart of the system. It's typically the size of a paperback book and is connected to the modem with an Ethernet cable. All your computers and other Wi-Fi devices send and receive their signals to and from the router. Prices vary for routers. At a site like Free After Rebate (freeafterrebate.info), you might be able to find a router that costs nothing except shipping costs. Or you can pay up to $200 for Apple's AirPort Extreme base station. If you have a Mac, you don't necessarily need an AirPort router; you can buy one from Belkin, Buffalo, D-Link, or LinkSys, because these companies make routers that use the same Wi-Fi chips as the AirPort Extreme and cost a lot less, often in the sub-$30 range. Look around Shopzilla (shopzilla.com) and Froogle (froogle.com) for deals.

When you get your router, read the instructions for setting it up. There's a good chance it will work out of the box, but there are some things you'll probably want to change, such as the SSID (service set identifier, a.k.a. the name of the network that appears on your computer when you want to connect to it), which typically has a default name like "linksys" or, even, "default." Next, you need to set up your computers for wireless. Most laptops come with Wi-Fi out of the box, and will instantly find and start using the first open wireless network it finds. On the Mac, you can select your wireless network by clicking on the antenna signal strength indicator on the menu bar (📶) and clicking on the name of your network. On Windows, right click "Network Connections" in the Control Panel, and click the "Wireless Network Connection" icon. In the Network Tasks panel on the left, click "View all available wireless networks." Then select your network.

▶ How Can I Tell if Someone Is Using My Wireless Network?

You can look in the logs of your router or install more sophisticated monitoring software

The software installed on your wireless router, which is usually accessed via a local Web address (consult the manual), usually has a logging function that lets you see what Web sites have been accessed recently. First off, make sure that it's enabled. By checking the logs periodically, you can see if there's any suspicious activity happening through your router. The next thing you can do is to check your computer security software (you do have security software, don't you?). Recent products, such as the popular (and recommended) Norton Security 2007 (symantec.com), have Intrusion Detection Software (IDS) built into them, which will alert you to any unwanted visitors on your network. There are also free and shareware programs, such as WallWatcher (sonic.net/wallwatcher), a popular logfiller program, that you can use. Securepoint Intrusion Detection (securepoint.cc) is another good program that's also free. A recommended software solution for the Mac is NetBarrier (intego.com). You can try it for free. It retails for $70. These programs offer many sophisticated tools for monitoring all of the incoming/outgoing traffic over your network. But rather than watch your uninvited guests traipsing around the inner sanctum of your electronic cottage, why not keep them out entirely (if you don't care to offer open access to your neighbors)? Your router software likely came with a WEP (Wired Equivalent Privacy) or WPA (Wi-Fi Protected Access) program built into it. See the next section to learn more about securing your network with encryption.

▶ How Can I Protect My Data When I Use a Wireless Network?

How to keep hackers from accessing data sent through a Wi-Fi network

Using a Wi-Fi network is a lot like using walkie-talkies. Anyone who has a walkie-talkie tuned to the same band can potentially listen in on your conversation.

A Wi-Fi signal has a maximum range of about 300 feet (though walls and foliage diminish Wi-Fi signals considerably.)

What can people who have access to your Wi-Fi network do with it? Theoretically, they can access your computers, use your Internet

service, and eavesdrop on everything—including passwords, bank
account information, credit card numbers, the contents of Web
pages you look at, and files you send and receive—that gets sent over
the wireless network.

It's not hard for a snoopy person to see the email you send and
receive and the photos and videos you download as they are being
transmitted back and forth between your computer and Wi-Fi
router. This has the potential to be embarrassing, but it's unlikely
they'll be able to harvest your credit card numbers and banking information as it zips through the air. That's because most online
stores and financial institutions use something called Secure Sockets Layer (SSL) to encrypt your data. (You can tell if a site uses SSL by
looking at the address bar. If the address starts with https://instead
of the normal http://then you're communicating securely.)

If you're concerned about the possibility of people accessing
your network, here are some ways to make it much more difficult
for them:

Hide your network. A Wi-Fi network can be "closed" or "open."
An open network can be detected by any wireless computer within
range of the Wi-Fi signal. If you close your network (the instructions for closing your network are in the user's manual for your Wi-
Fi router), computers within range will not be able to see the
network. This is a good way to stop most people from using your Internet connection if you don't want them to "freeload." (But if
someone uses your Wi-Fi once in a while to check his or her email or
go online, why should you care? After all, most Internet service
plans are "all you can eat," so it doesn't cost you anything.) A closed
network isn't a very effective way to stop a determined hacker, because they use programs that can sniff out closed systems.

Encrypt your network. All Wi-Fi routers have the option of en-
crypting the data sent over the network. That means only the computers that have the software "key" are able to decrypt the data being
sent over the network. The most common type of encryption is
called WEP (Wired Equivalent Privacy), but a much more secure
method of encryption, WPA (Wi-Fi Protected Access), is available
on all newer Wi-Fi routers. Your Wi-Fi router manual will explain

how to set up WEP or WPA on your network. Once you've configured it, only the people who know the password will be able to access the network.

▶ How Can I Extend the Range of My Wireless Network?

Some simple ways to boost a faint Wi-Fi signal

If you're suffering from a weak wireless signal, the first thing you want to do is to make sure you're doing everything you can to maximize the reach of the gear you already have. Ideally, your wireless router should be in the most central location relative to the computers and other wireless devices it serves. Try placing it as high in the room as possible. You can also buy a Wi-Fi sniffer, such as the Wi-Fi Seeker, a USB device for $20 (wifiseeker.com). It shows you when a wireless network is in range and its signal strength. Keep moving your router around the room until you find a spot and a height that's best. Don't forget that the position of the antennae on the router make a difference too, so play with them as well.

You can also replace the antenna(e) on your wireless router, if it allows for that. Brands that have the "rubber duck" type of antenna, which the majority of them do, can be easily swapped out for bigger antennae. This will cost you $8 on up, depending on how big and powerful the new antennas are. Some people have found great success in creating antenna reflectors from available materials such as wire mesh and cardboard. Here's a link to one project site about building simple antenna reflectors: www.freeantennas.com.

If you are feeling brave and are willing to deal with port settings and MAC addresses, you might try your hand at a WDS, or "Wireless Distribution System," which involves using multiple wireless routers set up as repeaters. Routers are cheap these days—I saw some advertised recently for $8 each! Unfortunately, different brands don't get along with each other, so if you go this route, get the same brand. A tutorial on creating a WDS can be found here: http://www.devicescape.com/docs/wip/admin_guide/WDS.php. Make sure

DEEPER

The potential dangers of an open network. Some people keep their networks open and unsecured because they like sharing their Internet access with passers-by who want to check on their email. I keep an open network myself. However, there are risks to doing this, above and beyond someone eavesdropping on your network traffic. For instance, in November 2003, Toronto police found a man in his car, naked from the waist down, watching child porn. He had downloaded the video over a Wi-Fi access point emanating from a nearby house. The man was arrested and charged with possession of child pornography and for "theft of communications" (the first time the new law had been put to use in Canada). The owner of the Wi-Fi access point had no idea that his network was responsible for transmitting the pornography and was not charged, but some lawyers say he took a legal risk for allowing his access point to run insecurely. Also, if authorities had been tapping the home-owner's network, they may have erroneously concluded that he was the one download-ing the porn, not the creep parked outside his house. Keep in mind that no one has been charged yet with the crime of having an unsecured Wi-Fi network that a criminal used to commit a crime.

you have plenty of aspirin (and maybe a good single-malt scotch) on hand before you strap on the propeller beanie and undertake this. Mac users have it easier: the AirPort Extreme base station and some versions of the AirPort Express base station do WDS auto-matically.

Beyond re-positioning your wireless router/base station and upgrading your antenna, the next thing to do that's easy but more costly is buying a range extender. Avoid the type that plugs into the wall and uses your home's electrical wiring as a data channel. These tend not to work as advertised. Extenders will cost from $40 to $140 each.

How Can I Share One Internet Connection with More Than One Computer at the Same Time?

Your computer has the ability to share its Internet connection with other computers. Here's how to do it.

Unless you live alone, there's probably more than one computer in your house. But you most likely have just one Internet connection. Does that mean only one person can get online at a time? Not at all. It's easy to share an Internet connection so that two or more people can be online at the same time.

The easiest way to do this is with a wireless network, which re-quires a wireless router (see "How Can I Set Up a Home Wireless Net-work?" on page 241). But if you don't want to set up a wireless network, or even a wired network, it's still possible for two computers to share an Internet connection. Here's how.

>Internet sharing with two Windows computers

1. You need a working Internet connection (DSL or cable—I wouldn't bother trying to share a dial-up connection because it'll be very slow when both computers are online at the same time), two computers, and two Ethernet cables. You probably already have one of the cables—a category-5 patch cable that

connects your main computer to the DSL or cable modem. You also need a category-5 crossover cable to connect the two computers together. The cables might be labeled 10base-T or 100base-T. Get the 100base-T, which is rated for higher speed, just to be safe. That's all you need in the way of equipment.

2. The host computer (that is, the computer that's connected directly to the cable or DSL modem) requires two Ethernet jacks. Most computers come with only one Ethernet connection, so you'll need to remedy that by adding another Ethernet jack. If you don't feel like opening up your computer and installing an Ethernet card, you can buy a USB-to-Ethernet adapter, which plugs into a spare USB port on your computer. It'll cost about $30. If you aren't afraid to remove your computer's case and plug a card into a slot, then buy an Ethernet card. It's less messy, and a lot cheaper: I've seen new ones on eBay going for a dollar. Whichever method you choose, the hardware will come with a CD-ROM containing a driver you need to install to make it work with your computer.

3. Now it's time to set up the host computer for sharing. First, make sure your Internet connection works by taking a test drive on the Web. Then connect the crossover cable from your host computer to the client. On the host, go to the Control Panel and double click "Network Connections." You'll see at least two icons in the window: one for your local area connection and one for your Internet connection.

4. Right-click the Internet connection icon and select "Properties." Make sure that both "Client for Microsoft Networks" and "Internet Protocol (TCP/IP)" are checked. (If you don't see these items, click "Install" and select them.) When you are finished, click "OK."

5. Now, it's time to turn on Internet sharing. Click the "Advanced" tab of the Internet connection properties window and check the box next to "Allow other network users to connect through this computer's Internet connection." Then click "OK."

6. The final step is to set up the client computer. Go to the Control Panel and double-click "Network Connections." You should see the icon for your local area connection. (If you don't, you'll need to reinstall the driver for the Ethernet hardware before proceeding.) Right-click the local area connection icon and select "Properties." Make sure both "Client for Microsoft Networks" and "Internet Protocol (TCP/IP)" are checked. (If you don't see these items, click "Install" and select them.)

Double-click "Internet Protocol (TCP/IP)" to bring up its properties settings. Make sure that the radio buttons for "Obtain an IP address automatically" and "Obtain DNS server address automatically" are chosen. Click "OK" and close the properties window. Test the Internet connection on the client computer and the host computer by opening a Web page on each.

>Internet sharing with more than two Windows computers

1. The steps for sharing an Internet connection with three or more computers are the same as the ones for the example above, with one difference: instead of a crossover cable, you'll need to get an Ethernet hub, which is an inexpensive box that sports several Ethernet jacks to connect computers and printers to each other. You can buy 4-, 5-, 8-, and sixteen-port hubs. You'll need one port (each jack corresponds to a port) for each device you connect to the network. If you have three computers and one (Ethernet-enabled) printer, you can get by with a 4-port hub. A 10base-T will set you back about $30, and a faster 100base-T will cost a bit more.

2. The host computer still needs two Ethernet jacks, but instead of connecting the host to the client with a crossover cable, you'll connect the host to the hub with a standard patch cable.

3. Set up the host and each client as explained above, and test your connection on each computer by trying to open a Web page.

4. Another option is to replace the hub with a router, which has built-in smarts to share the network with each computer. The router connects directly to the modem with an Ethernet cable, and each computer also connects to the router with an Ethernet cable. In this case, there's no host; every computer is a client.

>Internet sharing with two Macs

Sharing an Internet connection between two Macs is even easier than it is with two Windows machines. Why? Because your host computer (the one that's directly connected to the Internet with an Ethernet cable) doesn't need Internet jacks on it. Instead, you can use a FireWire cable to connect the host computer to the client computer.

1. Let's start with what you need in the hardware department: an Internet connection, an Ethernet cable, a FireWire cable, and two computers. Your host computer is already using the Ethernet cable, which is plugged into the cable TV or DSL modem that

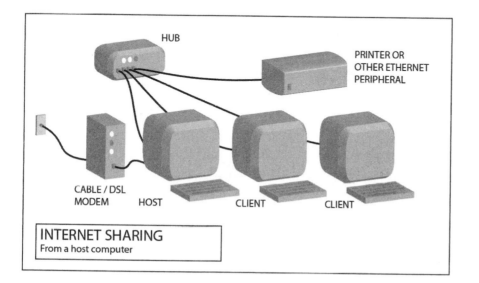

delivers Internet to your home. Connect the two computers together with a FireWire cable by plugging each end of the cable into the Macs' FireWire jacks.

2. Now you need to configure the sharing and network software on your Macs. Open "Network" in "Applications" → "System Preferences." Select "Network Port Configurations" from the "Show" menu and check "Built-in FireWire." On the host computer open "Sharing" in Applications → System Preferences. Click "Internet," and then select "Share your connection from: Built-in Ethernet" and "To computers using Built-in FireWire," then click "Start."

3. On the client computer open "Network" in "Applications" → "System Preferences." Select "Network Port Configurations" from the "Show" menu and check "Built-in FireWire." Click "Apply Now." Test your setup by opening a Web page on both computers.

>Internet sharing with more than two Macs

To share one Internet connection with three or more Macs, you should follow the same physical set-up as described in a three-or-more Windows network. On each of the computers open "Network" in "Applications" → "System Preferences." Select "Network Port Configurations" from the "Show" menu and check "Built-in Ethernet." Click "Apply Now." Test your setup by opening a Web page on all the computers.

You can also go the other direction, from wireless to a wire. If you connect to a fee-based wireless Internet service (like the kind T-Mobile offers at Starbucks), your friend can connect to your computer with a FireWire cable and use your connection along with you.

DEEPER

Hotel and coffee-house sharing. You can use sharing to save money on hotel Internet charges. When my wife and I need to be online at the same time in a hotel room that charges for Internet access, we'll connect one computer to the Ethernet cable that's connected to the hotel's Internet service. Then, we'll turn on Wi-Fi sharing for that computer. Now, anyone else who is in the room (or the rooms around us) can get free wireless Internet.

▶▶ CONNECTING ON THE ROAD

▶ How Can I Use My Bluetooth Mobile Phone and Laptop to Access the Internet?

You'll need a data plan for your phone, Bluetooth capability on your laptop, and a little patience

Wi-Fi wireless Internet has become so prevalent, at least in most urban areas, that we can take it for granted that we'll be able to access the Internet with our mobile computers when we want to. But what do you do when you have to grab a file or check your email and there is no wired or wireless access to be had? Well, if you have a Bluetooth-enabled phone and mobile computer, you can use your phone as a modem and access the Net that way. It's not high-speed, by any stretch of the imagination, but it's good enough in a pinch. Every setup is different, so we can't go into all of the variations here. You'll want to go onto the Web site of your wireless provider and search on "Bluetooth Dial-Up Networking" (or "Bluetooth DUN"). This should tell you all you need to know.

Basically, what you'll need is a Bluetooth-enabled mobile phone and you'll need to have Internet service available as part of your phone plan. On the PC side, you'll need to either have Bluetooth built into your laptop or a Bluetooth adapter. These are usually USB stick-type dongles that you can get for under $30. With these in place, you then need to get your phone and laptop talking to each other (known as "discovering" or "pairing"). Again, this process is slightly different, depending on your laptop, Bluetooth type, and operating system. On Windows XP, you'll likely go to "My Bluetooth Places." On a Mac, it'll be under the Bluetooth icon in the upper-right corner of your screen (or in "System Preferences" → "Hardware"). Check the docs for your hardware and software. When your laptop has found your phone and you double-click on the icon/listing for it, it'll likely ask for a name and password and a dialing number. What you enter here varies from carrier to carrier, so consult your provider's online info on Bluetooth DUN. Once the connection is made and the phone knows you want a connection (via the number you entered), you should be good to go.

▶ How Can I Find a Free Wi-Fi Connection When I'm Traveling?

Log into a public Wi-Fi hotspot and enjoy free Internet

A wireless Internet connection is a delight. I have a wireless network in my house, and it frees me from having to be tethered to an outlet. I can take my computer into any room of the house, and when the weather is nice (which is often here in Southern California) I can sit by the swimming pool and do my email or surf the Web. (If you'd like to set up a wireless network at home, see page 241.)

When I travel, a wireless connection is even more valuable. I subscribe to T-Mobile's HotSpot Internet service (hotspot.t-mobile.com), which costs $29.95 a month and is available at almost every U.S. Starbucks, Borders, and Kinkos in existence, as well as many airports and hotel chains. But there are lots of places I go where T-Mobile doesn't offer Wi-Fi, and that's when I start looking for an "open" Wi-Fi network.

There are basically two kinds of Wi-Fi networks: "closed" ones, which require a password to use, and "open" ones, which can be used by anyone without a password. The person or organization that owns the network can configure it to be closed or open with the flip of a software switch. I'm a believer in open access. If you are in my neighborhood (within a couple of hundred feet of my house) and you open your laptop (provided it has a wireless card installed), you'll see my open Wi-Fi network. You're free to use it to check email or a Web site. (You won't be able to see what's on my computers, though, because those are password-protected.)

Some people think it's unethical to use a stranger's Wi-Fi connection without their permission, and some states have made it illegal to use a wireless connection without the owner's permission. For example, in March 2006, a 32-year-old man in Rockford, Illinois, was spotted by a police officer late at night parked outside a nonprofit agency. The man had his laptop computer open and the officer questioned him, somehow surmising that he had been surfing the Net using the wireless connection. He was cited and fined $250, and warned that he could have been sentenced to a year in jail. Note that the man wasn't trying to break into the nonprofit's computer system. He was parked on a public street, using a wireless connection he had discovered. The fact that he was charged with a crime is, in my opinion, ridiculous.

Don't get me wrong. I don't think it's right to use someone's *closed* network (there are tools to crack the passwords to closed systems, but I'm not going to mention them by name) because they have kept it closed for a reason. I see no problem, though, in using someone's *open* Wi-Fi access point to download email or check a Web site. I consider it the owner's responsibility to keep the network locked if he or she doesn't want to share. Timothy Lee, a policy analyst at the Show-Me Institute, a nonpartisan research organization, likens the occasional sharing of a wireless access to be the "the 21st-century equivalent of lending a cup of sugar." (Now, I would have a problem with a neighbor who used my Wi-Fi connection to suck down huge multimedia files all day long, though, because it would slow my access to the Internet down. This kind of leeching is bad manners, and I would regrettably have to close my network to stop him.)

Now that you know what you're up against, you have to decide whether or not using strangers' open networks is OK for you. If you don't think it is, you can stop reading here. If you feel OK with it, here are some ways to find open networks.

First, pull out your laptop and look at the Wi-Fi signal strength indicator on the menu bar. (It's on the top right of both Mac and Windows.) If there's at least one colored bar on the icon it means there's Wi-Fi where you happen to be. But then you have to click the icon and then click the name of the network (on Windows, click the icon and then click "View Wireless Networks") to see if you can access it. If you are asked for a password, you're out of luck. If not, you'll be connected to the network and will probably be able to access the Internet (I say probably because in some cases a network will appear to be open, but will only work for registered computers).

		MacStumbler 0.7b						

Details: private
  MAC: 00:06:25:DF:9A:19
  Vendor: Linksys
  Type: Managed

Location: GPS Enabled
  Lat: W 3337.826904
  Lon: N 11739.685547

Comments:

My home network ;)

Save Open Clear   Status   Prefs Details

SSID	Chan	Signal	Noise	WEP	Vendor
default	6	21	6	No	D-Link
private	11	21	7	Yes	Linksys

Log:

SSID	Chan	Max Sig	WEP	Last Seen	Vendor
private	11	29	Yes	03:17PM 07/02/03	Linksys
default	6	27	No	03:17PM 07/02/03	D-Link

Searching for an open Wi-Fi signal with a "stumbler" utility.

Roaming Wi-Fi

Almost every business traveler needs an Internet connection, and more vacationers than ever are realizing the advantages of bringing a laptop along with them on holiday. With a computer and an Internet connection, you can store and upload digital photos, share your daily adventures on your blog, make free (or almost free) long-distance phone calls, use a Webcam for live videochats with your jealous friends and co-workers, and use Google to search for restaurants, look at schedules, get driving directions, and make reservations.

One of the best deals around for access to

45,000 Wi-Fi hotspots is Boingo (boingo.com), a company started by Sky Dayton, founder of Earthlink. Boingo has made revenue-sharing deals with hot-spot owners around the world. Customers pay $21.95 a month for full access and unlimited use of hotspots in Boingo's partner network, from a Kentucky Fried Chicken restaurant in Costa Rica to a nightclub in Moscow. The Boingo software (available for Mac, Windows, and Pocket Windows) helps you find a nearby hotspot.

The problem with this method is that it is inconvenient to have to try to log in to find out whether or not a network is available to you. You can make things a little simpler by using a "stumbler" application—NetStumbler for Windows (stumbler.net) or MacStumbler for Macintosh (macstumbler.com), which detects nearby wireless access points and lets you know if they're open or closed and how strong their signal is. With a stumbler you can see all the networks in your immediate area at the same time, which is much easier than clicking on each network's name one-at-a time under the Wi-Fi icon.

Mac users can install a nifty and free little app called Coconut Wi-Fi (coconut-flavor.com/coconutwifi) that adds a colored dot to their menu bar. A red dot means no networks are available. An amber dot means only encrypted networks are available. A green dot means you are in luck: at least one open and unencrypted network is available.

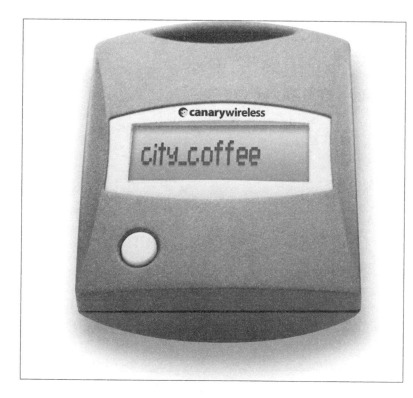

Wi-Fi finders show you available hotspots.

DEEPER

A better way to look for wireless networks. In all the above examples, the downside is that you have to take your notebook computer out of your backpack or case and open it up to check for a Wi-Fi signal. But there's a better way: get a handheld Wi-Fi detector. These are devices—ranging in size from a car-key fob to a mobile phone—that can alert you whenever you're in range of a Wi-Fi network. The cheapest ones (about $30, such as the Kensington Wifi Finder Plus) come with LEDs that light up when you're close to an access point. The more lights, the stronger the signal. On the positive side, they're tiny. On the negative side, they can't distinguish between an open and a closed network. The best one is the $60 Digital Hotspotter from Canary Wireless, which, at 2.5 inches × 2 inches, is a little larger than other Wi-Fi detectors, but comes with an LCD display that indicates whether or not a network is open or closed, along with other useful information, such as how many networks are in range. Don't leave home without one. Canary has stopped making the Digital Hotspotter (they are working on an updated version), but they're easy to find on eBay and froogle.com.

Here's another way to find out about free Wi-Fi access points: go to jiwire.com and search a directory of businesses, hotels, cafés, airports, and other places that offer free Wi-Fi (or will give you a password to use Wi-Fi if you buy a cup of coffee.)

How Can I Read My Email on Someone Else's Computer Anywhere in the World?

Use a Web-based email program to log onto your email account

Even if you don't have a Web-based email account like Gmail or Hotmail, you can still check your email on other people's computers or from an Internet café. My favorite service for getting email on the road is mail2Web.com, which is free and doesn't require registration. After going to the site, enter your email address and your password and click "Check Mail." You can also compose and send messages from mail2Web.com. It saves your mail on the server (unless you delete it on the Web site) so that when you get home, you'll have a copy for your records. Make sure you log out before leaving! Hint: before you hit the road, find out where the nearest cybercafé is by logging on to Cybercafes (netcafes.com).

▶▶ MOBILE PHONES

▶ How Can I Get Out of My Phone Contract?

A couple of Web sites can help you find someone willing to take over your phone contract

Mobile phone companies are not known for offering high-quality customer service. But if you're under contract with a carrier you can't stand, you're stuck with it, unless you fork over an "early termination fee" of between $150 and $250 per phone. If you have a family plan with more than one phone, it can add up to some real folding money.

Fortunately, the law says that if you can find someone willing to take over your contract, you can wash your hands of the whole deal. A couple of online services have sprouted up to create markets for buyers and sellers of cell phone contracts. Both CellTradeUSA (cell-tradeusa.com) and Cellswapper (cellswapper.com) let you list your contract for interested buyers.

Cellswapper charges $9.95 and CellTradeUSA charges $19.95 to list your phone and plan. The service is free for buyers, and for anyone interested in buying a mobile phone, these sites are a great place to look for deals, because sellers are often willing to give you their phone for free, and even offer you cash to take over the plan payments. As a buyer, you benefit from not having to pay an activation fee, and your contract will expire sooner than it would if you walked into a store and bought a new phone.

▶ Where Can I Shop for the Best Cell Phone Plan?

Use a phone plan comparison service to find the best plan for your needs

MyRatePlan.com is a convenient way to find the best deal on a mobile phone plan in your area. You start by entering your zip code number and a preference for a single phone or a family plan. Then you're presented with a page filled with photos of phones that are available. To narrow down the choices, adjust various slider bars and click different buttons to indicate the kind of phone you're looking for.

You can filter your choices by price, carrier, brand, size, weight, battery life, design style, camera resolution . . . you get the idea. As you become more specific in the kind of phone you want, the number of photos decreases. Once you narrow your choices down to two or three phones, click the "Compare" tab and drag the phone icons into the windows to compare the phones features side-by-side. Once you find a phone you like, click "Rate Plan" to go to the order page. (See page 258.)

Another excellent site for narrowing down your choices when looking for a mobile phone plan is Wirefly (wirefly.com). It's a

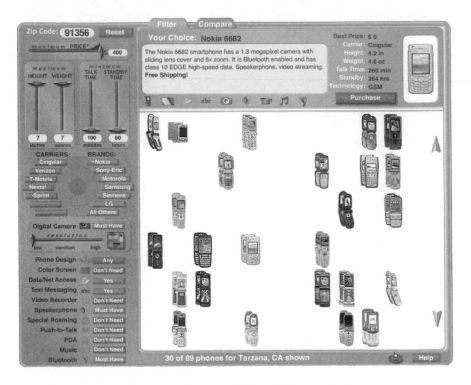

MyRatePlan.com lets you narrow down your choice of phones and plans.

good idea to use both MyRatePlan and Wirefly to find the best deal for you.

▶ How Can I Screen My Mobile Phone Calls?

Signing up for CallWave, a cell phone enhancement service, is free

Most people I know call me on my cell phone, because they know I carry it with me wherever I go. I don't really mind, but I prefer to use my landline. A free service called CallWave (callwave.com) lets me transfer calls to my landline, and even better, screen them. To sign up for CallWave, you fill out the online form as shown. The transfer number is the number you would like to transfer calls to. I entered my office number. (See page 259.)

Screen your phone calls with CallWave.

Next, the instructions will tell you to enter a string of characters into your phone (for Cingular phones, the string was *004*17756651234*11#), then press "Send" or "Dial." That's it! Like mutant limbs sprouting out of a movie monster, your phone has suddenly acquired a new set of functions.

The first new mutant limb, er, function, is call screening. When your phone rings and you don't recognize the person on the other end, you can either answer the call as usual, taking your chances that it is a telemarketer trying to sell you tickets to the Policemen's Benevolent Association, or you can press the "Ignore" button on your phone. Your phone will immediately start ringing again, and this time when you answer, you will be able to hear the person leaving a message on your voicemail. If you wish to talk to the caller, press "1."

If not, just hit the "Ignore" button again, and the message will be recorded. The caller will be none the wiser.

If you press "2," the call will be routed to the phone you specified in the transfer number. (See page 258.) Most phone carriers don't charge extra for this feature, but it's a good idea to check before going hog wild. Again, this happens without the caller knowing what's going on.

The way in which CallWave treats recorded messages is another cool function. You can access the message from your phone, but it will also be emailed to you as a sound file. That way, even if you aren't near your phone when someone leaves a message, you'll be able to listen to it on your computer.

Windows users have one extra nifty CallWave feature. By downloading a small program, you can screen calls right from your computer, even if your cellphone is turned off. You can choose from several numbers from which to transfer the call.

Why is CallWave offering this service for free? They're hoping you'll like the service enough to try some of the other services they offer, such as CallWave For Your Cell Pro, which lets callers leave longer messages, an "Internet answering machine" for home or office use, and an email fax service.

How Can I Make Free Ringtones for My Mobile Phone?

Don't waste money buying ringtones when you can roll your own

The international market for ringtones is in the billions of dollars. And every one of those dollars was needlessly spent. The cell phone carriers and the recorded industry love the ringtone business—where else can you sell something for $3 (the price of most ringtones) when you can buy a better version (the entire song, not just a snippet) for $1 on iTunes. If you have a teenager with a mobile phone in the house, check your phone bill carefully. It's not uncommon for kids to buy $50 worth of ringtones in a month. It's also not uncommon for cell phone carriers to bury those charges in the small print of your monthly bill.

I'm here to plead with you never to buy another ringtone again. They're a waste of money and, besides, it's more fun to make your own. Here are a few different ways.

>The super easy way

If your phone has a voice recorder function, you can record songs and other sounds by holding the phone next to the source of the sound, and then choosing the sound file as your ringtone. The quality isn't great by any standard, but you can't beat it for simplicity.

>The easy $20 way

If your phone accepts text messages, you can make ringtones the easy way, with a $20 program called the XingTone Ringtone Maker (xingtone.com). To see if your phone works with this application, visit xingtone.com/support/phoneTest.php and enter your phone number, carrier, and phone make and model. Then check your phone for a text message. If you see one from Xingtone, you're good to go. (If not, don't despair, just skip this method and try the "Not-as-easy free way," below.)

Before buying the application, you should first download the free demo, which allows you to create and upload one ringtone. If that's all the ringtone goodness you'll ever need, then you won't even need to buy the program.

>The not-as-easy free way

If you don't have a phone that can accept text messages, or you just don't want to spend $20 on a computer program, you can still get ringtones onto your phone. I'll assume you already have an audio file on your computer that you want to convert to a ringtone. Any MP3 file or audio CD track will do.

Next, you need to get a sound-editing file. I'm a huge fan of Audacity (audacity.sourceforge.net), a free audio-editing application that's available in Windows and Mac versions. You'll also need to download an additional piece of software called LAME

add information about the caller so that it shows up in caller ID the next time they call. You can also click a checkbox to always send calls from a certain number to spam, so you never have to take a call from that number or even hear their voicemail ever again.

(rarewares.org/mp3.html), which gives Audacity the ability to export sound files in the MP3 format. After installing and launching Audacity and LAME, you need to tell Audacity where LAME resides. Do this by going to the "Preferences" menu and clicking "Find Library." Click your way to the folder where LAME resides and select it. You can also select the bit rate in Preferences. A setting of 24 is perfectly adequate for a ringtone.

1. Using "File" → "Open," navigate to the song file you want. In this example, I've picked "Uncontrollable Urge," by Devo 2.0. (See top of page 263.)

2. We need to convert the song from stereo to mono. This requires a few steps. First, click the song title in the upper-left corner. This reveals a pull-down menu. Select "Split Stereo Track." (See bottom of page 263.)

3. Next, delete one of the now-split tracks by clicking on the "X" in the upper left corner. Click the title on the remaining track and select "Mono." (See top of page 264.)

4. We need to normalize the song to even out its volume range. Choose "Edit" → "Select" → "All" to highlight the entire song, then choose "Effect" → "Normalize." Go ahead and click "OK" in the pop-up window. (See bottom of page 264.)

5. Using the mouse cursor, select a 30-second sound clip. You can listen to it by pressing the green "Play" button. (See top of page 265.)

6. You're almost done! Now, select "File" → "Export Selection as MP3," as shown. Pick the location where you want to save the file and click Save. (See bottom of page 265.)

7. The only thing left is getting the file from your computer to your phone. There are a few ways you can do that.

    Email it. If your phone can accept email, then you can send the file to your phone as an attachment.

    Put it on the Web. If your phone has a built-in Web browser,

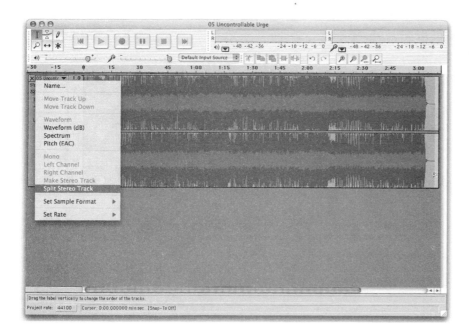

Audacity is an excellent, free, sound-editing application.

Splitting the stereo track into two mono tracks.

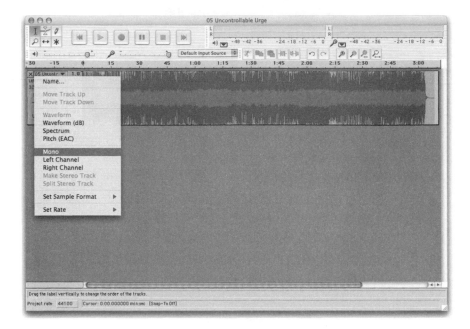

You need just one mono track to make your ringtone.

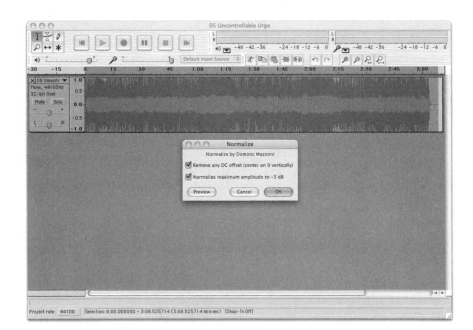

Normalize your sound clip to even out the volume range.

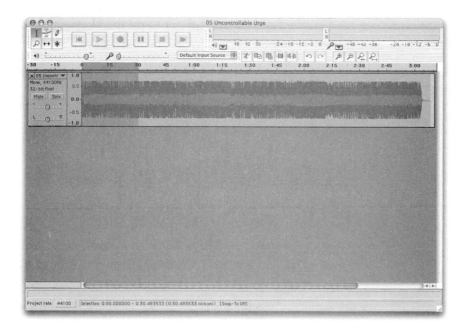

Selecting a 30-second sample.

Export your sample as an MP3 file.

you can upload the file to the Web (either your own Web site or to a free file storage service like dropload.com) and then click the link to the ringtone.

Use a USB cable. Many phones come with a cable to connect to a PC. If so, you can use that (they usually work on Windows computers only). If not, you can probably buy a cable as an accessory. Visit froogle.com and enter the name of your phone and "cable" in the search field.

Use Bluetooth. (See below.) If your phone and your computer both have Bluetooth (a short-range wireless connection technology, meant to replace all those cables snaking out of the back of your computer), this is an ideal way to get the song onto your phone. Mac has a built-in Bluetooth File Exchange Utility to transfer files from one Bluetooth-enabled device to another. Just navigate to the sound file and click "Send." When the file transfers to your phone, select it as the ringtone.

Note: Some phone carriers intentionally lock up Bluetooth file transfers because they don't want their subscribers to have the ability to make their own ringtones or put third-party software on their phones.

Transfer your ringtone to your phone via Bluetooth.

▶ What's the Best Way to Read Email on a Mobile Phone?

Use Gmail's mobile version for small screens

Most newer mobile phones have built-in email programs, but I have never found one that works as well as Gmail Mobile. To use it, you need a phone that can access the Web, along with a data plan. You also need a Gmail account. If you don't already have one, visit google.com/accounts/mobile and fill out the online form.

Once you've got a Gmail account, open your phone's browser, go to m.gmail.com, and enter your Gmail account name and password. Gmail formats itself to fit the size of your phone's display, and its spare, graphics-free interface loads quickly. If you get email with a Word file, PDF, or image attached, Gmail Mobile lets you click the link to view the attachment on the phone. And because it's hard to type in a reply using a phone's keypad, Gmail gives you the option of replying by phone to anyone in your Gmail contact list. Check out Google Mobile's other useful features at google.com/mobile.

▶ How Can I Send a Text Message to a Phone from My Computer?

It's easy to send a text message to someone's cell phone via iChat or AIM

Enter Ctrl-I (on iChat, use Cmd-Shift-N), enter the 10-digit number of the telephone you want to send the message to (in this format +12135551212), and type your brief message in the window. There are a couple of other useful ways to send a text message to a phone from your computer. You can do it from Google, by going to google.com/sendtophone and filling out the form. Or you can send a text message via email by sending it to teleflip.com (in this format: 213-555-1212@teleflip.com). Teleflip lets you send 100 free messages a month. After that, you can pay $4.95 to send an additional 150 messages per month.

▶**How Can I Receive AIM Messages on My Phone?**

You can use AIM to send and receive instant messages on any Web- or SMS-enabled phone

Here's how to use AIM via SMS (a feature on all modern cell phones):

1. If you don't have an AIM account, sign up for one (it's free) at aim.com.

2. Start a new text message on your phone. Address the message in this format: `screenname password`, where "screenname" is your AIM account name (don't use spaces) and "password" is your password (the password is case-sensitive, so don't forget to use capital letters where needed). Put a space between your screen name and your password.

3. Send the message to one of the following numbers, depending on your carrier:

   Alltel 265000
   Cingular 265000 or 4646
   Cingular (former ATT customers) 4646
   Cricket 265000
   T-Mobile 4646
   Verizon 4646

4. You'll get a message back from AIM with a list of your buddies who are online. To sign off, send a blank message to the same number as above plus one (e.g., Alltel would be 265001). If your phone won't let you send a blank message, send the letter "A."

5. If your phone is Web-enabled, your phone probably has built-in AIM software, which offers a richer set of features than the text-only version of AIM.

▶ How Can I Back Up My Cell Phone's Address Book?

You can spend from $2–7 a month on phone backup software/service from your carrier, or you can do it yourself, often for free

Most mobile phone carriers offer a backup service, usually for a set monthly fee. Some offer regular, automatic backups; with others, you have to back up manually via a small app on your phone. Service runs from $2 to $7 a month. Some services not only back up phone book content, but also photos, SMS text, etc. Check the Web site of your provider to see what they offer. What you get with these carrier-based services is convenience, but it costs you. If you're a little more tech savvy, you can do the backups yourself to your PC, and some of the software available lets you do much more between phone and PC. Several of the good ones are cheap, even free.

Probably the best Windows desktop app out there is MOBILedit! (mobiledit.com). It supports nearly every phone on the market. It allows you to connect between phone and PC via a sync cable, infrared (IrDA), or Bluetooth wireless. Besides backup of pretty much any sort of data you might have on your phone (phone book, calendar, email, text messages, photos, notes, games, and other Java apps), you can also import/export contacts into Microsoft Outlook and Outlook Express, edit your phonecam images, and more. Once connected to your computer and MOBILedit!, you can even answer calls via your PC, send them to voicemail, and send SMS. MOBILedit! sells for $25.

Another popular backup program for Windows is Float's Mobile Agent (fma.sourceforge.net/index2.htm). It has a similar set of features to MOBILedit! and is free. Unfortunately, it currently only works with Sony Ericsson phones. A new Web-based service called Zyb (zyb.com) is hopefully the future for this kind of mobile device backup. So far, the service is free. You simply register and then place a call from your mobile phone to the Zyb service (using the Web capabilities of your phone). It grabs your phone's contact list and converts it to Web-based files that you can then access via any Web browser. You can update your calendar and contact info on the Web, and it will

DEEPER

There are also hardware solutions for backing up your address book. If your phone has a Subscriber Identity Module, a.k.a. SIM Card—the postage stamp–sized card that contains your phone book, preferences, and other user-created data—you can get a SIM Card reader that plugs into your PC. Suntek Store (suntek-store.com) sells them for $30.

update the phone's data the next time you sync. Eventually, they'll offer premium services, such as integration with Outlook and scheduled syncing, for a small fee. Zyb works with many modern mobiles, but not all. Your phone has to be Web-capable and have SyncML software enabled (which most contemporary phones do). If you're looking for a backup technology that's not to hard to set up, is free, and allows Web-based access to your data, I'd check out Zyb first.

CellStik (sparktech.com) costs $40 and works with most phones. It's basically an adapter that connects your phone's connector jack to a USB port. It comes with software that not only lets you back up your data, but you can also edit your address book on your computer and then send it back to your phone. Unfortunately, the phone connector jack on the 'Stik is specific to the phone you have, so if you switch phones, you may have to get another CellStik to connect it.

▶ What Are the Best Web Sites for Use with Mobile Phones?

Get the best of the Web delivered to your handheld

In the past couple of years, most U.S. phone carriers have caught up with the rest of the world and are offering relatively high-speed Internet service for mobile phones. For an additional $20 a month or so, you can get unlimited access to the Web.

Of course, because phones have such tiny displays, they aren't suited for surfing the Web in the same way you do with your laptop or desktop computer. Regular Web sites look awful on a cell phone, and the pain of horizontal scrolling is enough to make anyone swear off using a cell phone's built-in browser.

Fortunately, many commercial Web sites have created small-screen versions for cell phone users, making it easy to look up movie show times, driving directions, traffic conditions, weather forecasts, sports scores, restaurant reviews, and other sites of interest to people out and about. Here's a rundown of the best of the mobile Web:

Yahoo! Go 2.0 (mobile.yahoo.com/go) offers a one-stop shopping version of the Mobile web. After entering your carrier, phone model, and mobile phone number, Yahoo! will send you everything you need to send email; send instant messages; play games; get sports scores, news, and stock quotes; look up phone numbers; find out about movie show times; get driving directions; access your address book and calendar; and more.

Google Mobile (google.com/xhtml). The front page of Google can't be more stripped down than it already is, but this mobile version of Google fits nicely on a mobile phone and the search results are configured for small screens. It's handy for finding restaurants near you—enter your desired cuisine along with the zip code. And the "Mobile Web" option returns Web sites that are configured for mobile devices.

AOL Mobile (mobile1.aol.com). In 2006, AOL stopped trying to sell subscriptions to its horrendous "walled garden" of online pabulum and has been attempting to survive as an advertising revenue–based service of online applications and, to its credit, it's doing a good job. The mobile suite of services is particularly impressive, including a mobile version of the venerable AOL Instant Messenger.

Use AIM on a computer that doesn't have the AIM application

Even if you're on the road and using a computer that doesn't have AOL's Instant Messenger installed, you can send and receive IMs by logging on at AIM Express: aim.com/get_aim/express. This Web-based version doesn't have all the fancy bells and whistles of the standalone application, but it'll get the job done.

▶▶ **INTERNET PHONES**

▶ **How Can I Make Free Long-Distance Calls Using the Internet?**

Use Skype to save on long-distance charges

When my parents went to Hong Kong for a couple of months, we stayed in touch without ever having to pick up the phone. But we talked at least a couple of times a week, using Skype, a free long-distance voice service that uses the Internet. Skype is a program that, once installed on your computer, lets you talk to any other Skype user in the world for free.

You can also use it to on your computer to talk to people on their ordinary phone lines, though you'll have to pay for that (but not much; we'll cover that later).

>**Getting started**

1. Download Skype (for Mac or Windows) at skype.com.

2. After installing Skype and launching it, you'll be asked to create a Skype name and password, along with your real name (which helps other Skype users when they want to look you up or add you to their contact list). I recommend that you configure Skype to launch automatically when you boot up your computer. If you don't, it's like unplugging your phone and taking the chance that you'll forget to plug it back in. You can also set your privacy preferences here, to allow calls and instant message from anyone, or from a list of buddies.

3. Once you're registered and logged in, you'll see a "Contacts window." Your contact list will be empty, however, because you have to add people to the list. That's easy to do. If you already know the Skype name of a person you want to call, select

"Contacts" → "Add a Contact" from the menu and enter the Skype name into the pop-up window and click "Continue." (You can also enter a name using their Skype phone number, which I'll get to a little later on.)

If you don't know the Skype name of the person you want to add to Skype, click the little magnifying glass icon. You can then try to find your friend based on a number of criteria. If you can't find your friend by either method, then that probably means he or she doesn't have a Skype account. Skype makes it easy to invite them to join for free. Visit skype.com/share/tellafriend, fill out the form with your friend's email address, and click "Send this." Your friend will receive an email letting him or her know that you want them to join Skype.

>Your first Skype call

Once you've added some names to your contact list, you'll probably want to call someone to try out the new service. But before you do that, you should test your setup by calling Echo 123, which is Skype's sound-check service. Just enter Echo123 into the field next to the icon of a telephone handset at the bottom of the "Contacts" window, and press the green "Call" button. In a moment you should hear a recorded message. If you don't, that means something is wrong with your setup. First, make sure your computer speakers are turned on and try calling Echo 123 again. If that doesn't work, go to "Preferences" → "Audio" and try changing your audio output. The recorded message will ask you to speak for 10 seconds while it records what you say. It then plays back what you just said. If you can hear it, great. If not, make sure the microphone is working. Most computers come with built-in microphones. If your computer doesn't come with a microphone, you'll need to buy one.

>Using a handset or headset with Skype

An Internet headset with a microphone costs as little as $25. Some have a USB jack; others come with two jacks, one to plug into your computer's microphone receptacle and one for the headphone

A handheld phone for Skype.

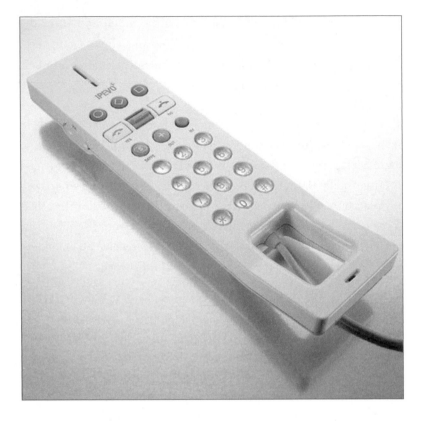

receptacle. I get better sound with the USB models. A headset is really important to have if you plan on using Skype regularly. Otherwise, your caller's voice will come out of your computer's speaker and your caller will hear his own voice play back through your microphone after a one- or two-second delay. Your caller should also use a microphone-headset combination, too, so you don't get confused hearing your own voice echo everything you say.

Another option is to get a USB phone, like the one shown here. These plug right into your computer's USB port, and function much like a regular phone. The low-end ones cost $40 or so, and the keypads can be used to make calls to regular (non-Skype) phone numbers, provided you've signed up for the SkypeOut service (more about that later).

If you aren't ready to invest in an Internet headset, a cheaper route is the $10 Skype Starter Kit which comes with an earbud and mic headset and a 30-minute SkypeOut card. You can buy the starter kit, as well as headsets and handsets, from skype.com.

If you're dead set against buying anything, then you can still improve the quality of your calls if both you and the person you are talking to wear a pair of ordinary headphones. If you have an extra set of headphones, you can plug those into your computer's microphone jack and use it as a makeshift microphone. You might look a little silly with this setup, but at least you didn't have to spend any money.

>Making conference calls

One of the neatest features of Skype is the ability to make conference calls. Select "Call/Start Conference Call" from the menu, and start dragging in the names of the people you want to have in the conference call. Then click "Start." If you're the person who started the conference call (the "host"), then you are the only one who can add people to the call. Because of the way Skype operates, the host's computer and Internet connection will have to supply most of the bandwidth and processing power to manage the call, so it's a good idea to designate the person with the fastest Internet connection as the host.

>Receiving calls from non-Skype users with SkypeIn

SkypeIn is a sweet deal if you're traveling and want to let your friends call you on the cheap. For about $4 a month, you can sign up for a SkypeIn number in any area code in any of the following countries: United States, United Kingdom, Brazil, Denmark, Estonia, Finland, France, Germany, Hong Kong, Poland, Sweden, and Switzerland. As long as you have a broadband computer connection in whatever far-flung outpost you happen to be in, the call will be routed to your computer. If you aren't available, the call will get routed to voicemail, which is stored on your computer, so you can retrieve it when you're back at the keyboard. (You can also buy Skype Voicemail without a SkypeIn subscription for about $2 a month). If you are constantly on the go, you should consider SkypeZones, which, for $8 a month, lets you make free Skype calls at thousands of Wi-Fi access points (managed by Boingo.com) around the world.

DEEPER

Making calls to non-Skype users with SkypeOut.

At the time I'm writing this, 7,044,042 Skype users around the world are online. That's a lot of people, but compared to the number of people around the world who have ordinary phone connections, that's a drop in the bucket. But you can still use Skype to call non-Skype users on their regular phones. The first question you might ask is, why not just use your regular phone to call them? Well, if you're making a toll-free call, then you might as well use your regular phone. But if you want to call anyone else anywhere in the world, you can save a lot of money with Skype. For instance, calls to anywhere in the continental United States, Mexico, Canada, Australia, and most of Europe and China cost only a few cents a minute. Other places are more expensive; check out skype.com/products/skypeout/rates for prices around the world. (The most expensive place to make a call? The tiny island of Diego Garcia, a UK/U.S. military compound in the Indian Ocean. With Skype, it'll cost you $1.86 a minute to call your buddy stationed there.]

▶ How Can I Make Skype Calls and Regular Calls Using the Same Phone?

This little gadget lets your landline phone do double duty as a Skype phone

The $50 VoSKY Internet Phone Wizard from.Actiontec.com lets you make phone calls using Skype on your ordinary phone. The unit itself is tiny—smaller than a paperback notebook. You plug it into a Windows computer with the included USB cable. The USB connection powers the device, so there's no need for a power adapter, which is excellent (the world needs fewer power adapters, if you ask me).

You have to install the included software on your PC, which works with Skype to let you make calls. Then you plug your phone and phone line into the device. To make a regular phone call, just dial the number. To make a Skype call, Press ## first and then the speed-dial number of your Skype buddy.

Use a cheap Webcam with iChat

Apple's iChat AV is a great way to have a video chat over a high-speed Internet connection anywhere in the world. Newer Macs come with a built-in iSight Camera. If you have an older Mac, you can buy an iSight for about $140. But if you already have a Webcam, there's an even cheaper option.

Buy a copy of iChatUSBcam ($10, ecamm.com/ mac/ichatusbcam) and use your USB Webcam to videochat. The quality isn't as nice as an iSight, but my sister's kids use it to chat with my kids, and they are having too much fun to complain about grainy images and washed-out colors.

▶ What's the Best Way to Get to a Human When I Call a Company for Customer Support

Stuck in a voicemail maze? Reach a real person using gethuman.com

Computer technology has made life more convenient in many ways, but in the arena of phone support, it has fallen flat. It's bad enough to have to call customer service to get help with something that should work in the first place, but it's even worse to be greeted by a computerized voice offering a menu of options that never seem to apply to the particular problem at hand. And if you want to talk to a real person, you usually must wait to find out which button to press, or you have to go hunting through a maze of options to get to one.

Penny-pinching companies must hate Gethuman (gethuman.com), which tells you how to reach a live human in the customer service and phone support departments of hundreds of companies, including banks, airlines, insurance companies, Internet companies, etc.

The tried-and-true methods listed on this site have been contributed by real people like you who have stumbled across the secret combinations of key presses and voice commands that will put you in touch with a real person. For instance, to reach a human at Verizon DSL after calling the toll-free number (800-567-6789), you need to say "real person" at every prompt, no matter what the instructions tell you to do.

I recommend printing out this wonderful list and giving a copy to your parents.

▶ What Do I Need to Know Before Switching to an Internet Phone?

While an Internet phone will save you money, it'll come at a few other costs

Internet telephony, or VoIP (Voiceover Internet Protocol) in geek-speak, has been on the drawing board, and on the desktops of brave early adopters, for nearly a decade. VoIP devices, networks, and technology standards have come, promised that true VoIP was finally here, and then collapsed back into the roiling sea of ones and zeros whence they came. We have a closet shelf full of the digital dodo devices to prove it (anybody remember the Aplio?). But with the full embrace of VoIP in recent years by communications giants like Comcast, and the emergence of serious new players like Vonage (vonage.com), Internet telephony has finally gained a solid toehold in the telecom market. Now you can get a system and service that allows you to use your existing phone, existing phone number, and you don't even have to go through your computer. So, should you take the plunge? It depends on what you value more, saving money or saving time and headaches. Let's be clear: Internet telephony is worlds better than it used to be. It's right on the cusp of true widespread usability, but there are still some problems with which to contend. First off, how it actually works. Different services work slightly differently, but with basic similarities.

We'll use the example of Vonage, as it's probably the best of the bunch to date. You sign up, get a VoIP adapter box that you plug into your cable or DSL modem, hook your phone into the adapter, and you're good to go. Actually, if you just hooked your Vonage box to a DSL modem, there's already a problem. Vonage needs the phone number to not be on the same wire as the DSL connection. Confusing, but what this means is that you'll have to get a second phone line for your DSL (which sort of defeats the purpose of the VoIP connection in the first place). Cable customers are okay. There's also the issue of keeping your old number. Most numbers can be transferred. Some can't. And the ones that can sometimes take a frustratingly long time (as much as a month) to get switched and can involve hassle calls to shiftless corporate drones. Providers like Vonage give you a temporary number you can use to make outgoing calls so you can keep your landline number and phone in business until the switch happens. We've heard of people's numbers getting lost in the void (the landline phone gets shut off and the VoIP phone service fumbles the hand-off) for a few stress-filled days before everything is fixed.

The other big drawback to VoIP concerns emergencies. The traditional 911 service (which gives the 911 call center your name and address as soon as you call) doesn't work with VoIP. Internet phone carriers are now required, as mandated by the FCC, to register their customers with the e911 (Enhanced 911) system (which handles VoIP and mobile phones), but there have been technical hurdles. If you get a VoIP service, you want to not only make sure you give your correct address and emergency information to your provider, but you want to check up on the latest details of e911 implementation to make sure this info is getting to your local emergency call center. Go to the FCC's consumer page (voip911.gov) and make sure the service is completely operational in your area. You may want to do this before subscribing to VoIP service.

The next emergency issue is power and network outages. If your power goes out a lot or your Internet connection gets dropped, you need to realize that you won't have phoning ability during these times.

Well, that's plenty of cold water, don't ya think? But if you overcome all of this what you get is a BIG drop in your phone bill, unlimited calls anytime to U.S., Canada, Europe, and Puerto Rico, nearly every premium feature offered by traditional phone companies, all for free (three-way calling, call waiting, voice mail, caller ID, etc), and lots more, all for a flat fee of $25 per month. The general feeling about VoIP is still mixed. Fans of it are thrilled, especially with the savings and the fat feature set, while detractors claim it's still not ready for primetime, and besides the hurdles to getting in, the quality seems to vary with the wind direction (though again, these problems seem to get smoother by the day). One other thing to be careful of is pricing. Cable providers and other traditional communications companies are getting into the act, and they charge more than providers like Comcast (and have hidden fees). Take away the significant savings of VoIP, and there's definitely little reason to switch.

▶ How Can I Record My Skype Phone Calls?

Keep a record of all your Internet phone conversations

Being a journalist, a podcaster, and a Skype user, I needed to find a way to record my Skype conversations. The best solution I could find for my Mac was Call Recorder (ecamm.com/mac/callrecorder), a $14.95 add-on that works flawlessly with Skype. (See below.) You can tweak settings, including file compression and sound quality, by opening the "Preferences" window in Skype. The recorded files are saved on your hard drive. When you buy Call Recorder, it comes with a utility application to convert the files to the MP3 format (I wish the files could be recorded as MP3s, because they wouldn't take up so much room.) Windows users can get a similar program called Pamela Pro for $24.95 from pamela-systems.com. (Recording a call without permission is illegal in some states.)

Use Call Recorder to save Skype Calls.

►How Can I Get a Free Disposable Phone Number?

Avoid pests by getting a free phone number that goes straight to voicemail

There are times when you want to give out a phone number, but you don't want to give your home, office, or mobile number because you don't want to be pestered. For these occasions, you need a disposable phone number—one that callers can leave messages on, but won't be able to speak to you directly unless you call them back. I use a disposable phone number on my Web site instead of my home phone number. When someone calls me at the number (it's 818-475-1350) they are asked to leave a message. That message is emailed to me as an audio file attachment. If I feel like calling the person back, I do, and if I don't I just delete the message. So where can you get one of these disposable phone numbers? Visit AIM Phoneline (aimphoneline.com) and register for a free number in your area code. Once you get it, you can start publishing it on your Web site and giving it to car dealers you don't necessarily want to talk to. Then, check dashboard.aimphonline.com or your email for messages.

LANDLINE PHONES

►Who Keeps Calling Me?

You can look up the number on whocalled.us and see what experiences others may have had with calls from that number

Whocalled.us is another great example of the power of the aggregated intelligence and eyeballs of the Internet. The site maintains a database of numbers entered in by others annoyed by the same sorts of calls you're getting, maybe from the same pest. Once a number has been entered into the database, the next person to search on it can see a record that contains notes left by others who've received calls, see the frequency of calls, and even see the calls plotted on a map. Over time, the comments begin to work like a collective detective investigation, as people share information and clues that sometimes lead to a phone spammer, heavy breather, etc. being chased out into the open. The site also has an ongoing contest where they give away Phone Interceptors to the best stories posted to the site. The Interceptor is a device that can be used to route specified calls to an answering machine that then delivers the "We're sorry, you have reached a number that is no longer in service" message and special tone, tricking dialing robots into thinking the number is no longer valid. Take that, strong-arming collection agents and pesky telemarketers!

Foil a telemarketer

Don't you hate getting those dinner-time calls from telemarketers intent on selling you something you don't want? Especially infuriating is the way they use a script to counter any argument you give them. I've gotten to the point where I just say "no thank you" and hang up the phone right in the middle of their script recitation, but I'm tempted to try this "anti-telemarketing counterscript" (xs4all.nl/~egbg/counterscript.html). Print it out and keep it in a drawer next to your phone. The next time you get a call from a telemarketer, pull it out and read from the script. The aim is to ask the telemarketer questions until he becomes exhausted and realizes that he is wasting his time with you. Maybe if enough people use this script, telemarketers will give up and look for a new job. (How's that for wishful thinking?)

▶▶ EMAIL

▶ Help! I'm Drowning in Email. What Can I Do?

Use this system to stay on top of an unruly inbox

When I got my first email account in 1989, it was a rare treat to get email. If I was lucky, I'd get three or four messages and I'd excitedly write back replies, adding comments like, "Isn't e-mail cool!?" (Back then, everyone hyphenated email).

But by 1993, the magic had worn off, and I was getting 100 emails a day. Today, I get about 1,000 per day. If I don't stay on top of my email, I feel like I'm being buried alive. With so many other things to do, how can I possibly deal with so many email messages?

Even if you don't get as many emails as I do, you probably get the same panicked feeling when you think about the email in your inbox. I'll bet you've got a lot of what I call "sticky" emails sitting around, taunting you every time you open your email application. A sticky email is one that you can't answer for one reason or another. It could be that you don't have the information you need to answer it. It could be a long letter from a friend or relative telling you about the things that are going on in their lives, and you probably feel it would be rude to send a one- or two-sentence reply. Instead of answering it, you just keep the messages in your inbox in the vain hope that one day you'll have time to compose an equally long response.

>One simple rule

Keeping sticky email in your inbox is a mistake. To keep your inbox manageable, you have to obey the "only handle it once" rule. Never open an email, glance at it for a moment and then move to the next one. That's wasted time, because odds are you'll do that again and again to the same email message, making you feel worse every time.

As soon as you open an email and read it, you need to decide what to do with it. I learned how to handle email from Merlin Mann's fantastic personal productivity blog, 43 Folders (43folders.com).

When you open an email, you should do one of five things with it:

1. **Delete it.** Email that can be disposed of immediately is my favorite kind, because it requires no effort on my part beyond pressing the "Delete" key. Emails that fit into this category include spam, forwarded jokes and urban legends, most email that I'm cc'd on, mailing lists, and inquiries that don't interest me. Just because a stranger sends me email, I'm under no obligation to reply. This may seem rude, but when you get a lot of email, it's the only way to deal with it.

2. **Answer it.** If you can answer the email in two minutes or less (including the time it takes to conduct any research needed to supply the answer) then go ahead and take care of it on the spot. Today, a guy who sent me a DVD showcase of his work asked me if I could return it to him. I threw the DVD in an envelope, addressed it, weighed it, checked usps.com to calculate the postage, stuck stamps on it, ran it to the mailbox, and replied to the guy that I'd put it in the mail—all in under two minutes. Then I deleted the email.

3. **Let someone else deal with it.** This is my second favorite way to get a message out of my inbox—make it someone else's problem. When you get an email with a request for information or your time to help out on something, think about the other people in your organization who are better suited to dealing with the request than you are. Then redirect the message their way (cc the requestor as well so they know that you've delegated things—otherwise, they might come a-knocking a month later thinking you dropped the ball) and forget about it.

4. **Save it for reference.** Some emails you'll want to save: receipts, passwords, useful URLs, or other information you might want

to refer to later. I move these into an appropriately labeled folder, knowing I'll be able to search for it if I need it later.

5. **Tag it for later action**. This is my last resort. If I can't delete, delegate, or deal with it immediately, I move the email into a folder labeled "Action" and then add an entry to my to-do list. Today, a Web site offered to give me space for a free banner ad. I put the email into my action folder and added "Make a banner ad for Steve's site" on my to-do list. When I get a chance to make the ad, I'll email it to him in my reply.

>Prioritizing your email as it comes in

Another important trick I've learned is to color-code my email as it arrives. All email applications have automatic filtering built in. I set up my filters to change the colors of the subject lines of emails. Any email sent to me from a person in my address book gets colored green. Email that I'm cc'd on gets colored blue. Email from mailing lists gets colored purple. My mail program sorts all the mail in my box based on color. I always go through my green email first, because it's from people I know well enough to have in my address book. Then I go through the blue email, which I can almost always delete. I never have to reply to purple mail, and sometimes I delete it without even reading it. The mail that stays black means it has come from a stranger, or at least someone who isn't in my email box. Most of it is spam and a pleasure to get rid of.

There's one other filter I use, the "killfile." This is a list of people whom I don't want to hear from: pests, cranks, obnoxious public relations flacks, and so on. When my mail filter detects a message from someone on my bozolist, it goes straight into the trash without my knowing it. I enjoy thinking of the energy the people on my bozolist have wasted in composing a message I'll never see.

>Life with an empty inbox

Even if you don't follow these rules religiously, you'll realize the benefits of not having to worry about dozens or hundreds of unanswered emails. But don't fall into the trap of becoming obsessed with processing your email the second it arrives in your email box. It's crazy to set your email preferences to check for new email every five minutes. Research has shown than when you are interrupted by a co-worker, phone call, or the "ding!" of a new email landing in your box, it can take 25 minutes to get back up to speed on the project you had been working on. I suggest checking your email once every couple of hours throughout the day if you can help it.

▶ I Have So Much Email That I Can't Even Begin to Dig My Way Out. What Can I Do?

As a last resort, here's how to declare email bankruptcy

Lawrence Lessig, a well-known copyright lawyer, gets 200 email messages a day (not including spam). In June, after spending over eighty hours in one week trying to catch up with his email, he decided to do something drastic: he declared email bankruptcy. He sent an email message to all the folks in his address book to let them know that if they were waiting for a response to an email message they had sent him, it was unlikely that they'd get one. He asked his contacts to resend any urgent messages, with the promise that he would attend to those first.

   If you're brave enough to declare email bankruptcy, here's the way to do it:

1. Move all your unanswered email into a folder. Give the folder a name. (Choose something other than bankruptcy, otherwise you might get depressed every time you see it.) If you are especially brave, just delete all the messages. (You might not die as a result.)

2. Send a message to everyone in your address book (put their addresses in the bcc field so the recipients can't see everyone else on the list). The message should politely explain your predicament.

3. Now that you have an empty inbox, use the technique described in the previous section ("Help! I'm Drowning in Email. What Can I Do?") to stay on top of your inbox. Good luck. You'll need it.

▶ How Can I Archive My Email?

Save your email in a searchable database

I save most of my email messages because they are loaded with valuable information that I find myself searching for months, or even years, after receiving them. But with close to 50,000 saved email messages, my email program was starting to bog down. I didn't want to save the email by burning it to a DVD and then deleting it from my email program, because that would make it inconvenient to search. Instead, I invested $50 in a mail-archiving program called Mail-Steward for Macintosh (mailsteward.com). It works with most popular mail programs, including Entourage, Eudora, and Apple's Mail application. It took a long time for MailSteward to chew through my email and convert it into its database, but once it was finished, all my emails (and their attachments) were easily searchable by specifying a date range and entering keywords in the "To," "From," "Subject," "Mailbox," and "Body" fields. For Windows, FastMailBase is a pricey option at $97 (manybases.com). Rather than fork over a Ben Franklin for this, consider switching over to a free Gmail account instead and ditching your current email application (see below to learn more about Gmail).

▶ What's the Best Web-Based Email Service?

For my money (which is $0), the best Web-based email service is Google's Gmail

Gmail was introduced in April 2004 with a massive 1,000 MB of storage (enough to store a half-million pages of text)—compare this to the measly 10 MB or so that competitors like Hotmail and Yahoo! were offering at the time. (Yahoo! has since upped the capacity for

free accounts to 1,000 MB, but Google has upped theirs to 2.8 GB—
and it grows by the second.)

>What makes Gmail different

Once you start using Gmail, you'll never want to use another Web-
based mail system again. You may even want to ditch your regular email
address, or better yet, do what I do—incorporate your regular email
into your Gmail account.

Besides offering more free storage capacity than any other major
Webmail provider, Google is loaded with powerful features, the
most important being searchability. Google applies its awesome
Web search technology to your email database, making it lightning
fast to find any email message, as long as you can remember the
name or address of the sender or recipient of the email, or any of the
words in the email. This means you don't have to bother setting up
folders to organize your email. After you've read an email, just click
"Archive" to move it out of your inbox.

Gmail organizes your email messages as "conversations," so that
back-and-forth messages on the same subject are grouped together
in an organized, logical way. As new messages on the same subject
are sent and received, they're added to the conversation.

If you decide to use Gmail, I recommend installing the Google
Toolbar (toolbar.google.com), which lets you search your Gmail
messages without having to first go to the Gmail site. Plenty of other
goodies abound in the toolbar, including an auto—form filler and
something called Auto-Link, which makes it easy to track packages
and display addresses on a map.

>Privacy concerns

All Webmail programs have ads, but Gmail's ads are different. You'll
notice that they're related to the subject of whatever email message
is currently open. For example, an email about an upcoming art
show will likely trigger Gmail to display ads for online art dealers.
Now, this has some people understandably concerned. Does this
mean that Google is reading your email in order to figure out what

it's about? The answer is yes, but there's no reason to panic. Google employees don't read your email (that would be way too costly); computers do the scanning. Google's software scans the email in your inbox and looks for keywords that trigger pertinent ads to be displayed.

If that makes you uncomfortable, consider this: all major Web-mail services scan your email, in order to delete spam and viruses, conduct spell checking, and filter messages. In addition, Internet service providers that handle regular email accounts regularly scan email for spam and viruses, and back up subscriber's email.

The truth of the matter is, if you use email, you should use it with the idea that everything you send and receive is available to anyone with a court order. In fact, in early 2006, a U.S. Magistrate Judge sent a subpoena to Google, demanding all Gmail email messages from a man involved in a Federal Trade Commission lawsuit, "including but not limited to all emails and messages stored in all mailboxes, folders, inboxes, sent items, and deleted items, and all links to related Web pages contained in such email messages." Google was required to comply with the request. If you take a look at Gmail's privacy policy, you'll see that Google states that "Residual copies of deleted messages and accounts may take up to 60 days to be deleted from our active servers and may remain in our offline backup systems." In other words, even if you delete your email, or even quit the service, your email messages may never vanish from the face of the earth. (If you are truly concerned with privacy, consider scrambling your email with an encryption program before you send it. I recommend the GNU Privacy Guard, available at gnupg.org).

When Gmail scans your messages, it also looks for addresses and package tracking numbers, and generates potentially helpful links as shown on page 290.

>Getting Gmail

It's easy to sign up for a free Gmail account. Visit www.google.com/accounts/NewAccount and fill out the form. Note that when you sign

Gmail scans your mail and offers useful services based on what it finds.

up for a Gmail account, Google gives you the option of saving your Google search history. That means you can log on to any computer and look at the previous searches you've made on Google. This is a handy way to go to a site that you want to return to, but can't remember the name or address of, but it also can be potentially embarrassing if someone else sees the kinds of things you search for. This is yet another example of the trade-off between online convenience and privacy. The more convenience you opt for, the less privacy you get, and vice versa. The choice is yours.

>Using Gmail

Once you've signed up for your Gmail account, you can access it in a number of different ways. The easiest way is to just use the Web interface at gmail.com. You can read and compose messages from it, just like any other Webmail service. I prefer to use Gmail in my regular email application, however, because I have several email addresses and I like them all to come to one place. I do this in the "Forwarding and POP" section of Gmail's "Settings" panel, as shown on page 291.

There are two different ways to use Gmail with another email application. One is by forwarding all your messages to any email address you wish. For example, say you have the email address moonshine-nematode@earthlink.net. You can instruct Gmail to forward all incoming messages to that address (except for the messages that Gmail thinks are spam). You can specify whether or not to keep copies of the messages in Gmail or delete them. I recommend

Gmail's settings for forwarding email to another account.

selecting "archive Gmail's copy" (as shown on page 292) because it's
a good way to back up your incoming email, and you can use Gmail to
search for messages. (See page 292.)

A more powerful way to use Gmail on another email application is
to enable POP (Post Office Protocol, the standard method for receiving
email) so that you can read email you've downloaded from Gmail even
when you aren't online. To do this, you have to configure your email
application to download Gmail messages. There are too many email
applications out there for me to explain how to set this up on every one
of them. Fortunately, Gmail has an excellent step-by-step guide for
all the major email apps, including Outlook, Outlook Express, Entourage, Eudora, Netscape Mail, Apple Mail, Thunderbird, and
Blackberry Internet Service. The guides are available here: mail
.google.com/support/bin/answer.py?answer=12103. (These guides
also show you how to send email messages using Gmail's outgoing
mail server. This is important, because your existing email provider

*Archiving G-mail that is for-
warded to another account.*

probably won't let you use their outgoing mail server to send mail
from any account other than their own.)

With Google's POP option enabled, you are also allowed to save
your messages on Gmail for backup and search.

Another way some people use Gmail is to automatically forward
all their email from their other accounts to Gmail (you'll have to find
out from your email service provider how to have your email forwarded). You can then send messages from Gmail designed to look
like they come from any address you own. It's the simplest way to
handle the multiple addresses situation and lets you work from one
interface on every computer.

>My Gmail setup

Here's how I use Gmail. I have an email address, mark@boing
boing.net. I went to the Web site of the company that I used to register
the boingboing.net domain and filled out a mail forwarding form,
shown in the figure below. (Most domain name registrars offer this
service for no additional charge.) (See page 293.)

Now, all email sent to mark@boingboing.net goes straight to
markfrauenfelder@gmail.com. I've set up my mail application to
download my Gmail and, in Gmail's Settings, I've also set up my
reply-to address to be mark@boingboing.net, as seen in the figure
on page 294.

I've set up my account options to make it look like all the email
I send, whether it be sent from Gmail's Web interface or my Apple
Mail applications, appears to have come from mark@boing
boing.net. The people I correspond with won't even know that I'm

Example			
you	@boingboing.net	to	you@yourisp.com
mark	@boingboing.net	to	markfrauenfelder@gmail.cc

☐ delete account

Save Changes   Cancel

How I forward my email to Gmail.

using markfrauenfelder@gmail.com. Why is this important? For one thing, I try to keep the number of different email addresses I use to a minimum. More importantly, if I decide to switch to a new Gmail address (because, believe it or not, my 2.7 GB account is almost half-full after only a year or so), or another mail provider, I can keep using mark@boingboing.net. (It's good to have an email address that you own, not one that you might lose if a company goes out of business or changes their policy or business plan.)

Here's the beauty of this setup:

1. All incoming mail to mark@boingboing.net gets automatically archived in a searchable database.

2. I can use Gmail's outgoing mail server wherever I am, even at a wireless hotspot.

3. If I want to check my email from someone else's computer, it's all there at gmail.com.

But what if you've been using Hotmail for years and everyone you know sends email to your Hotmail account? You can still switch with relatively little pain. Here's how to do it: (1) open a Gmail account as described above and (2) export your Hotmail contacts to a CSV file. Hotmail doesn't offer an easy way to export your email contacts, but Google has detailed instructions. Go to Gmail Help and search for "Hotmail." Now, send an email to your contacts informing them that you've switched email accounts. Keep your Hotmail account and

DEEPER

Import your contact file from another email program to Gmail. Are you still using Hotmail? There are so many reasons why you should switch over to Gmail. For starters, Hotmail accounts only allow you to store 1 GB in your inbox. Gmail gives almost three times as much storage. For another thing, you can't download your Hotmail email to another email program. You can't search your Hotmail, either. The Hotmail interface displays annoying advertsing. The list goes on. Gmail is much better in every way. (See "What's the Best Web-Based Email Service?" on page 287).

Settings

General   **Accounts**   Labels   Filters   Forwarding and POP   Chat   Web Clips

Send mail as: (Use Gmail to send from your other email addresses) Learn more	Mark Frauenfelder <markfrauenfelder@gmail.com> Reply-to address: mark@boingboing.net	make default edit info
	Mark Frauenfelder <mark@boingboing.net>	default edit info delete
	Add another email address	
	When I receive a message sent to one of my addresses: ○ Reply from the same address the message was sent to. ⊙ Always reply from my default address (currently mark@boingboing.net) (Note: You can change the address at the time of your reply. Learn more)	
Google Account settings:	Visit your Google Account settings to reset your password, change your security question, or learn about access to other Google services	

My Gmail account's return address is mark@boingboing.net.

check it from time to time. When you get an email sent to your Hotmail account, send that person a message from your Gmail account, letting them know about the switch. Eventually everyone will start sending mail to your Gmail account.

▶ What's the Best Way to Keep from Getting Spam?

A list of tips for keeping spammers at bay

Spam exists because it's profitable. Believe it or not, there are people out there foolish enough to give their credit card numbers to online hustlers hawking Vicodin and Xanax, weight-loss patches, mortgages with 1 percent fixed rates, Web casinos with odds in favor of the player, herbs guaranteed to permanently enlarge certain body parts, and all manner of get-rich-quick schemes. It's sad that some people actually believe in things that are too good to be true.

Spamming is a numbers game. A spammer knows he can make more money hooking in ten or twenty suckers out of a mass mailing to millions of email addresses than it costs to send those emails, so he will continue to send out spam. Spamming is unstoppable. You can pass laws against spamming; you can sue spammers; you can mail them live scorpions. But as long as there is a dollar to be made from spamming, it will never go away.

What can you do about it? First, accept the fact that no matter what you do—short of canceling your Internet service—you will never be able to completely eliminate spam from your mailbox. Think of spam as a germ, one that evolves to get around your body's immune system. Spam mutates, too—the reason spam uses so many misspelled words is because it's trying to get past the filters people have set up to stop it.

That said, there's a lot you can do to greatly reduce the amount of spam that arrives in your email box. Here's a list of spam-killing tips:

1. **Don't let spammers know you exist.** The best way to prevent being spammed is by not letting the spammers find out you exist. If spammers don't know your email address, they can't spam you.* You shouldn't post your email address anywhere online, because spammers use software that scans the Internet for email addresses to add to their junk email lists. If you must disclose or post your email address online, you might want to use a disposable email address (see page 297). Some people write "Email me at nancy (at) hotmail (dot) com," but some spam-harvesting software is smart enough to decode these masking attempts.

2. **Don't ever reply to a spam or click the "unsubscribe" link.** This will only increase the number of spams you receive because the spammer will know that there is a real person attached to that email address.

3. **Don't ever buy anything advertised via spam.** Your name will be added to a "suckers list" and the amount of spam you'll get as a result will bury you.

---

*An exception: if your email uses a common word or name, you will get spammed, because spammers often conduct full dictionary attacks on particular domains. For instance, they'll send spam to nancy@hotmail.com, sales@camerasandlaptops.com, or tiger@gmail.com simply because they know that people will be using these email addresses. It's better to use two words in your email address—nancyrealtor@hotmail.com, sales_info@camerasandlaptops.com, tigereyes@gmail.com.

4. **Use your Internet service provider's spam-filtering options.**
   Almost every email provider offers junk-mail protection. Go to
   your provider's site and search on "spam." Some providers, such
   as Google's Gmail, incorporate excellent spam filtering by default.

5. **Use the spam-filtering capability that comes with your email
   program.** If you use Entourage, or Mac's Mail application, Eudora, or most any email application, it will include some kind of
   spam filtering. You can usually adjust the strength of the filter—if
   you set it on the low side, you'll get more spam but decrease the

DEEPER: A SPAM SOLUTION TO BE AVOIDED

There's one spam-blocking system that I don't recommend: the so-called "challenge-response system." In theory, it sounds like a foolproof way to block spam: the system creates and maintains a "white list" of everyone in your address book, allowing email from anyone on the white list to pass through the gates. Any email that isn't on the white list gets quarantined. The system then sends "challenge" emails to the senders of the quarantined emails. If the email was sent by a spammer, the chances are great that the return email address is phony, and it will trigger a "bounce" notice, which tells the system to move the email associated with it from the quarantine folder to the trash.

Any real person who receives the challenge email will be asked to solve some kind of problem, called a captcha, which is easy for a human to do but time-consuming and costly for a computer. Typically, the captcha involves looking at an image of warped and discolored characters and typing them into a field. If the person can successfully solve the captcha, his email leaves quarantine and gets sent to the recipient. The sender is also added to the white list so that he doesn't have to go through the process again.

There are three problems with challenge response systems. The first is that they make it very difficult for the millions of sight-impaired people who use the Internet. Text-to-voice machines can't decode the images because the images were designed specifically to confound computers. People who are totally blind, and people with poor eyesight can't see well enough to tell what the characters are. The second problem is that captchas put the burden of the problem on the wrong person—spam is the recipient's problem, not the sender's. It is a hassle having to go to a Web site to solve a captcha just to send an email. The third problem is that these systems don't work as well as they used to because spammers are now using viruses to infect innocent people's computers to do their spamming for them. Not only do these "zombie" computers spew out thousands of spam email messages right under the unwitting noses of their owners, they also find the address books on the computers and send spam to them. Sometimes this spam has the zombie computer owner's name in the "from" field, and if it appears on the recipient's white list, the spam will sail right through the filter.

risk of filtering out legitimate email. If you set the filter on the high side, you'll keep more spam out of your inbox but you risk losing some genuine emails as well. I usually keep my filter on the low side, because I don't want to miss out on a legit message.

6. Use a third-party filter. For a couple of dollars a month, you can run your email through a system that filters it for spam. My favorite is SpamCop (spamcop.net), which costs $30 a year and checks for viruses and spam. It hangs onto the suspect messages and releases the legitimate email to your account.

You don't need to follow all the six steps here to establish an effective spam-blocking system. I've found that using steps 2–5 are enough to get rid of all but five or six spams a day. Here's how I've set up my system: I have a Gmail account, to which all my email is automatically forwarded (for more about Gmail, see page 287). Every day, Gmail captures over 200 spam emails sent to my email addresses. I never have to see them because they go straight into the spam folder. When I first signed up for Gmail, I checked the spam folder every day to look for false positives (legit emails inadvertently tagged as spam) but I have never seen a single one, so I don't bother looking any longer.

Next, I download the mail to my computer using the Mail application that comes with Macintosh OS X. It has a built in "Junk" filter that you help train to recognize spam. It catches between 10–20 spams a day, and I might find a false positive a few times a week, so I usually scan the subject lines and "from" addresses every day to check. And that's it. I get so little spam that it's no longer a problem.

▶ How Can I Give Out My Email Address and Still Protect Myself from Spam?

Use a disposable email address

Anytime you give out your email address online, you put yourself at risk of getting lots of spam. Many Web sites require you to register with your name and address before they give you access, and it's likely those Web sites will turn around and sell your information to a bulk emailer. There are a lot of applications and services you can use to filter out spam (See "What's the Best Way to Keep from Getting Spam?" on page 294), but the best way to keep from getting inundated by junk mail is by keeping off the spammers' email lists in the first place.

An excellent way to keep your email address away from spammers is to use a temporary email address to sign up for a service. Spamgourmet (spamgourmet.com) is a free disposable email service. You start out by creating an account with Spamgourmet. It's as simple as entering a username, password, and your real email account. Spamgourmet will send a confirmation message to your email account. Click the link in the message to complete your registration process.

Now, you are free to create a self-destructing, disposable email address that you can use to foil any would-be spammers. Here's how you do it.

The next time you are required to divulge your email address in order to gain access to an online newspaper, enter a contest, or register for a newsletter, use a Spamgourmet address. You can make up any address you like, as long as it's in the following format: someword.x.user@spamgourmet.com.

Someword can be any word you like, as long as you've not used it before. x is the maximum number of emails you are willing to receive from this address. user is your Spamgourmet user name. So, if your username is astrochimp, and you want to allow up to five messages to reach you at this address, you could create the following email address: ipodcontest.7.astrochimp@spamgourmet.com. The first seven times anyone sends something to this email, it will be forwarded to your protected account. After that, Spamgourmet will "eat" subsequent emails. I just checked my message stats (which you can see at Spamgourmet when you log on to the site). I've created 6 disposable addresses, to which 18 messages have been forwarded, and 242 eaten. I love the idea that spammers are sending email to a black hole. Spamgourmet also offers an "advanced mode," which, among other options, allows you to add a list of "trusted senders" who are allowed to send email to a disposable address without advancing the message count.

DEEPER

Publish your real email address on your Web site without getting spam. One of the most common ways to end up on a spammer's list is by leaving your email address on a Web site. If you have a home page with your address on it, or if you leave a comment on a message board, it's a sure bet that a spammer's harvester program will grab it in a matter of days and add it to a spam list.

A less sophisticated but simpler disposable email address service is Dodgeit (dodgeit.com). When a Web site requires an email address, enter `someword@dodgeit.com`, and then go to dodgeit.com to pick up the mail, simple as that.

Some people add characters to their email to prevent this from happening: markremovethis@removethisboingboing.net is one way to do it. A human being is smart enough to figure out what your email address is, but an email harvester usually won't be able to remove the unnecessary characters.

Here's another, better way to hide your email address from harvesting agents: obfuscate it using the form provided at u.arizona.edu/~trw/spam/spam2.htm. This form converts standard characters into the hex code equivalent. For example the hex code equivalent of "a" is %61, the hex code for "b" is %62, the hex code for "c" is %63, and so on. The hex code for my email address, mark@boingboing.net, is %6D%61%72%6B%40%62%6F%69%6E%67%62%6F%69%6E%67%2E%6E%65%74. If I put this on my Web site, it will appear as mark@boingboing.net, but a spam harvester will only see the hex code, and won't bother harvesting it.

As the creator of this email obfuscator points out, it is possible that some spam harvesting agents might be able to convert the hex code back into your email address. If you want to make sure your email is invisible to harvesting agents, use the form at u.arizona.edu/~trw/spam/spam.htm, which makes it all but impossible for agents to harvest your email address. It creates a small script that you can add to a Web page that will bewilder spam harvesters. This will only work for visitors to your site who have Javascript enabled on their browsers, though.

▶ How Can I Get Rid of the ">>" Characters That Show Up in Forwarded Email?

Clean up your email with Text Monkey

Email messages that are forwarded and reforwarded several times get awfully ugly looking, what with all the ">>" characters at the beginning of every line. Mac Mail users can remove binary marks by highlighting the text and entering Cmd-' as many times as needed. Windows users can download a free copy of Text Monkey Lite from boxersoftware.com. To use Text Monkey Lite, just copy text in the clipboard and paste it right back.

The $30 Text Monkey Pro comes with a host of other very useful text-handling features. For instance, you can copy text and paste it as formatted HTML code ready to add to your Web page.

▶ I Often Forget to Add Attachments to Email. Is There a Way to Remind Me Before I Send the Email?

Be automatically reminded to attach files to your email

I'm not the only one who frequently forgets to attach files to email messages. It's common enough that there's a free utility that reminds

Send anonymous prank email

Why would you want to send anonymous email? The number one reason is to play a prank on a friend or enemy. That's where Sharp Mail (sharp-mail.co.uk) comes in, a site that lets you send email that looks like it is coming from another person (real or fictitious).

To use Sharp Mail, you have to register using a real email address, because your activation code will be sent there. (Sharp Mail wants a real email address because if you use the service for illegal purposes, it will hand over your contact information to the authorities.)

To make things easy for lazy pranksters, Sharp Mail has a library of pre-written prank email to send to your target. (I like the one that purports to be from a couple of campers thanking you for inviting them to pitch a tent in your backyard for a couple of weeks.)

you. For Windows, Attach! (kmgi.com/attach) scans the text of your outgoing email messages, looking for certain words that indicate you are intending to send an attachment along with your email message (this list of trigger words is customizable). If your email message contains one of these trigger words and you attempt to email it without an attachment, a window will pop up asking you if you are forgetting to attach a message. You can then go back and attach the file or click "Send anyway."

Mac users can download a similar utility, the Attachment Scanner Plug-in for Mail (home.cc.gatech.edu/eaganj/49).

For Gmail, there's an attachment reminder script for Greasemonkey (userscripts.org/scripts/show/2419). For more information on how Greasemonkey can make Firefox even more powerful, go to greasemonkey.mozdev.org.

▶ Why Can't I Send Email from My Laptop When I'm Traveling?

Make sure your email gets sent no matter where you are

If you've ever connected your computer to a hotel, airport, café, or other public place's network (wired or wireless) you may have noticed that you can receive email messages, but that you can't send them. That because the network has blocked unauthorized users from using their email server to send mail. It wasn't always this way. In the pre-spam days of the Internet, most Internet service providers allowed "relaying" of email on their outgoing email servers. But those rotten spammers abused the kindness and openness of system administrators by pumping tons of junk mail through other people's SMTP servers. (SMTP stands for Simple Mail Transfer Protocol, which is the way email gets delivered across the Net.) Now, it's almost impossible to find an SMTP server that allows relaying, and if you do happen to find one, chances are the service provider of the person you are sending the email to will have long ago blacklisted the server in order to stop the gusher of spam pouring out if it.

So what can you do about it? You have several options. You can

Using Gmail to send emails from anywhere.

ask the proprietor of the business that owns the network you are using to tell you what the outgoing mail server is (it is usually a name
like smtp.somename.com). Usually, you'll get a blank stare from the
person you're asking.

If you're on Windows, you can buy a program called 1st SMTP
Server for $49 (emailarms.com/products/1st_smtp.html), which al-
lows you to relay email messages directly to their destination. You can
download a fully functional 30-day trial version for free. Another
method is to pay to use a portable SMTP server like smtp.com, which
charges $10 a month to relay up to 50 emails per day. But I don't think
it's worth it. The method I use is free. I have a Gmail account from

Google, and I use its SMTP server to send all my email, no matter where I happen to be. (To learn more about Gmail, see page 287).

See page 302 to see how I've set up Gmail's outgoing mail server.

Most email applications have a similar setup window. Make sure you set the SMTP server to smtp.gmail.com. Choose "Password Authentication" and enter your complete Gmail address as your user name and your Gmail password as your authentication password. If you are asked for a server port, enter 587.

I've found the Gmail method to be extremely reliable.

How Can I Prevent Creeps from Sending Email to Me?

How to create a killfile so you'll never see email from someone you don't like

Anyone who has participated on an Internet message board has probably gotten into an argument with other users of the board. If

Remind yourself of an important event that will take place months or even years in the future

You can send a message to your future self up to five years in the future at futuremail.bensinclair.com. Choose a time and date, write a message, click the "Email this message to me" box, and click "Save." If the service is still working on that day, and you still have that email address, FutureMail will send you the message. FutureMail is better for one-time events than it is for recurring ones, such as birthdays, anniversaries, annual doctor appointments, and so on. For those, try Google Calendar at calendar.google.com.

email addresses of the users are public, the argument often migrates over to email, where a one-on-one flame war ensues.

I always try to be polite when I reply to email, even though it's hard to resist the temptation to reply in kind to an invective-filled missive or other abusive email. But I've learned from experience that sending an angry response to angry email only fuels the anger on both sides. In recent years, I've developed a different way to deal with flames. Now when I get an email that brims with hostility, I refrain from replying to it and instead add the sender of the email message to my killfile. No, this isn't a list of people that I intend to hunt down and strangle, it's merely a record of email addresses that my email program uses to delete messages sent to me from people on the list. Less ominous-sounding names for killfile include "bozo bin" and "twit list," but I prefer the finality of "killfile."

When my mail application sees an incoming message sent from a killfile member, it instantly zaps the message. I'm not even notified that a message from a killfilee was sent, and I like it that way. It's fun to think that a creep on my killfile list wasted energy composing a message that no one will ever read or even know was sent.

Almost every email program will let you create a killfile. To set up a killfile in Apple's mail program, select "Mail" → "Preferences" → "Rules" and click "Add Rule." Give the rule a name in the "Description" field and set the rule to apply "If any of the following conditions are met." From the pull-down menus, select "From" and "Contains" and enter the email address of the killee in the blank field. (If you opened the "Rule" settings after opening an email from a person you want to killfile, the email address will be automatically added to the blank field.) Select "Delete Message" from the actions menu. To add another person to the killfile, click the + sign next to the blank field and enter the address of that killee. See page 305 for an example setup.

In Microsoft Office Outlook 2007, adding a person to your killfile is easy. Just select "Tools" → "Options" → "Preferences" → "E-mail" → "Junk E-mail" → "Blocked Senders" → "Add" and then add the email address you want to block.

Creating a killfile to rid yourself of email pests.

In some cases, it might be better to fool an email pest into thinking that your email address no longer exists. You can do this by sending a phony bounce message, which informs the person who sent you the message that your email address isn't valid. I sometimes use fake bounces to get off mailing lists that I never subscribed to but which started appearing in my inbox anyway. The software that manages mailing lists looks for bounced email and removes the addresses. It's an easier way to unsubscribe than by clicking on the unsubscribe link and filling out a form on a Web site. (Keep in mind that fake bounces will do nothing to curb spam because spammers never use valid return email addresses.)

Apple Mail makes it dead simple to send a bounce. Just highlight or open the message and select "Message" → "Bounce," and you're done. If you want to automate bouncing for a persistent pest, download a copy of Bounce Mail (scriptbuilders.net/files/bounce-mail1.0.html). Copy it to "Library" → "Scripts" → "Mail Scripts," select "Mail" → "Preferences" → "Rules" and click "Add Rule." Set up your rule as described above, but instead of selecting "Delete Message" from the actions menu, select "Run AppleScript" and click "Choose" to navigate to Library/Scripts/Mail Scripts/Bounce Mail 1.0.scpt. See page 306 for an example of a rule that bounces

Description: Bounce and Kill

If [any ‡] of the following conditions are met:

[From ‡] [Contains ‡] [Ima_Pest@trollheaven.c] ⊖ ⊕

Perform the following actions:

[Run AppleScript ‡] [/Library/Scripts/Mail Scripts/Bou] [Choose...] ⊖ ⊕

[Delete Message ‡] [   ] ⊖ ⊕

(Cancel) (OK)

The bouncer script returns email to pests as if it never reached you.

Retrieve an email message after you've sent it

Email is a wonderful way to communicate because it allows you to send archivable messages to anyone, instantly. It can also be very dangerous for those same reasons. Who hasn't regretted hitting the "Send" button just seconds after composing an email written in anger? There's also the problem of mis-addressed email. When I was working for a magazine, one of my colleagues forwarded a bunch of us in the office an email she'd gotten from our boss, to which she added: "Can you believe how stupid this is?"

A minute later, we all got an email from the boss, which read, "Who's stupider—me for writing that, or you for forgetting to take my name off the recipient list?"

Lucky for her, she kept her job. Still, I'll bet she wished she had something like YankBack (yankback.com). The service (which costs $25 a year), holds all your sent email in a queue with a timer for each message. You can take a look at all the emails in the queue and see to whom they're addressed and how much time you have before they're automatically sent (you can set the default delay to whatever length of time you wish). You can pause any email by clicking a button or pause them all by clicking the big red "Panic" button.

YankBack is good for preventing embarrassing email, but it's also useful when you've forgotten to send an attachment or to include additional information in your message.

and then deletes any email sent from a (fictional) bozo named Ima_Pest@trollheaven.ck.

Windows users can download a utility called Bounce Bully (bouncebully.com) that works with any email program. Just copy and paste an offending email message into Bounce Bully's window, and click "Bounce." If you are feeling especially vengeful, you can click "Punish," which will send the bounce message back to the creep up to five times.

CHAPTER 9

TOOLBOX

Think of this section as a place to find new tools and to sharpen the ones you already have. You'll learn how to get rid of junk files and programs that needlessly bloat your computer system, as well as tricks and tips to access and manage the files you do want to keep.

▶▶ SYSTEM TUNE-UP

▶ How Can I Clean Up the Crap That Gunks Up My Hard Drive and Slows My Online Activities to a Crawl?

Use free and inexpensive utilities to keep your computer from grinding to a halt

Like the backseat of a car occupied by toddlers, your computer collects lots of junk over time: unneeded fonts, unwanted programs, mysterious orphan files, duplicate files, and lots of other detritus accumulated over years of wanton downloading.

Unlike spilled milkshakes and cheese-puff powder, computer gunk is less conspicuous. But even though you can't see most of it, this virtual garbage ends up being a big drag on your computer's performance, threatens the integrity of your data, and compromises your security. Naturally, you'll want to get rid of all this clutter, but you need to do it in a way that doesn't make things worse and that protects your computer from getting fouled up again later on down the road. Here's how to clean the junk out of your computer and, more importantly, keep it out.

>Windows

Use a junk-cleaning program. The easiest way to keep your machine free of obsolete, duplicate, and unnecessary files is by using a junk-cleaning program. Download a trial version of Disk Medic (iomatic.com). To get an idea of how many useless files you have on your hard drive, run the program, click "My Files" on the top row of buttons, then click "Junk Files," and then click "Start Scan." Disk Medic will probably find hundreds of junk files representing tens of megabytes that you can safely delete. The trial version of Disk Medic only lets you delete five files at a time. Then you have to rescan and delete the next five. It's well worth forking over $20 for the full-featured version of the program.

If you've been online for more than a few months and downloaded programs from the Internet, you've probably noticed that mysterious program icons are showing up in Window's system tray without your consent. This is generally a bad thing, because these little programs are like parasites, sucking performance from your computer's microprocessor and slowing everything down. If you'd like to take a look at all the programs that are running on your computer, press Ctrl-Alt-Delete and see for yourself. Where do all these memory- and processor-hogging programs come from? Well, lots of different places, but mainly from companies you'd think you could trust. America Online, Real Networks (maker of RealPlayer), and other Internet companies are infamous for their sneaky program planting. To get rid of them and prevent new ones from infecting your machine, get yourself a copy of WinPatrol Plus ($25 from winpatrol.com). After you install it, WinPatrol will monitor any program that attempts to launch itself when you boot up Windows. An icon of a little dog, Scotty, warns you whenever a new program is added to the Startup list, giving you the option to keep it or prevent it from loading. For stubborn programs that won't go away no matter how many times you've tried to zap them, you can right-click the Program icon and select "Delete File on Reboot." When you re-launch Windows, WinPatrol will delete the file before Windows starts up and gives another sneaky program the opportunity to prevent the deletion of the file.

Another good dejunker is Ccleaner (short for Crap Cleaner, ccleaner.com). It does a fantastic job of getting rid of temporary files, orphaned files, relics left behind after uninstalling software, invalid icons, and so on, and it's free. I run Ccleaner once a month in order to knock all the sludge out of my computer.

Use Windows' Disk Cleanup utility. It's good to have lots of unused space—5 GB or more on your hard drive. Your computer uses the extra storage to perform housekeeping duties, and your applications use it like scratch paper. When your hard drive gets dangerously bloated, it'll display a pop-up window warning that you are too low on free space. You probably don't need a bigger hard drive. Chances are, you can reclaim a lot of free space by using Window's built-in Cleanup utility. Go to your Start menu, select "My Computer" and right-click your hard drive—usually called Local Disk (C:). Select "Properties," then click "Disk Cleanup." You can safely delete a bunch of no-longer-needed files by clicking on all the checkboxes and clicking "OK." You can get rid of even more junk by clicking the "More Options" tag in the "Disk Cleanup" window and removing unwanted programs and Windows components. For instance, I don't plan on ever using my computer to send faxes over the modem, so I got rid of it and saved about 4 MB. Another prime candidate for removal is the MSN Explorer component. While you're here, get rid of your restore points, which are settings Windows can use to restore your operating system to a earlier point in time, should problems occur. Don't worry, your most recent restore point won't be deleted.

>Macintosh

Get rid of unwanted applications. If you're like me, you probably enjoy trying out demo and shareware versions of software

(macupdate.com is my favorite source for freeware and software).
Nine times out of ten, I'll toy with the application for a few minutes and never use it again. Usually I remember to delete the file.
However, simply dragging an application into the trash doesn't
always wipe away all its vestiges. Often, a number of support files
and cache files belonging to the application remain on your hard
drive, needlessly taking up room and slowing down your system
performance. A $13 utility called AppZapper (appzapper.com)
does a great job of finding and zapping all the components of an
application. Just drag an unwanted application into AppZapper's
window, and it'll display the files it's about to delete. Then click
the "Zap" button. You'll hear a ray-gun sound effect, indicating
the program and all its support files have been vaporized. Even
easier, select "Show Genie" from the file menu and sort your applications by date. You'll be surprised at how many applications
are on your computer that you haven't used in years. Zap 'em. (See
page 313.)

Delete files you no longer need. Do you ever wonder where all
your hard-disk space went? There's a good chance your computer is
loaded with unneeded gargantuan movie and sound files. It's good to
get rid of them, because your computer needs plenty of unused storage space so it can perform routine maintenance tasks, and so your
applications can have the scratch space they need to store temporary
backups and behind-the-scene files. My favorite way of uncovering
disk-hogging files is with a free program called Disk Inventory X
(derlien.com). Using a unique visual representation of the files and
folders on your disk, called "treemaps," this handy utility lets you
quickly uncover the largest files on your computer and toss them
into the trash if you don't need them.

Disk Inventory X sorts all your files and folders by size, making
it easy to find the biggest files. You can also click the larger rec-
tangles in the visual representation of your hard drive, to see what
they are. Likely candidates for dumping are: AIFF files (which are
uncompressed sound files that might be hanging out in iTunes) and
no-longer-needed movie project files from iMovie. I'm usually

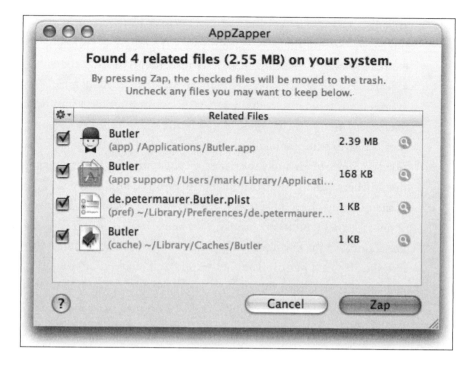

AppZapper for Mac deletes unwanted applications along with their support files.

able to recover at least a gigabyte of disk space every time I use Disk Inventory X.

Not everyone likes the visual format of Disk Inventory X. Another great utility for finding large files is WhatSize (id-design.com/software/whatsize). This program scans your hard drive and then sorts your folders and files by size, color coding them (anything over 1GB is red, files between 1MB and 1GB are purple, and anything smaller is green). WhatSize also displays "invisible" files that your operating system purposely keeps hidden from view. The application denotes a hidden file by displaying it with gray text. Be careful about deleting hidden files, because some of them are needed to keep your operating system intact.

Use a maintenance utility. Your Mac operating system performs regular housekeeping tasks to keep your computer running smoothly. But if you shut down your computer every day, it won't get the chance to run these tasks. But you can force it to complete its chores by using a cleaning utility. My favorite program is the $8.99 Macaroni (atomicbird.com), which takes care of regular Mac OS X system maintenance, such as repairing support files, rebuilding databases, managing log files, and deleting old temporary files, old Mac OS X installer logs, old crash logs, and old printer spool files. What's more, Macaroni looks for language support files and zaps them. Many Mac applications have files for many different languages. iTunes, for instance, has support files for Chinese, Danish, Dutch, English, Finnish, French, German, Italian, Korean, Japanese, Norwegian, Portuguese, Spanish, and Swedish versions. Unless you live in a multilingual household and share your computer, you can tell Macaroni to remove "Localized files." You'll probably recover at least 250 MB by doing this. The first time I removed all my localized files, I saved a whopping 2.1GB by removing 214,767 localization files!

Another useful and free—donations accepted—utility (www .titanium.free.fr/pgs/english.html) is called OnyX. It has lots of features to keep your system running smoothly, but is not as easy to use as Macaroni, which pretty much runs in the background. But if you're willing to roll up your sleeves and get under the hood, OnyX is an excellent utility. It verifies and repairs permission files (which often get messed up when you install new applications or experience a system crash), optimizes your operating system by updating the System libraries, and runs the daily, weekly, and monthly maintenance scripts. You can use it to clean cache, log, cookie, and history files. It also allows you to customize certain aspects of the operating system's appearance, such as scroll bars and label lines, and can show hidden files.

Delete duplicated files. Over time, your hard drive will accumulate duplicated files. This is especially true of digital photos and music files. Not only do duplicate files unnecessarily take up a lot of disk space, they also slow down searching and system maintenance tasks. Several utilities exist to help you track down and delete duplicate files, but for my money (all $30 of it), the best one is Tidy Up! by Hyperbolic Software (hyperbolicsoftware.com/TidyUp.html). This powerful program lets you create customized searches for any type of file. The best thing about Tidy Up! is the way it lets you preview sound, font, media, PDF, text, and image files from within the application, so you can decide whether or not a suspected duplicate file really is a clone.

Delete printer drivers you don't need. The Mac operating system comes with over 1 GB of printer drivers for all the major brands of printers. You only need to keep the ones for which you have printers. You can find the driver folders by opening a "Finder" window and navigating to "Library/Printers." Delete folders named with printer brands you don't use. Don't worry if you end up buying a printer later on that used a driver you deleted. Chances are the printer comes with a disc that has the driver on it, and even if it doesn't, you'll be able to download it from the manufacturer's Web site.

Fix your toilet without a plumber

Who hasn't had a toilet that, one time or another, flushed sluggishly, wouldn't stop refilling, made strange noises, or, horror of horrors, wouldn't unclog no matter what you tried? You might have tried to fix it yourself, only to call the plumber after breaking a rusted bolt or flooding the bathroom. Toiletology 101 (toiletology.com) not only shows you how a toilet does its thing, it helps you troubleshoot your problem and tells you how to fix it. If Toiletology can't help you, here are two more Web sites with good advice: Fix a Toilet (fixatoilet.com) and How Stuff Works (home.howstuffworks.com/how-to-repair-a-toilet.htm).

▶ How Do I Clean All the Junk Software Off of My New PC?

Use the PC De-Crapifier to delete useless crippleware from your new computer

I know people who have actually purchased a new computer because they say their old one was filled with so many buggy programs, corrupted files, spyware, and viruses that they felt their only option was to throw it out and get a new one. This is silly. If you ever get completely fed up with your computer's strange behavior, you can just reformat the hard drive and start over. In fact, that's a better option than buying a new PC, because manufacturers load the hard drives of their new computers with all sorts of junk programs that make it harder to use. Why do they do this? Because they're hoping you'll sign up with AOL or Earthlink as your ISP, or that you'll pay to upgrade an application from the demo version to the full-featured version. When you do, the PC manufacturer gets a bounty. And so they pre-clutter your computer with all sorts of come-ons. I'm telling you, you don't need any of it. The sooner you get it off your computer, the better. The easiest way to do that is with the free and fabulous PC-DeCrapifier (yorkspace.com/pc-de-crapifier). When it starts up, you're given the option to delete a bunch of pre-installed applications and utilities, such as Corel Word-Perfect, QuickBooks Trial, Dell Search Assistant, and many others. I even recommend that you get rid of the installed version of Google Desktop, because who knows what kind of version it is and whether or not it has any privacy-violating hooks in it? Maybe I'm paranoid, but it's a simple matter to re-install a clean copy of Google Desktop from desktop.google.com.

▶ How Can I Use Two Computers with the Same Monitor and Keyboard?

Two computers on one desk? Here's how to save room by consolidating peripherals

Do you switch back and forth between two computers? Some people have a laptop and a desktop PC, and some use a Mac and a Windows computer, switching back and forth throughout the day. If you're one of these switch hitters, you can save valuable desk space by getting a KVR switch, which lets you share a monitor and keyboard with two computers. The coolest KVR switch is the Belkin Flip (belkin.com/flip), a wireless button that looks like a little round cake of hotel soap. You attach the supplied cable to your laptop and desktop computers, and to a monitor, keyboard, mouse, and optionally, a set of speakers. Whenever you press the switch, the cable will connect one of the two computers to the monitor, keyboard, and mouse. (It only works with analog monitors, which rules out Apple Cinema displays, unfortunately.) Each time you press the button, the other computer connects to the peripherals.

▶ How Can I Tell If My Hard Drive Is in Good Shape?

Get a jump start on potential hard drive trouble by using a S.M.A.R.T. utility

When it comes to hard-drive failure, it's a question of when, not if. Hard drives are delicate mechanisms with two motors and read/write heads that fly a tiny fraction of an inch over the surface of the disks, which are spinning around a hundred times a second. One of these days, a speck of dust is going to get caught between the read/write head and the disk. The head will drag the dust speck into the surface of the disk, scraping away the material that stores your data. The material will get stuck under all the read/write heads and in a split second the inside of your hard drive will be a dust storm of magnetic particles. You will then be the proud owner of an expensive paperweight.

That's why it's essential that you back up your hard drive every single day. That way, you'll never lose more than one day's work. It's also important to monitor the health of your hard drive. Today's hard drives support something called S.M.A.R.T. (Self-Monitoring Analysis and Reporting Technology). S.M.A.R.T. drives are able to self-evaluate the condition of their motors, disks, read/write heads, and control circuitry. And they're able to warn you when something is about to go on the fritz.

You can check your S.M.A.R.T. status on the Mac by going to "Applications" → "Utilities" and running Disk Utility. Select a drive from the list on the left and then look at the S.M.A.R.T. Status message at the bottom of the window. If it doesn't say "Verified," then you should back up your data as soon as possible and get a new hard drive installed. (If your Mac is still under warranty, they'll probably replace the drive for you at no charge.) An even better way to check the S.M.A.R.T. status on your Mac is to let your computer do it for you, and tell you if there's a problem. Download a free copy of SMARTReporter (homepage.mac.com/julianmayer). After launching, you see an icon of a hard drive in the menu bar. A green icon means everything checks out. Red means it's time to get a new hard drive.

An icon of a hard drive should appear in your menu bar (right top of your screen). It turns green when your hard drives are verified, turns red when they are failing, or stays grey if no status has been determined (you can also choose other "styles" in the preferences). If you don't want to clutter your menu bar with icons, you can set up SMARTReporter to pop up an alert or send an email when it detects a failure.

To monitor the S.M.A.R.T. status of your Windows computer, download a free copy of HDD Health (panterasoft.com), which sits in your system tray monitoring your drive's vital statistics. If it detects a problem, it will alert you by email, sound, or pop-up message.

▶ Does My Computer Need More Memory?

Insufficient memory could be one reason your computer might not be as perky as you'd like it to be

Your computer has two ways to store all the ones and zeros it processes: on its hard drive and in its random access memory (RAM). When you launch a program, the ones and zeros that make up that program are loaded from the relatively slow hard drive to the very speedy RAM chips. You can find out how much memory your Windows computer has by right-clicking on "My Computer" in the Start menu and selecting "Properties." The amount is displayed in the lower right corner of the General window. On a Mac, select "About This Mac" from the Apple menu. When you have a lot of programs and files open at the same time, the RAM isn't sufficient to store them all, and some of them have to be temporarily offloaded to the disk drive. As you switch from one application to another, data is swapped back and forth between the disk drive and the RAM. This takes a lot of time, and that's why your computer slows down when it's running a lot of programs.

You can perk up your PC by adding more RAM. Most computers come with 512 MB of RAM, which is enough to smoothly handle several programs at once. But if you have lots of programs open that work with large data files, such as video editing, music editing, or photograph retouching, 512 MB might not cut the mustard. Before sending your Windows computer to the dealer to have more RAM installed, however, you can try to free up more of your computer's existing RAM with a free utility called FreeRAM XP Pro (yourwaresolutions.com). FreeRAM XP Pro finds RAM that applications have borrowed and forgotten to return. It also finds little-used data residing in RAM and moves it to the hard drive. After installing and launching FreeRAM XP Pro, you'll see an icon in your system tray with a number on it, which represents the amount of computer's unused RAM. Right-click the icon, select "AutoFree Now," and let the program go to work. In a matter of seconds, it'll find the incorrectly allocated RAM, clean it up, and make it available to the programs currently running.

DEEPER

Installing RAM yourself. If FreeRAM XP Pro doesn't make your computer zippier, then you should buy more RAM. You can take it to a dealer and have them install it, but it's easy enough to do yourself—all you need is a Philips head screwdriver and an anti-static wrist strap, which prevents you from destroying the RAM with a jolt of static electricity. Most online RAM dealers will walk you through the process. For example, Maverick Memory (maverickmemory.com) has an Autodetect Tool that determines what kind of computer you are using, what kind and how much RAM it has, and how much additional RAM you can install. The Web site will let you know the right kind of RAM you need. After you order the RAM, go back to the Web site and follow the instructions for desktop or laptop computers. Also, you might want to compare prices with dealram.com before you buy.

Before you install the new RAM, you should make a special CD-ROM that tests your computer's RAM. (You might not need it, but if the new RAM is faulty it'll help you diagnose the problem.) Go to and download the ISO image of Memtest86. You need to burn this onto a CD-ROM using a CD-burning program, making sure to select the "Make Bootable" option. Then restart your computer with the CD-ROM (usually by holding down the F12 key when you restart and selecting "CD-ROM Device"). After you're sure that Memtest86 works, go ahead and install the RAM.

If the computer doesn't start up properly or refuses to recognize the newly installed RAM, check to make sure that all cables you may have unplugged during installation are plugged back in. Also make sure that your new RAM cards have been properly installed into their sockets. Take them out and reinsert, making sure they go all the way in. If that doesn't solve the problem, reboot your computer using the Memtest86 disk. It will tell you whether or not the RAM is faulty. If it turns out to be bad, take it out and send it back to the dealer for a replacement.

 # MUSIC

▶How Can I Play MP3s on My Home Stereo?

Liberate your digital music from your PC

Like the Sony Walkman, the iPod was designed as a personal music player, but because it can store thousands of songs, it's only natural that people have started to think of it as home base for all their digital music. And so, it makes sense to connect it to your home and car stereos, so that the songs on it can be played through full-size speakers. I've tried many different ways to get big sound out of the little iPod, and have come to the conclusion that no solution exists that's cheap, good, and easy. But many methods are good enough. Here's a rundown:

>Battery-powered speakers

For about $25, you can pick up a small set of battery-powered speakers that connect to your iPod's headphone jack. I use my portable speakers in the bedroom to play music and old radio plays.

Advantages: Portable, inexpensive, and easy to use.

Disadvantages: Mediocre sound quality and limited to low volume use.

>FM transmitter

The FCC allows individuals to transmit a signal over the FM radio band, provided the transmitter is 0.25 watts or less. (By way of comparison, major FM radio stations transmit at 10,000 watts.) You can buy a tiny FM radio transmitter for $20 or so that plugs into your iPod's FM headphone jack and then tune a nearby FM radio to pick up the signal. I use my transmitter to play my iPod through the car stereo system, through a boombox at outdoor barbecues, and though a hotel room's stereo or clock radio.

Advantages: Portable, inexpensive.

Disadvantages: Range is limited to 50 feet or so and prone to static. If you're in an area with a lot of FM stations, the interference might make it not work at all.

>Wired to stereo

For about $70, The HiFi Link for iPod (xitel.com) is a nice solution for playing your iPod through your home stereo system. You plug the cables coming out of the dock into the AUX jack of your stereo. (You also have to plug an AC converter into the dock in order to keep the iPod charged.) I appreciate the ease of use—I didn't even need to refer to the manual to use it. The remote allows you to jump from one playlist to another, and skip forward or back by track, but there's no

AirLink wireless audio transmitter.

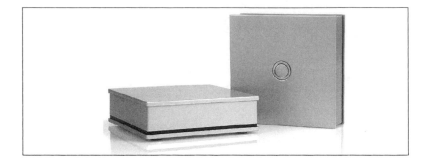

volume control. Also, the remote uses infrared, not RF, so you need a line-of-sight to the dock to skip songs, which is not ideal for my setup (I hide the stereo system and HiFi Link in a cabinet, which means I need to keep the cabinet doors open if I want to be able to change a song.)

The HiFi Link also hooks up to a TV, so you can view photos and videos (if you have an iPod Video) with it.

Advantages: Excellent sound quality, thanks to direct connection between iPod's line-out port and stereo system; remote makes it easy to switch songs; cradle keeps iPod fully charged and ready to go.

Disadvantages: Remote control needs line-of-sight to dock in order to work.

>Digital wireless

The $65 MP3 AirLink Wireless Audio Transmitter and Receiver (startech.com) uses the same frequency spectrum as a Wi-Fi network to transit your music from an iPod or computer to a stereo. The system comes with two palm-sized rectangular cubes—a transmitter and a receiver. The transmitter has a button to let you scroll through eight channels, helping you get a clear signal.

Startech advertises the range to be 100 feet in the clear, and 30 feet through walls, and that seems about right to me. When I connected the transmitter to my desktop computer in one room and the stereo in another, I experienced some dropouts, until I moved the transmitter and receiver around. (See above.)

Advantages: You can control the songs from your iPod or computer; sound quality is good.

Disadvantages: Each device is powered with an AC adapter, but if you don't need portability, this isn't a problem; getting good reception can be tricky, range is limited to 30 feet through walls.

>Top end

Experiencing the Sonos after struggling with these other systems for years was astonishingly pleasant. Finally, somebody has done digital music right. Sonos is a beautiful system that matches Apple's products in terms of slickness and ease-of-use. I got the ZonePlayer 80 Bundle, a $999 package that comes with two ZonePlayers—white cubes that are approximately the size of a Mac Mini. These can be connected into any stereo, radio, or home theater system. The ZonePlayers don't require an AC adapter—the power supply is built in, so all you have to do is plug the ZonePlayer into the wall. One ZonePlayer must be directly connected to your home router, but the other ZonePlayers can communicate with the system wirelessly. (There is a way to use Sonos completely wirelessly, but it's an unsupported feature.) You can use up to 32 ZonePlayers on one network.

The controller looks and acts a lot like an iPod, with a 3.5-inch full-color display and a touch wheel. It has a motion detector, so it comes to life when you pick it up, and a light sensor to illuminate the buttons when it's dark. Even with these energy-saving features, the battery life isn't great. I have to recharge the remote controller every two or three days, but that's a small price to pay for having complete control of your home music system in your hand.

I've set up several wireless networks over the years, and each time, I got snagged on some arcane configuration detail that had me running to Google for help. Not so with the Sonos. I installed the Sonos software on an old eMac I keep running in the laundry room. (Sonos works with Mac and Windows). The software slurped up all the MP3s on the machine as well as the iTunes playlists. (Sonos can't play songs purchased from the iTunes music store, because Apple does not allow other hardware makers to decode the DRM it uses to scrambles the songs with. No matter—I don't buy songs from the iTunes music store because I don't like being prevented from playing my music on non-Apple players. People are nuts to buy music from the iTunes Store, if you ask me.)

I attached one of the ZonePlayers to my Ethernet router and pressed two buttons on it. The Sonos software recognized it and prompted me to give it a name (I chose "TV Room"). I attached the other ZonePlayer to my home stereo system, pressed the buttons, and Sonos asked me to give it a name ("Living Room"). I also got a Zone-Player 100, which has a built-in 50 W amplifier and a pair of speakers, and I put that in the kitchen and called that zone "Kitchen."

I was expecting that there'd be more to the set-up process, but that was it. I didn't need to consult the manual to use the controller because the interface, controls, and display are very well thought out. It's very easy to select any one of the three zones and start playing music. You can have different playlists going in different zones, or you can link zones together to play them from the same queue. You can control the volume of each Zone separately or all at once.

You can play Internet radio with Sonos, and add stations that aren't already on its list. It also plays Rhapsody if you have a subscription. I signed up, and love having access to 2.5 million Sonos. I also have a 500 GB NAS hard drive to store the music that the Sonos system plays. My wife usually complains when I introduce a new technology into our lives. This is the first thing since TiVo that she really digs. My daughters like it, too—I have a playlist for my seven-year-old and one for my three-year-old. I'm listening to as much music as I did when I was in college. Sonos really has brought back music into my life.

Advantages: You can control the songs from a remote player that works like an iPod; can play different songs in different rooms around the house.

Disadvantages: At $750 for a starter system, it's more expensive than other solutions.

If you don't want to shell out the money for an iPod–car interface, but you have a car stereo that plays MP3s on disc, you can burn about 200 songs on one CD using iTunes and play that. At less than a quarter per blank CD, it's a great way to enjoy your digital music collection

DEEPER

Play your iPod in the car.
Most solutions for playing your iPod in your car involve cables, adapters, or tiny FM transmitters. I've tried them all, and none of them are ideal. To listen to—and control—an iPod in a car, it's best to get a professionally installed system. These allow you to insert your iPod into a cradle and control your iPod with your car radio knobs and buttons. Most new cars come with iPod dealer options, too. Visit apple.com/ipod/ipodyourcar to find out about factory-installed iPod interfaces and after-let systems.

in your car without spending any money. (See page 327 to learn how to make an MP3 CD).

How Can I Convert Windows Media Files to MP3s?

Convert music files from Microsoft's proprietary format to the universal MP3 standard

I don't like proprietary music formats because they limit your ability to play your music on different devices. Whenever I can, I take my song files as plain old MP3s. iTunes has a built-in MP3 encoder, but it's not as versatile as Switch, a free sound-file conversion application (nch.com.au/switch/index.html) that works on Macs and Windows. Use it to batch convert songs from wav, ogg, flac, aac, wma, au, aiff, msv, and other formats into MP3s. You can set the encoder to output MP3s in a variety of formats (you'll probably want to use the default 128 kbps setting) and you can preview songs with the built-in player.

How Can I Convert My LP Collection to MP3s?

Use a special turntable to rip vinyl to digital files

I have a nice collection of LPs from my high school and college days, but for years I didn't have a turntable to play them on. A few years ago I bought a record player meant for elementary school use, and while I liked the retro charm, I had to run the audio through the record player's mono headphone jack to my computer, which meant I lost the stereo signal. Today, the best way to convert LPs and 45s to MP3s is with the Ion Audio iTTUSB turntable (search for them on froogle.com), which has a USB port that lets you plug it directly into your computer. This nifty-looking turntable (which costs $139) comes with the excellent Audacity software or you can use any other audio software you like. Audio Technica also makes a turntable for digitizing LPs, the AT-LP2D LP-to-Digital Recording System, which costs a little over $100.

Sadly, no company has announced an eight-track-tape-to-MP3 converter yet.

DEEPER

Convert cassette tapes to MP3s. What are you going to do with that shoebox full of cassette tapes that you haven't listened to since the Bush, Sr., era? You don't want to throw them away because those hundreds of linear feet of magnetic tape contain an instant trip down memory lane. But with cassette players a relic of the past, it's a hassle listening to them. With the Plusdeck (plusdeck.com), you can have the best of both worlds. This $150 cassette player fits into the standard 5.25-inch drive bay of a PC and converts music on cassette tapes into MP3s.

Keep your iPod screen from getting scratched in the first place. The next order of business was finding out how to prevent my display from becoming scratched again. As much as I liked the Applesauce Polish, I'd rather not have a reason to use it. For $5, I bought a clear plastic sticker that wrapped around the iPod like a burrito. There were a few bubbles under the plastic, but I managed to squeegee them away by sliding my thumb across them. When I wrote about the plastic wrapper on my blog, someone commented that they found a better, and cheaper solution: clear thin vinyl purchased at a craft store. "It sticks great to a clean iPod and itself without any adhesive," he said. "I used the same approach to my first iPod, and it died after five years of use without a scratch on it." Since then, I've been using the craft store vinyl on my iPod, too, and it's better, and cheaper, than the specialty iPod protective cover I bought.

▶ How Can I Remove Scratches on My iPod Display?

Keep your iPod's display crystal clear with special polish

I never paid attention to the scratches and nicks that accumulated on my iPod. After all, the thing was made to be listened to, not looked at. I thought the great lengths people went to keep their iPods in pristine condition was a little silly, on the order of plastic carpet runners and vinyl couch covers.

But my attitude changed with the introduction of the iPod video player. As soon as I got mine, I made a habit of keeping it in the cloth bag that Apple shipped with it. I didn't want the screen to get scratched, because I used it to watch movies while using the equipment at the gym (see "How Can I Watch Videos on My iPod or PSP?," page 171). But one day, I noticed a nasty scratch on the display. And it was in a spot right over the place where people's faces often appear in medium-length shots in movies. It really bugged me, and I promised myself I'd be more careful.

A few days later, I discovered a bunch of new scratches on my iPod. What was going on? I did a little searching on Google and found that lots of people were complaining about the same problem. "The screen scratches if you look at it," wrote one disgruntled iPod Video owner. I felt the same way.

My Google searches also led me to a number of companies offering liquid polishes designed to remove scratches from iPod displays. Curious, I ordered the potions from several different companies. The only one that really did the job for me was Applesauce Polish (applesaucepolish.com), a $20 kit that contained two small plastic bottles and several polishing cloths. One bottle was labeled "Microfinishing Polish" and was to be used to remove larger scratches and the other bottle, labeled "Microfinishing Glaze" was designed to restore the screen to its store-bought luster. I dripped a drop of the first bottle of polish onto the display and started rubbing it with the cloth. After being disappointed by the other polishes I'd tried, this one really seemed to be working. Several drops and several minutes later, most of the scratches were gone. I then applied the glaze, and ended up with a screen that looked almost, but not quite, as good as new. It was much better than before, though.

▶How Can I Make an MP3 CD?

How to put 200 songs on one disc

Most newer CD players made will play a special CD format called MP3 CDs. Now, these aren't simply audio CDs that you've burned. An MP3 CD stores the songs as MP3s and you can fit 200 or more MP3 songs on an MP3 CD. With the price of a blank CD as low as a dime, you won't find a cheaper way to create portable music.

iTunes is the easiest and (since it's free) cheapest way to make an MP3 CD. Here's how you do it:

1. Select "Preferences" → "Advanced" → "Burning" and click the "MP3 CD" radio button. While you're here, you might consider changing the Preferred Speed to something slower than the maximum rate. I find that my MP3 CDs have fewer errors when I don't burn them at the maximum possible rate. (See page 328.)

2. Select "File" → "New Playlist" and give your playlist a name. Now, start dragging songs and podcasts from the library into the playlist folder.

   Most writable CDs have a maximum capacity of 700 MB. To be safe, don't drag more than 690 MB into the playlist, otherwise you might run into playback problems. You can see how big your playlist is by clicking on it and looking at the line of information on the bottom of the iTunes window.

3. If you want, you can change the play order of the songs by clicking on the playlist, and then clicking on the columns to sort by Name, Artist, Genre, Album, etc.

Advanced

General   iPod   Podcasts   Playback   Sharing   Store   Advanced   Parental

General | Importing | Burning

CD Burner: MATSHITA DVD-R UJ-835E

Preferred Speed: | 16x ▲▼ |

Disc Format: ○ Audio CD

Gap Between Songs: | 2 seconds ▲▼ |

☐ Use Sound Check

● MP3 CD

○ Data CD or DVD

Data discs include all files in the playlist. These
discs may not play in some players.

(?)   (Cancel) (OK)

Making an MP3 CD to store 200 songs or more on one CD.

4. Make sure your playlist is highlighted and then click the "Burn
   Disk" icon in the upper-right corner. iTunes will check all the
   songs in your playlist to make sure they're valid MP3 files. It
   will let you know if it finds any that it can't burn, and will give
   the option of canceling or continuing with the files that are
   burnable.

5. When your MP3 CD has finished burning, take it out and try it
   in your player. If your player has a display, it might be able to
   show the song and artist information.

▶ How Can I Liberate iTunes Songs So I Can Play Them on Different Computers and Handheld Players?

How to play iTunes-purchased songs on non-Apple players

Songs purchased on iTunes are not MP3 files. They use a file format called AAC (Apple Audio Codec). You can't play iTunes-protected AAC songs on computers or devices not supported by Apple. In addition, Apple imposes a five-computer limit on any iTunes song you purchase. This represents a big step backward in customer convenience. I certainly don't think people should steal music, but I also don't think they should be prevented from listening to their purchased music on any music player they choose to use. It's unfair for Apple and other technology companies to prevent you from making backups.

However, there's an easy way to convert iTunes-purchased songs into the MP3 format. When you buy a song from iTunes, you're allowed to burn it to a CD. You can burn any particular playlist five times, after which Apple shuts the door. So here's the trick: highlight the "Purchased Music" folder on iTunes and click the "Burn" icon in the upper right corner. iTunes will prompt you to insert a CD and begin burning the files to the disc. If there are more songs than can fit on a single CD, iTunes will prompt you to insert additional CDs.

Now you have your songs stored as standard audio files (which are about 10 times larger than MP3 files). You can play these on any CD player. But if you want to play them on an MP3 player, you have to rip them to MP3 files. That's as simple as sticking the disc back into your computer and clicking the "Import CD" icon (which is in the same spot where the Burn icon was in the previous step). iTunes will convert the audio files into MP3s.

There are three other drawbacks to this method: you'll lose the album art image that appears on your iPod and iTunes when you play the song; you'll often lose the song information, such as artist, album, and title, and the audio quality of the song becomes a little worse as a result of the conversion process. I don't have a problem with this last drawback because I don't mind (and usually can't even tell) the difference between an MP3 file and a higher quality version of a song. But if you're an audiophile, it's something to take into consideration before converting all your purchased iTunes songs. (Circumventing this protection may violate the law and Apple's terms. The risk and ethical decision are yours.)

▶ How Can I Get Rid of Duplicate Music Files in iTunes?

Use a free utility to clean redundant songs from your music library

From some reason, digital music files seem to enjoy breeding inside computers. There have been times—especially after moving my iTunes library to a new hard drive or importing an iTunes library from another computer—where I've had four copies of each song. It's not easy getting rid of the duplicate songs either, even with the iTunes "Show Duplicate Songs" command. That's because you still have to select each song you want to get rid of. If you have thousands of songs in your library, that represents hours of carpal-tunnel-syndrome-inducing mouse clicks to clean your hard drive of the duplicates. And it's not really safe to delete songs this way because you can't really be sure whether or not you are getting rid of the actual song and keeping a "dead" track (dead tracks are songs that are listed in the iTunes database but are not associated to corresponding song files.)

I've tried several different song file duplicate-eradication utilities, and the best one I've come across for Macintosh is a free program called Seek and Destroy Music Duplicates (SDMD), available from pekarna.si. It's not the easiest program to use, but it gets the job done, quickly and accurately. For Windows, try Dupe Eliminator (markelsoft.com). It costs $30, but you can try it for 30 days for free, which ought to be enough time to clean up the largest iTunes library.

```
┌─────────────────────────────────────────────────────────────┐
│                       Smart Playlist                        │
├─────────────────────────────────────────────────────────────┤
│  ☑ Match the following rule:                                │
│  ┌──────────────┐  ┌──────┐  ┌────────────────────┐         │
│  │ Play Count ▲▼│  │ is ▲▼│  │ 0                  │  ⊖ ⊕    │
│  └──────────────┘  └──────┘  └────────────────────┘         │
│                                                             │
│  ☐ Limit to  25   songs ▲▼   selected by  random    ▲▼      │
│  ☐ Match only checked songs                                 │
│  ☑ Live updating                                            │
│                                                             │
│                                  ( Cancel )  ( OK )         │
└─────────────────────────────────────────────────────────────┘
```

Smart Playlists are a great way to organize songs on iTunes.

▶ How Do I Use iTunes Smart Playlists?

iTunes smart playlists are an excellent way to manage large music libraries

They're easy to set up and use, too. Here's an example. Say you'd like to listen to songs that iTunes hasn't played before.

1. Select "New Smart Playlist" from the "File" menu.

2. From the pull-down menus in the "Smart Playlist" window, select "Play Count," "is," and "0." (See above.)

3. Click OK and give the playlist (which will show up in the Source list on the left of the main iTunes window) a name, like "Never Played."

You can create more complex playlists as well. If you'd like to find out which songs have been added to iTunes in the last week but have never been played, build a smart playlist like so:

```
Date Added—is in the last—1—weeks
Play Count—is—0
```

(Be sure to select "Match all of the following rules," not "Match any of the following rules.")

Smart playlist for finding songs that you have added to iTunes in the last week but haven't played yet.

How about creating smart playlists to filter out music you don't want to hear? Here's one I use to avoid listening to kids' music, podcasts, holiday music, and audiobooks:

Smart Playlist filters out unwanted music genres, leaving only "pure" music.

```
Genre—is not—Children's Music
Genre—is not—Holiday
Genre—is not—Podcast
Genre—is not—Speech
Genre—is not—Spoken Word
```

To find out about other smart playlists that iTunes' listeners have created, visit Smart Playlists (smartplaylists.com).

▶ How Can I Use iTunes as an Alarm Clock?

Wake to the beautiful sounds of your iTunes library

I fear and loathe hotel room clock radios. Far too often, they have jarred me from my sleep at 3:30 AM with static-filled classic rock because the previous guests either had to catch an early flight or they possessed a sadistic sense of humor. And because alarm clocks are nearly impossible to program, what with all the buttons, switches, and knobs scattered across every exposed surface, I now simply pull the plug on these radios as soon as I enter a new hotel room. iTunes serves as my clock radio, thanks to a nifty utility for the Mac called PowerController from keakaj.com/powercontroller.htm. It costs $9.95, but you can try it out for 30 days for free.

PowerController's alarm schedules stay active even if you reboot your Mac, and the alarm will still work if your Mac is in sleep mode. But if your Mac is turned off, the application won't be able to turn your computer on for you, so don't forget to keep it on before you go to sleep. You don't have to worry about your volume setting with PowerController. Even if you mute your volume before going to sleep, PowerController will turn on the volume at the appointed time and slowly increase the volume until you either click the "Snooze" button or the "Acknowledge Alarm" button. In the "Event Editor" window, choose "iTunes alarm" from the pull-down menu, give the alarm a name, and set the time and days of the week that you want the alarm to go off.

A simpler, but effective, iTunes alarm clock is Alarm Clock, free

PowerController turns your Mac into an alarm clock.

PowerController: The Daily Grind

Wake up!

Snooze   Acknowledge Alarm

from robbiehanson.com/alarmclock. Unlike PowerController, you can only set one alarm and you can't direct it to open applications or scripts, but if all you need to do is get out of bed at an appointed time, Alarm Clock is perfect.

Windows users can join in the fun with Alarm Clock Pro (koingosw.com/products/alarmclockpro.php) a $19.95 utility with a 15-day free trial. The program is loaded with bells and whistles—you can trigger an alarm to wake you up with an iTunes message, send an email, open a Web site, send a text message to a mobile phone, and perform many other tasks. Alarm Clock Pro is available on the Mac, too.

▶ What Are Some Neat iTunes Tricks I Should Know About?

Learn a few shortcuts for the best digital music player around

Nothing does the job like iTunes for storing, organizing, and playing your MP3 library. One great thing about iTunes is the way you don't need to read the instructions to use it. But iTunes has a lot more going for it than an easy-to-use interface. Hidden in the menus and behind keystroke combinations are a bevy of useful features for music lovers who want to go one step further than pressing the play and next track buttons. Here's a rundown:

To pause iTunes while it is playing press the space bar. To resume, press the space bar again.

To control which columns appear in the player window, press Ctrl-J (Cmd-J on Mac). I like to include the "Date Added" column so I can sort the songs by the most recent ones I've added to iTunes. It comes in handy when you want to add new songs to a playlist or add track, album, and artist information to the songs.

To fast forward/fast reverse through a track press Ctrl-Alt-right arrow / Ctrl-Alt-left arrow (Option-⌘-right arrow / Option-⌘-left arrow on Mac).

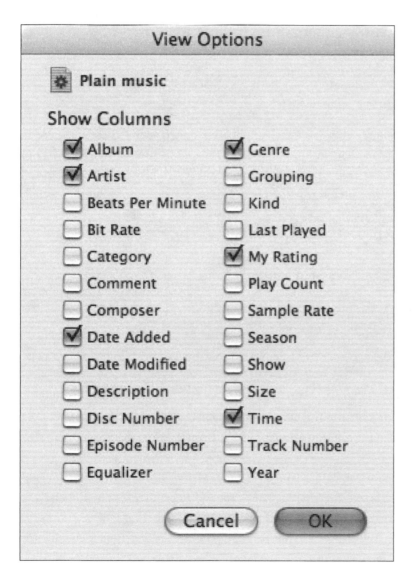

iTunes' view options allow you to select whatever information appears in the music browser.

To share your songs on your home network, so that every computer in the network can play songs from one iTune's library, click the "Sharing" tab in iTunes' preferences and activate the "Share my music" checkbox. To make the sharing feature even more useful, download a free copy of Blue Coconut (husk.org/apps/blue_coconut) which lets Mac users actually copy a song file from one computer to another, rather than simply play it.

▶ What Are Some Neat Scripts I Can Use to Improve iTunes?

Extend the abilities of iTunes by adding scripts to perform automated tasks

AppleScripts are small applications that perform tasks on Macs. They're not hard to write, and many people like to share the scripts they've created by posting them on the Web. Doug's AppleScripts for iTunes (dougscripts.com/itunes) has over 400 scripts specially made for taking care of iTune's housekeeping chores.

Here's how to install a script:

1. Make sure iTunes isn't running.

2. Open a finder window and go to Library/iTunes in your home folder.

3. Create a new folder called "Scripts" in the iTunes folder.

4. Move the script(s) you've downloaded into this folder.

5. Launch iTunes. You will see a script icon in the menu bar. To run a script, simply select it from the menu.

I use a bunch of scripts to keep my iTunes library clean and easy-to-use. Here are my favorites. To download them, visit the site and search for the name of the script.

Artist - Name Corrector. If you have a large library of songs on iTunes, you probably have noticed that some of the songs have the artist name and the song title together in iTunes' "Name" field, like this: "Cliff Edwards - A Great Big Bunch of You." It's easy enough to change one or two songs that are labeled this way by cutting and pasting the name into the "Artist" field, and deleting the dash, but when there are tens or hundreds of songs like this, you should let a script do the work for you. "Artist - Name Corrector" does it automatically. Highlight the songs you want to correct and select the script from the pull-down script menu.

Proper English Title Capitalization. To fix song information screaming at you in ALL CAPS or all lowercase, download a "Proper English Title Capitalization." Highlight the songs you want to correct and select the script from the script menu.

Google Lyric Search. The Web has the lyrics for almost every popular song you can think of. This script searches Google for the lyrics to the current song on iTunes. You can copy the lyrics into the song's information window by pressing Cmd-I in iTunes, clicking the lyrics tag, and pasting them in the window, or you can download another script called Clipboard to Lyrics Scripts and automatically insert the text from your clipboard into the "Lyrics" section of the song's information window.

▶ How Should I Use the Graphic Equalizer on iTunes?

You can adjust the levels of different frequencies with iTunes equalizer

You can improve the way music sounds on different kinds of speakers by adjusting iTunes' graphic equalizer. To bring up the equalizer, select "Show Equalizer" from the "View" menu. You can either adjust the frequencies by dragging the sliders with your mouse or choose settings from the pull-down menu. The effect the equalizer has on a song is subtle but worth the time it takes to adjust it.

If you really want to get hardcore about it, you can assign a preset to each song in your library. To do that, highlight a song in the iTunes player window and press Ctrl-I (Cmd-I for Mac). Click the "Options" tab and choose an equalizer preset from the pull-down menu and click "OK." Alternatively, you can add the equalizer settings to the

DEEPER

AppleScript shortcut keys. You can assign shortcut keystroke combinations to any Applescript in iTunes. (In fact you can create menu shortcut keys for almost any application.) Here's how to do it:

1. First, make sure iTunes isn't running. Open "System Preferences" in the Apple menu and click the Keyboard and Mouse icon.

2. Click the "Keyboard Shortcuts" tab.

3. Click the + button to add a new shortcut.

4. Select "iTunes" from the pull-down menu and enter the name of the script in the "Menu Title" field. Make sure you have spelled it correctly or the keyboard shortcut won't work. (See page 338.)

5. Click in the "Keyboard Shortcut" field and press the key combination you want to assign to the script.

6. Click "Add."

7. Restart iTunes and try out your script!

Application:	iTunes
Menu Title:	Find Album Artwork With Goo
	Enter the exact name of the menu command you want to add.
Keyboard Shortcut:	⌘⇧G

Cancel   Add

column view by pressing Ctrl-J (Cmd-J on Mac), activating the Equalizer checkbox, and then using the pull-down to assign a preset equalizer value to each song. (See below.)

Over the years, iTunes aficionados have worked on developing a "perfect" equalizer preset that makes all songs that have been encoded into MP3s sound better when played over iTunes on relatively small speakers. In 2004, MacFormat (macformat.co.uk) published its version of a perfect equalizer setting. To try it yourself, open the equalizer window and adjust the slider bars like so: db +3, +6, +9, +7, +6, +5, +7, +9, +11, +8 db. (See page 339.)

Equalizer settings are subjective, but to my ears, "perfect" equalization makes my tiny PowerBook speakers sound much better than the default "flat" equalizer setting.

The so-called "perfect" equalizer setting is supposed to make the best use of a computer's tiny speakers.

Genre	My Rating ▼	Equalizer
60's Garag...	★★★★	"Perfect"
60's Garag...	★★★	"Perfect"
60's Garag...	★★★	"Perfect"
60's Garag...	★★★	"Perfect"

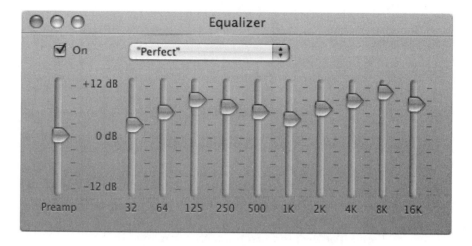

Slider bar positions for the perfect equalizer setting.

▶ How Can I Move Songs From My iPod Back onto My Computer?

Use a utility to copy your iPod library back to your computer

If you've ever plugged your iPod into your computer and tried to copy the songs from it onto iTunes, you know what it's like to be locked out. Even though it is pleasantly simple to copy songs from iTunes to your iPod, vice versa is a no go.

And if you click the iPod icon on your desktop, hoping to get to the songs that way, you'll discover that they aren't there. Your iPod is hiding your music from you. Why? Is it some kind of cruel prank cooked up by Apple? Maybe. But it's also Apple's way of soothing record company execs who have nightmares of losing their vacation estates in St. Barts because everyone in the world is trading music with each other instead of buying it. So Apple has made computer-to-iPod transfer a one-way street.

This doesn't do much to stem peer-to-peer file-sharing online, but it does plenty to frustrate average, honest music fans that simply want to listen to the music they've legally acquired on different computers. All too often, a computer hard drive will catastrophically fail. If you haven't backed it up, you'll lose all the music you have on it.

While Apple and the record industry aren't interested in helping you solve this common problem, a few smart people on the Internet are happy to help by creating useful utilities that let you drag songs off your iPod and onto your computer.

My favorite utility of this kind is called iPodDisk (ipoddisk .ourbiti.com). When you run iPodDisk while your iPod is connected to your Macintosh, it will mount your iPod as a regular hard disk, giving you full access to your music folder. From there, you can copy files to iTunes or to another hard drive.

I used iPodDisk to consolidate the different iTunes libraries on the three Macs in my house. It was the easiest way to get all the songs I own onto a single hard drive.

For Windows users, a free utility called iPod → Folder (longfingers.com/ipodfolder/) will backup an iPod's entire music catalog to a computer.

▶▶ VIDEO AND MOVIES

▶ Why Can't I Take a Screen Capture of a DVD Movie on My Mac?

>How to fix this intentionally broken feature

Here's how paranoid the movie industry is—they've convinced Apple to disable the screen capture utility while a DVD is playing. If you try to capture an image (Shift-Cmd-3) with the DVD Player running, you'll see a message such as the one on the next page. Hollywood is terrified by the idea of movie fans grabbing still shots of movies and posting them to their blog. It doesn't make any sense—why would the movie industry want to prevent movie fans from promoting their movies?

I guess it doesn't have to make any sense; after all, this is the industry that spent millions of dollars trying to stop people from being able to buy and use VCRs. In 1982, Jack Valenti, then head of the Motion Picture Agency of America, testified to the House of

Screen grabs are unavailable during DVD playback.

Please quit DVD Player first.

OK

The Mac operating system forbids screen grabs while the DVD Player is open.

Representatives that "the VCR is to the American film producer and the American public as the Boston Strangler is to the woman home alone." Luckily for everyone, the movie industry included, Valenti's fear-mongering tactics didn't work. Today, video and DVD sales account for far more revenue than box office receipts.

Fine, Hollywood once again wants to shoot itself in the foot by stopping movie fans from taking a screen grab of Harry Potter zapping Lord Voldemort with a lightning bolt. That would be bad enough, but Apple has taken the extra step of disabling the screen capture function on DVDs that you have made yourself, using Apple's very own iDVD application. That means I can't take a screenshot of the video I made of my daughter's third-birthday party, because Hollywood says I can't.

The inanity doesn't stop there, though. When you are playing a DVD on your Mac, you can't even use the screen capture function to take a snapshot of an entirely different application window, such as a spreadsheet, or a Web site. Think about it—the entertainment industry gets to dictate how you use your computer even when you aren't watching or listening to entertainment content.

In the meantime, of course, people have taken the problem into their own hands and have fixed what Apple and Hollywood had broken. A freeware program called ScreenCaptureGUI (homepage.mac .com/wii5on/1/screencapturegui.htm) lets you grab screen shots of anything that appears on your Mac's display. (Make sure only to capture screenshots that you are legally entitled to.) Here's how to use it:

1. Start playing your DVD with Apple's DVD Player program.

ScreenCaptureGUI lets you take screen shots while the DVD player is running.

2. When you get close to the frame of the movie you want to grab, use the DVD Player's controls to pause the action, then use the right arrow key to step through the frames until you get to the one you want to capture.

3. Launch ScreenCaptureGui. (See above.) I like to give myself at least a 20-second countdown (you'll see why in step 5). In the same window, choose an image file format and the folder you want the screen grab to be saved to.

4. Click "Start Countdown."

5. Go back to the DVD player and press Cmd-zero to enter full-screen mode. If the controller is visible, press option-Cmd-C to hide it. (Making the screen full-size and hiding the controller are the reasons why you need a countdown timer).

6. When the countdown timer runs out, ScreenCaptureGui will take a shot of the entire screen.

Do you feel like the Boston Strangler for doing this?

▶ How Can I Rotate a Video I Shot Sideways?

Learn how to rotate movies that you've shot with a digital camera you accidentally held sideways

This has happened to me more times that I care to admit—using my digital camera to make a video recording of my daughter

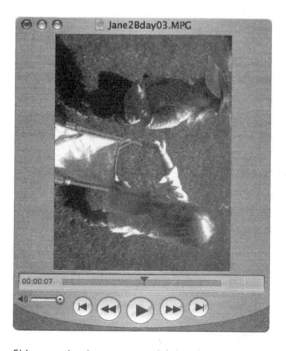

Sideways view is a common mistake when you use a digital camera.

Using QuickTime Pro to rotate a video.

Be sure to save your rotated video as a self-contained movie.

snowboarding, or a squirrel behaving bizarrely after eating fermented fruit, only to find out that I had held the camera on its side, so the resulting video is rotated 90 degrees.

One way to solve the problem is by turning your monitor on its side to compensate, but a safer way is to use QuickTime Pro (apple.com/quicktime). QuickTime Pro costs $29, but it offers plenty of useful features, including full-screen viewing and conversion options.

Here's how to rotate a video using QuickTime Pro:

1. Open the video in QuickTime Pro. (See page 343.)

2. Select "Window" → "Show Movie Properties."

3. Highlight the track in the "Properties" window and then click the "Visual Settings" tab. (See page 344.)

4. Click either the clockwise or counterclockwise button to rotate the movie. (If you really screwed up and held the camera upside down, click either button twice.)

5. Save the clip as a "self-contained movie." (See bottom of page 344.)

PERSONAL PRODUCTIVITY

▶ How Can I Turn My Documents into PDF Files?

Adobe's Portable Document Format is an excellent way to share documents over the Internet because it can handle complex layouts, including images and unusual fonts

Both Windows and Macs can read PDF documents with the free Adobe Acrobat Reader (adobe.com/products/acrobat/readermain.html). If you want to turn your Microsoft Word (or any other) document into a PDF file, you can fork over $300 for Adobe Acrobat Standard, or you can do it for free, using the following methods.

>Creating PDFs on the Macintosh

You don't need any special software to make PDF files out of your documents on the Mac, because the operating system has PDF tools baked right into it.

1. First, open the document you want to convert. It can be almost any kind of document—a Word file, a Web page, a Photoshop image—anything that can be printed.

The PDF button in the Mac "Print" dialog box offers several options for creating PDFs.

2. Select "File" → "Print" from the application menu.

3. Click the "PDF" button in the Print window and select "Save as PDF." (See page 346.)

4. From the PDF menu, you can also choose to email the PDF file. This menu selection will open your email program and attach a PDF of the file to the message.

>Creating PDFs on Windows computers

Windows users can download a free program called PDFCreator from pdfforge.org. Once installed, it sets itself up as a printer. When you want to create a PDF from a document, select "Print" and choose PDFCreator as the printer. Then just follow the prompts and save the PDF.

▶How Can I Quickly Open Recently Accessed Files and Programs?

A faster way to access frequently used documents and applications

Instead of hunting through folders every time you want to open a frequently used document, it's easier to create a folder of recently accessed files on your desktop. On Windows, this is easy enough: just click the "Start" button and select "My Recent Documents." But if you're willing to fork over $20, you can buy a handy utility called RecentX (conceptworld.com), which puts unobtrusive tags on the perimeter of your PC's display to give you access to your recent files, folders, applications, and Web sites. After using it for a few days, it will remember enough of the things you do on your computer that you'll rarely need to use the "Smart" menu to go digging after a file or application. You can try it free for 30 days.

Macs have a "Recent Items" button under the Apple menu, which shows recently used applications, documents, and servers. If you want a more customizable solution, select "New Smart Folder" from the "File" menu in the Finder. Then you can set up criteria for filtering your files, images, text, folders, applications, and so on. When you're done, click "Save" and check the "Add to Sidebar" box. Now you can access your smart folder from any Finder window.

Once you use QuickSilver for a while, you'll grow so used to it that you'll use it to open files without even thinking about it. In fact, you'll try to invoke QuickSilver when you're using someone else's computer, and you'll be frustrated when you have to open files and navigate your way to the item you need.

A Windows equivalent to Quicksilver is called Launchy (launchy.net). To trigger Launchy, press Alt + Space. Then start entering the first letters of the program you want to open. It will display the name of the program it thinks you want. If it's right, click "Enter." If not, wait a second and Launchy will display a list of possible alternatives. Scroll down to the application you want and press "Enter." Launchy is configured to look for applications only by default To add other types of items, such as movies, images, documents, etc., trigger Launchy, then right-click the window, select "Directories," and click "Add" under the "File Types" window. Then add the file type extension you wish to add: .mp3, .pdf, .avi, etc.

If you trigger Launchy by mistake, back out by entering Esc.

How Can I Keep My Computer Desktop Clean?

Use a catch-all folder to store all the stuff you don't care enough about to file

When my physical desktop gets too cluttered for me to set down my espresso cup, I clean it. When my computer desktop gets too cluttered to add a document to it without covering another icon, I know it's time to clean it, too. When I'm too busy to bother sorting all the stray files into labeled folders on my hard disk, I just throw them all into a folder on the desktop called "desktop junk." Sure, it's a bit like sweeping dust under the carpet, but with tools like Google Desktop or Apple's Spotlight, finding files is easy. And you'll be surprised at how

DEEPER

Launch folders and applications with keystrokes.
For the ultimate in instant access, get a program that lets you open files without having to use your mouse. For Mac, the amazing and free Quicksilver (blacktree.com) opens items with a keystroke combination, called a trigger, followed by the first couple of letters of the item (a folder, an application, a Web site address, a contact from your address book, etc.). Quicksilver will find that item and open it when you press return. I've set up Quicksilver to trigger when I type Cmd-Space.

much better you feel after cleaning your desktop this way. It reminds me of design consultant Donald Norman's observation that a freshly washed car seems to run better than a dirty car. For some reason, a clean desktop makes my computer seem to run more smoothly, and I feel more productive. (Isn't self-delusion a wonderful thing?)

PROTECTING AND MAINTAINING

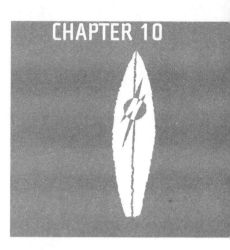

CHAPTER 10

SECURITY AND PRIVACY

▶How Do I Keep My Files Safe?

Here's how to lock your computer up tight

Your computer has probably got your bank account information, email correspondence, passwords, tax records, Web site bookmarks, and plenty of other personal information that could be embarrassing or financially devastating should it fall into the hands of the wrong type of person. If you travel with a laptop computer, you're taking a chance that someone might steal your computer from your car, office, or hotel room. That's why it's important to keep your computer safe from snoops. Locking down the information in your computer isn't convenient but, believe me, it's worth the hassle. Here are some methods you can use to ensure that your private information stays that way.

Protect your computer account with a log-on password. I like being able to walk over to my computer, hit the spacebar to wake it up, and start working. Since I work from home and I trust everyone in my house, I don't worry about a password protecting my computer. But when I step outside with my laptop, I activate password control of my machine. On a Mac, you can do this by selecting "System

The Mac offers a variety of security settings.

Preferences" from the Apple menu and clicking "Security." You can
see my setup above. I've checked "Require password to wake this
computer from sleep or screensaver," "Disable automatic login,"
and "Logout after 30 minutes of activity." This means that whenever I put my computer to sleep, either by closing the cover, selecting "Sleep" from the Apple menu, or not using my computer for 30
minutes, no one will be able to snoop around on my computer unless they have the password.

   To activate a screen saver password on Windows, open the "Display" control panel and click "Screen Savers." Choose a screen

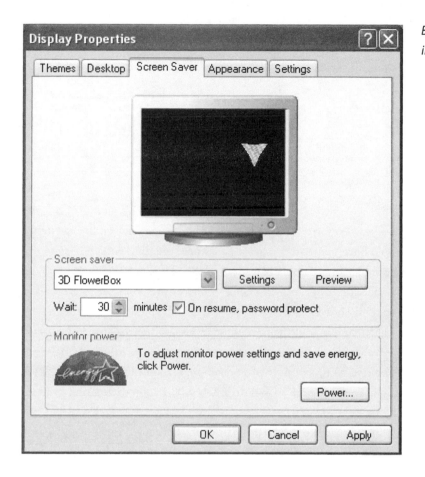

Enabling password protection in Windows.

saver, select a wait time and check the "On resume, password protect" box as shown above.

Encrypt your hard drive. The step above is fine for thwarting
casual snoopers, but doesn't offer enough protection against someone who steals your computer or has time to sit in front of your
desktop computer while you're at lunch. To foil these more determined snoops, you'll need to encrypt your files with a password.
When you encrypt a file, the data is scrambled so that only people
who know the password are able to unscramble it.

Mac users can use OS X's built-in encryption software, called
FileVault, which scrambles everything in your "Home" folder. Select

You need plenty of drive space to use the Mac's FileVault.

There isn't enough space on your hard disk to turn on FileVault.

Turning on FileVault requires an additional 4072.2 GB of free disk space to create an encrypted copy of the home folder. Try emptying the Trash or deleting files you don't need.

OK

"System Preferences" from the Apple menu and click "Security." You'll have to create a master password, one that you can use to unscramble any of the files on the Mac. Then, click "Turn on File-Vault." The program will check to make sure you have enough extra room on your hard drive to store the encrypted files. If there's not enough room, you'll get an error message like the one shown here (see above) telling you how much extra space FileVault needs to complete its mission. If there is enough room, FileVault will let you know. You can click "Turn on FileVault" in the dialog box to begin the encryption.

Should you decide to use FileVault, here are a few things to keep in mind. First, unless you are logged out of your account, or your computer is shut down, your files can be accessed by anyone. Second, FileVault may not play nice with the backup software you use. Before using FileVault, I recommend that you first backup your entire hard drive to an external drive. Finally, if you forget your password and master password, you're out of luck. Apple's help documentation says it bluntly: "[If] you can't remember the master password, the information in your home folder is lost forever." In other words, you will never be able to get your data back. You'll have to erase your hard drive and start over.

FileVault isn't for everyone. I don't use it because I like to keep my computer logged onto my account all the time, making it useless. Instead, I use a $10 program called Crypt (dekorte.com/projects/shareware/Crypt/). The free version allows you to encrypt

Crypt offers drag and drop file encryption.

and decrypt files, but not folders. It's brilliantly simple to use. Just drag any file or folder you want to scramble into the Crypt window. (See above.) Then, enter a password (one that you won't forget—Crypt plays for keeps!). You also have the option of deleting the original file or folder, and going another step by shredding the file or folder, which makes it impossible for someone to unerase using a file-recovery utility. (See below.)

Windows users can encrypt files and folders with a similar program called Winguard Pro (winguardpro.com). Like Crypt for the Mac, the free version of Winguard Pro allows you to encrypt and decrypt files, but not folders. To encrypt a file or folder, right-click an

Crypt lets you know when your password is strong enough.

icon and select "Encrypt" or "Decrypt" from the menu, enter the password (it has to be the same as the password you use when you set up Winguard Pro). Winguard Pro also lets you password-protect programs to prevent other people from running them.

Encrypt Microsoft Office documents. Maybe you don't need to encrypt many different kinds of files and folders. If it's just sensitive Microsoft Word and Excel documents you'd like to keep safe, then you don't need to buy a third-party program to protect files. Microsoft Office applications have built-in encryption. On any open Word document on the Mac, choose "Save As" from the "File" menu, select "Options" and then click "Security." Enter a password in the "Password to Open" field and click "OK." In Windows, select "File" → "Save As" and then click "Tools" → "Security Options." Enter a password in the "Password to Open" field and click "OK." The procedure is similar for Excel files.

Lock your portable devices. The PDAs, cell phones, iPods and other gadgets you carry with you are convenient ways to access addresses, passwords, and other information when you're away from your home or office. But losing a device can cause a world of trouble, unless you protect it with a password. Many newer cell phones come with a keypad lock function that renders your phone unusable unless you type in the correct password. PDAs usually have the same functionality. It's a good idea to start locking your keypads if you don't already.

USB thumb drives are a convenient way to store hundreds of megabytes of data, but because they're so small they're easily lost. You don't want to store sensitive documents on them unless they are encrypted. You can scramble the files using a program described above, or better yet, you can buy a password-protected USB thumb drive. When you plug one of these thumb drives into the USB port of your computer, you'll be asked to enter a password before you can see any of the files stored on it. A 1 GB password-protected thumb drive costs less than $30.

While iPods let you store your address book and calendar on them, I don't recommend you do it. There's no way to password-protect your iPod. If you use your iPod as a portable hard drive, however, you can encrypt the files you keep on it using the software I mentioned above, or you can buy a program like PodLock (Mac, micromat.com) or Icon Lock-iT XP (Windows, iconlockit.com) that hides your iPod's files.

I Want to Sell My Computer. How Can I Wipe All the Data Off the Hard Drive?

Make sure you wipe your hard drive's slate clean before selling or recycling your computer

When you delete a file on your computer, the computer doesn't really erase it from the hard drive. All it does is remove a few bytes of information from the file that's there to keep it from being written over by another program. In fact, if you accidentally erase a program from your computer by emptying the trash icon, you can use one of many different kinds of utilities to recover the file. Even formatting a disk drive won't get rid of the data. All the information is still on the drive.

As an experiment for an article he was writing, one of my journalist friends bought a dozen used hard drives for sale at a second-hand computer store. These drives were all pulled from used personal computers. When my friend attached them to his computer and fired them up, he was surprised to discover that their former owners hadn't erased some of the drives. And even the drives that had been erased were still full of easily recoverable data. In the interest of science, he undeleted the contents of the drives, discovering a wealth of financial data, personal correspondence, and a huge amount of pornography. In the hands of an unscrupulous person, this information could have been used for blackmailing their former owners or worse. Fortunately, my friend is the honest sort, and after filing his article he did to the drives what their former owners should have done before they sold them: he scrubbed the data.

Data-scrubbing involves not only erasing the files, but also writing over them with ones and zeros so that the magnetic particles that store the information lose all record of what they once held.

It's not hard to scrub an entire disk (or even just a selected file or folder than you don't ever want anyone to see, including yourself, ever again). On the Macintosh, you can use the built-in Disk Utility program to securely delete a disk. First, you need to boot up using a drive other than the one you want to zap. Your OS X install disk will work. Just stick the CD into the slot and restart the computer with the "C" key pressed. Then open "Disk Utility" from the "Go" menu, and select the disk drive to be erased. From there, click the "Erase" button and then the "Security Options" near the bottom of the window. If you select the Defense Department Standard, you can be assured that no one will ever be able to undelete the files on your hard drive.

Windows users can download a free copy of Darik's Boot and Nuke (dban.sourceforge.net). Copy the program to a CD, then boot your computer with it to "nuke" everything on the hard drive.

▶ What Are "Cookies" and What Do I Need to Do About Them?

Control the information that Web sites collect about you while you're online

When you visit most commercial Web sites, they embed a little text file, called a cookie, on your computer. Most Web sites use cookies responsibly. For instance, when you visit Amazon.com on your home computer, Amazon.com looks at the cookie file on your computer (which it placed there the last time you signed onto the site) and is able to tell who you are, greeting you by name and showing you recommended products. This kind of cookie is convenient.

But cookies aren't always good. In some cases, advertising networks have been known to track people by name as they go from Web site to Web site, making a record of the sites belonging to the network that they've visited. See page 359, my cookies control panel in the Firefox Web browser.

The cookie on my computer for DoubleClick, an advertising

The "Privacy" tab in Firefox lets you adjust your cookie settings.

tracking service, is 800000687cb152d, which uniquely identifies my computer (and supposedly not my name) when I visit any Web sites with a DoubleClick ad on it. So, when I go to a site that DoubleClick tracks, its software says, "Here's 800000687cb152d again. I'll make a note that he or she visited here on March 31, 2007."

If you use a computer at work, it's important to note that the names of the Web sites that you've visited will show up in your cookies file. Snoopy employers might scan your computer to find out which sites you've visited.

>Control your cookies

Fortunately, today's Web browser applications—Internet Explorer, Firefox, Safari, and Opera—have excellent cookie management tools. I'm going to show you how to manage your cookies on Firefox,

You can delete cookies one at a time or all at once.

because it's the best browser, and there are few reasons why you'd want to use another one. (In fact, if you are interested in keeping your computer virus- and spyware-free, then you should stop using Internet Explorer and switch over to Firefox.)

In Firefox, select the Privacy settings by choosing "Tools" → "Options" → "Privacy" on Windows or "Firefox" → "Preferences" → "Privacy" on the Mac.

I recommend that you activate the checkbox next to "Accept cookie from sites."

This shows the cookie viewer window that appears when you click "Show Cookies." If you highlight a cookie, you can get rid of it by clicking "Remove Cookie." If you want to nuke all your cookies, click "Remove All Cookies." I don't do this, because I don't want to lose my automatic registration with a bunch of sites I visit frequently, like eBay, *The New York Times*, and so on. But if you really want to clean your tracks and you don't mind re-entering your user names and passwords, click away.

Whether or not you've activated "Accept cookies from sites," you can click "Exceptions" to tell Firefox which sites are allowed to embed cookies on your computer (if you are keeping "Accept cookies from sites" unchecked) or to tell Firefox which sites to block (if you've got the "Accept cookies from sites" checked). In either case, just enter the URL of the Web sites to allow or block, and click the appropriate button. Then close the Exceptions window.

For the truly paranoid, select "Keep until I close Firefox." This will flush all cookies every time you quit the application.

Remember, all cookies aren't inherently bad. But it's important to know which ones are on your computer and how to manage them.

Before you answer that, consider this: In early 2006, the U.S. government demanded that AOL, MSN, Yahoo!, and Google hand over the search requests of millions of random people (it's part of an investigation by the Justice Department to prove its case that there ought to be a law against Internet pornography). AOL, MSN, Yahoo! (all of whom use cookies like the ones Google uses) handed over the data without a fight, and the government's request for the data may not have gone public if it hadn't been for Google putting up a fight. In the end, Google was forced to hand over a smaller sample set of data.

In January 2006, my friend John Battelle, who wrote a book about Google called *The Search*, asked his contacts at Google two simple questions:

1. "Given a list of search terms, can Google produce a list of people who searched for that term, identified by IP address and/or Google cookie value?"

2. "Given an IP address or Google cookie value, can Google produce a list of the terms searched by the user of that IP address or cookie value?"

John said that his contacts at Google "rapidly replied that the answer in both cases is 'yes.' "

DEEPER

Dealing with Google's cookies. If you've used Google, and you don't block cookies, then you undoubtedly have Google cookies on your computer that keep a record of the searches you've made. (How far back? Google's not saying, but it's possible that they're saving every search you've ever made). I took a look at the Google cookies that are stored on my computer. Most of them won't expire until January 17, 2038. Do you want every search you make for the next 30 years or so to be saved in a database that you can't control?

Are you interested in using Google without Google knowing who you are? You have several options. One is to use the GoogleAnon bookmarket (imilly.com/google-cookie.htm) To use it, grab the icon from the site and drag it into your links bar at the top of your Web browser application window. Also, make sure that your Web browser is set to accept cookies—because GoogleAnon needs to be able to add the anonymized cookie to your computer when you request it. Then, once in a while (it's up to you) go to the Google Web site and click the GoogleAnon link. This will "zero out" your cookie, and then redirect you to Google's preference page, so you can reset your Google preferences (I always set my number of results to 100 per page). If you do this often, you won't have to worry about Google keeping a historical record of your search requests.

This same site also has a bookmarklet called ZapCookie that will delete any cookie from the Web site you are currently visiting.

▶ How Can I Use Someone Else's Computer and Keep My Activity Private?

Use portable apps to keep all your favorite applications on a USB flash drive or iPod

There are times when I'm not sure whether to bring my notebook computer with me on a trip. For instance, if I'm visiting my parents for a weekend, I know I probably won't be doing any work, but it would be nice to have my own computer so I could access my Web browser bookmarks, consult my address book and calendar, do instant messaging with the folks on my buddy list, and so on.

With a USB drive or an iPod loaded with "portable apps," I can keep everything I need in my pocket, save the computer itself. But since all my friends and relatives have computers, that's not a problem.

Portable apps (portableapps.com) are free computer programs that are usually smaller than their full-featured brethren, and which store all of their support files (such as preferences and data) on the portable media device.

You can install a Web browser, a Microsoft Office–compatible suite of apps, an instant message application, an email client, and a calendar and task list on a 256 MB flash drive. Just insert it into the USB of any PC and you've got everything you need, with all your passwords, bookmarks, and data right there. Your friends will love you for using portable apps too, because you won't have to monkey around with the system settings on their computers to access your online information.

When you're done, you don't need to worry about having left any personal information on the computer—it's all stored on the flash drive. The computer won't have a trace of your activities on it. When you get home, you can transfer the data back to your main computer.

▶How Can I Encrypt My Email?

Scramble your email using public key encryption

Did you know that it is perfectly legal for your employer to read your email at work, and even eavesdrop on your phone calls? You pretty much leave your privacy out the door when you enter the workplace. It's a good thing to remember when you send email from the office. Even when you send an email from home, there are plenty of points along the way where a snoop can intercept the email and take your credit card number or learn personal information about you that could be used for nefarious purposes.

If you send sensitive emails, you should start scrambling them with a method called public key encryption. Public key encryption is an amazing mathematical trick. Basically, it involves two keys: a public key, which you can share with the world, and a private key, which you must never share with anyone. If someone wants to send you a scrambled message they can use your public key to encrypt it. The encrypted message can be sent across your employer's network or any unsecured network and you can be confident that anyone who intercepts the message won't be able to unscramble the message, because you and only you have the private key that's associated with the public key used to scramble it.

An excellent "strong encryption" utility that you can use with Web-mail services (such as Gmail, Yahoo! mail, and Hotmail) is freenigma (freenigma.com). After registering, you can install the freenigma Fire-fox extension (see page 100 to learn about Firefox extensions and how to use them), and then start inviting your friends to join the free service.

When you want to send an encrypted email to someone on your buddy list, just click the "Encrypt" button in the freenigma graphic and enter your password. The text of your message will be automatically encrypted and you can click the "Send" button with the assurance that no one but your intended recipient will be able to read the message.

▶ How Can I Create a False Identity?

There are times when it's reasonable to assume a false identity online—here's how to do it

I often use BugMeNot (see page 146) to access news and information Web sites without having to disclose my personal information. I don't feel that an online newspaper has the right to know who I am and what articles I read. After all, when I drop two quarters into a newspaper vending machine, I don't have to swipe my driver's license into a card reader.

When BugMeNot doesn't work, I'll sometimes just enter a fake name and address information into the form. The best way to obtain a fake identity is to visit the False Identity Generator at fake-namegenerator.com. The information it generates includes a name, address, phone number, email address, mother's maiden name, credit card number, and more. Not only is this good for accessing snoopy newspaper sites, it's also a great way to infuriate spammers and scam artists. There are other legitimate reasons why you might need to generate fake names: to test a software application by populating it with fake user data, to log into a message board from a foreign country that uses an address form that doesn't work with the

Your Randomly Generated Identity

Gender:	random ▾ Go	**Name set:**	American ▾ Go	
Save As:	permanent URL	**Country:**	United States ▾ Go	

These name sets apply to this country: American, Hispanic

Jerry R. Mitten
1400 Jerome Avenue
Harlingen, TX 78550

Email Address: Jerry.R.Mitten@dodgeit.com

Phone: 956-265-6373
Mother's maiden name: Janise
Birthday: September 7, 1967

Visa: 4485 0241 9174 4057
Expires: 11/2007

SSN: *Only available with bulk name orders.*

With the click of a button you can generate a false identity.

local address format, to create a pseudonym on the Internet so that you can maintain a separate online identity from your life in the real world, and so on.

Once you go to the site, and accept the terms of service (basically promising that you won't abuse the service to commit fraud, which would be a very bad thing to do), all you have to do is click the "Go" button to get a page of fake information that can fool almost any form. (See above.)

> **Here's the bookmarklet:** <u>Generate password</u> You can drag it to your browser's book
> just click it right now to test it on the form
>
> | Bookmark This Link... |
> | Copy Link Location |
> | Cache View ▶ |
> | ⬇ Save link with dTa on... |
> | ⬇ Start link with dTaOneClick! |
> | |
> | Properties |
>
> **How does it work?** It gets the hostname from
> cryptographic magic we call <u>MD5</u>. It will alway
> that result if either changes. (Well, once in a fe
>
> **Note that this bookmarklet works on Safari an
> trained otters. (<u>Here</u>'s an IE version someone
>
> Oh, and the MD5 Javascript code is © <u>Paul Joh</u>

This password bookmarklet generates strong passwords and remembers them so you don't have to.

▶ How Can I Create Passwords That Are Difficult to Crack?

Don't give a bad guy the keys to your online kingdom—use this simple method to generate unique passwords that you don't need to remember or write down

Computer security experts offer two pieces of excellent advice about online passwords: use a combination of letters, numbers, and punctuation (to foil hackers who use "brute force" attempts to break into accounts using every word in the dictionary) and to use a different password for every site you are registered to (to prevent a hacker who gets one password from visiting and cleaning out your bank accounts, eBay account, and stock portfolio). Excellent advice indeed. Too bad no one follows it. Who can remember 25 different passwords that read like a cat stepping across the keyboard? No wonder so many people use the name of a loved one or a pet for their password, and use it for every Web site that requires a password to visit.

Fortunately, a fellow named Nic Wolff has created a password generator that creates unique passwords that will stump even the most determined sleazebag. Here's how to use it.:

1. Visit angel.net/~nic/passwdlet.html and right-click the "Generate password" link. Select "Bookmark the link" from the contextual menu, as shown above.

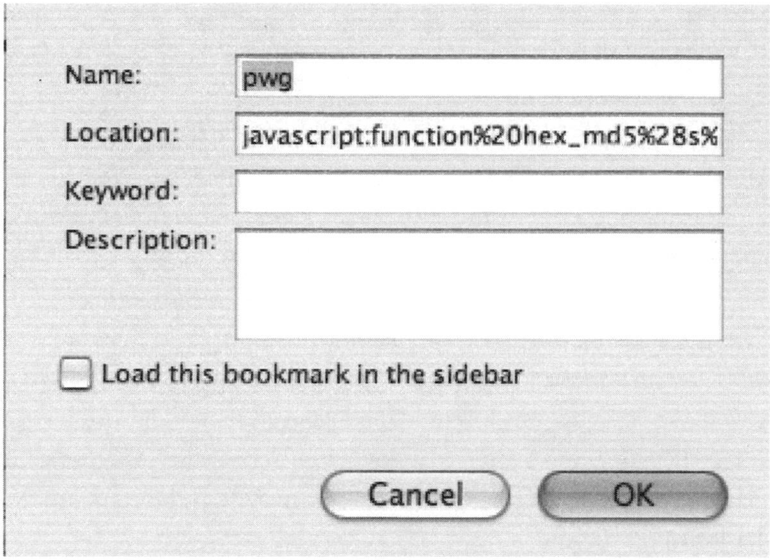

Name:
pwg
Location:
javascript:function%20hex_md5%28s%
Keyword:
Description:
Load this bookmark in the sidebar
Cancel
OK

Saving the bookmarklet in your toolbar.

2. Choose "Bookmarks toolbar" as the place to save this bookmarklet.

3. From the toolbar, right-click "Generate Password" and select "Properties" from the pull-down menu. Rename it to something short, like "pwg," as shown above. (The reason for doing this is to save real estate on your precious bookmarks toolbar.)

4. Now, the next time you visit a site that requires registration, click the "pwg" bookmarklet. It will ask you for your master password, which can be anything. Just make sure it's something easy to remember, and that you use the same master password for every site you visit. (See, this is the opposite advice that an online security expert would give you, but in this case you are safe, because the master password used to generate the unique password is never transmitted online—the generation is done locally on your computer.) The bookmarklet will automatically fill in the password fields for you with a unique password.

5. From now on, whenever you revisit a site that you registered with using Password Generator, use the bookmarklet to fill in the password field.

The downside to this is that you won't be able to access your password-protected sites from another computer, so keep that in mind if you travel and use cybercafés or friends' computers.

Once you've got Greasemonkey (see sidebar) running, visit xs4all .nl/~jlpoutre/BoT/Javascript/PasswordComposer/greasemonkey .html and install the Password Composer script. Now, when you visit a Web site, the password field will be colored green and will have a small "P" in the upper right corner. Double-click the "P," enter your master password, and Password Composer will enter your unique password for the site.

Now you have no excuse for not practicing safe security.

▶ How Do I Clean Spyware Off My PC?

Download free spyware and adware removal software

DEEPER

Using a Greasemonkey script for even easier passwords. Greasemonkey is a Firefox extension that lets you run powerful scripts that change the behavior of Web sites. Download it from greasemonkey.mozdev.org. When installed, you'll see a smiling simian head at the bottom of Firefox's browser window.

Besides viruses (which are programs that make copies of themselves and hide inside other programs in an attempt to infect as many computers as possible) there are lots of other types of bad programs which all fall under the category known as malware. One of the worst kinds of malware is spyware, which is software that secretly collects your personal information and Web activities and then sends this information to third parties without your knowledge. Similar products include annoyware (software that generates lots of pop-up and pop-under ads—usually for porn, gambling, or scams—when you use a Web browser), keyloggers (programs that record every keystroke you make and email the file to the hacker, who will sift through the logfiles for passwords, banking information, and credit card numbers), and dialers (programs that secretly instruct your modem to silently dial an expensive overseas telephone number so you get hit with a huge bill, which the hacker splits with the sleazy long-distance company). You need to protect yourself from malware.

One of the best malware detectors and removers is Lavasoft's Ad-Aware Personal, which you can download for personal use for free from lavasoft.de. Lavasoft is an excellent utility, but its main shortcoming is that it doesn't prevent spyware and adware from infiltrating your system—it only catches it after the fact. Microsoft's Windows Defender (search Microsoft.com for "windows defender") does perform real-time scanning. It's not a bad idea to install both programs, and run Ad-Aware on a regular basis to detect and delete the stuff Windows Defender misses.

The best way to protect yourself against adware and spyware is by investing a little money on a commercial anti-spyware utility. The highly regarded Webroot Spy Sweeper constantly monitors your system for malicious software and catches more malicious software than the free utilities can.

Before downloading and installing a spyware removal program not listed above, here's some advice: Many of the companies offering free anti-spyware software are actually spyware promulgators. Before installing any program that advertises itself as an adware or spyware removal tool, search for the name of the product at symantec.com, a company that monitors malware threats.

▶ How Can I Use a Firewall on My Home Network?

Start by turning on the firewall features on your router and/or PCs, or consider a stand-alone firewall program

Taken from the building industry, as the name implies, a firewall is a barrier between two things, in this case, your home network and the Internet, which prevents destruction (or other bad news) on one side of the wall from affecting things on the other. Many users seem unaware of the fact that most home network routers come with firewalls built in, as do home computer operating systems, such as Windows XP and Apple OS X. Make sure these are turned on and set up properly (consult the docs for your router and operating system).

▶ How Can I Keep My Kids Away From Objectionable Stuff Online?

Use a kid-friendly browser to prevent your kids from stumbling upon inappropriate content

The great thing about the Internet is that anyone can create content for it and offer it up to a potential audience of over a billion people. Today, you can walk into a consumer electronics store and buy a computer, a Web camera, a microphone headset, and software for $1,000, giving you the power of a TV station, and a larger potential audience to boot.

The dark lining to this silver cloud is that there is plenty of adults-only content that I wouldn't want my eight-year-old daughter to come across while she surfs the Web for games and homework research.

Some people think the answer to the problem is establishing laws that would make it a crime to publish objectionable content on the Web. I think such laws do more harm than good. First of all, from a First Amendment standpoint, any law that gives the government the power to censor the press (and anyone who has a blog, or posts a comment on a message board, is a member of the press, in my opinion) is unconstitutional. Second, laws that attempt to stem the flow of information simply won't work on the Internet, because the Internet is a global network, and people in the U.S. would still be able to access content from other countries. Third, there are already anti-obscenity and child-protection laws on the books. We don't need any more laws along these lines.

A far better way to keep children safe from the seamy side of the Internet is a home- or school-based filtering system. At my house, we use a kid-friendly Web browser called Bumpercar ($29.55 from freeverse.com/bumpercar2) for Macintosh computers that allows parents to create lists of sites that their kids can access. The application comes pre-loaded with a great list of destinations, including Yahooligans (Yahoo's Web directory for kids), and other educational and entertainment sites. When my daughter uses it, I feel confident that she won't accidentally end up in the Web's red-light district.

Windows users can use a similar, and free, kid-friendly Web browser called Kid Rocket (kidrocket.org).

▶ How Can I Safely Store All My Passwords?

Keep your passwords in one place for quick access

If you've been on the Net for any length of time, you've undoubtedly signed up for several services that require a user name and a password, such as online banking services, email accounts, brokerages, eBay, Web sites that require registration to access, certain online magazines and newspapers, gaming sites, and so on.

You've probably been told not to use the same password at each site, and it's good advice. It's not hard for some ne'er-do-well system administrator at one of the Web sites you are registered on to get your password and try to use it to open your eBay or bank account. If that happens, you'll have a time-consuming mess to clean up. It's much better to use a completely different password at each Web site you are registered on.

Of course, the problem then becomes how to remember all those different passwords. If you write them down on a piece of paper, then you're taking the risk that someone can steal the paper or copy the information on it. An even worse idea is keeping a list of passwords stored in a document on your computer. If you keep this on a laptop computer and you lose it, it's like handing over the keys to your house and a combination to your safe.

I recommend using a keychain application to store all your passwords. My favorite is Password Plus, a $29.99 utility (dataviz .com/products/passwordsplus/index_win_mac.html), which lets you store not only usernames and passwords, but also credit card numbers, driver's license numbers, and just about any other kind of personal information you need to keep safe. To open the application, you have to enter your master password, which means a laptop thief won't be able to get to the information stored inside. One neat feature of Password Plus is the way it synchronizes to a Palm handheld computer. You can enter a new password on either your computer or your

Palm and it'll appear on both machines the next time you sync them up. This came in handy a while back when I went to pick up some food at a Chinese restaurant. When it came time to pay, I discovered that I'd left my wallet at home. I pulled out my Palm and looked up the record with my credit card number and expiration date information. The restaurant manager accepted this for payment, saving me a trip home and back again.

▶ What Is Phishing, and How Do I Protect Myself?

Don't be fooled by phony requests to update your bank account

I was almost the victim of a phishing scam. It happened a few years ago. I opened an email, purportedly from eBay, warning me that my account was about to be frozen due to "suspicious activity," and that I had 24 hours to validate my account before eBay would lock it up. I clicked on the link and started filling out the information: my name, eBay username, password, and credit card. But when I saw a field for entering my driver's license number, and another for my bank-account number and routing number, I lifted my fingers from the keyboard as it dawned on me that I was about to be scammed. eBay had never asked for this information before. Why would they want it now? My suspicions were confirmed when I looked at the Web site address at the top of my browser. It wasn't for eBay—it was for an un-recognizable site with an Eastern European domain. Fortunately, I hadn't yet clicked on the submit button, or I'd have sent enough personal information to the thief to wipe out my bank accounts.

Today I get one or more of these scam letters every day. They're called phishing expeditions because the perpetrator sends identical emails to hundreds or thousands of potential fish, in the hopes that he catches one or two suckers. (Why "phishing" instead of "fishing?" Because in the early days of computer hacking, people who broke into phone company networks were called "phone phreaks." Now, replacing the "f" with a "ph" is common in hacking circles.) So how do you tell the difference between a legitimate email and a phishing email? Start by assuming that any email that asks you to click a link to update your information is bogus. Phishers have gotten better at hiding telltale Web addresses, making it easier to fool their victims into thinking they're at the real site, and not one designed to wipe out their net worth in the blink of an eye.

One dead giveaway that the email is a phishing message is that it won't refer to you by your user name. Instead, it'll say "Dear eBay user," or something like that. Legitimate email from eBay will always be addressed to your user name. Another easy way to spot phishing messages is a preponderance of spelling and grammatical errors in the email. That's because almost all phishing scams originate from outside of the U.S. (Phishers may have gotten better at masking their identity, but they need to sign up for English as a Second Language classes if they want to net more victims.)

Whenever you get an email from eBay, your bank, PayPal, or any financial institution, don't click any links. Instead, open your Web browser and manually enter the site's URL. When you log in, you'll be able to check for any messages the company wants you to read.

▶ What Is Pharming, and How Can I Avoid It?

Pharming is a type of identity theft committed when you land on a phony Web site

You're likely already familiar with phishing, the criminal use of counterfeit email that looks like it's from your bank, eBay, PayPal, or some other e-commerce or financial institution. If you click on a link in one of these messages, you're taken to a phony Web site and asked to enter your credit card info, Social Security number, or other personal information. Since most Web users have now been taught not to click on links in such emails, crooks have moved on to other means, including the ability to spoof Web addresses so that you go to what you think is your bank, PayPal, whatever, via the Web, not through an email link, and you still end up at a dummy site designed to capture personal data.

There's an easy way to guard against this. All browser software has a security feature built into it that shows you when you've landed on a secure Web page that uses data encryption software and that looks for a certificate ID that verifies the banking or e-commerce site is what it says it is. If the certificate doesn't add up, your browser will tell you. Never accept a certificate mismatch. Call the organization in question and find out why this happened. All popular browsers also have a padlock icon that appears in the browser window when you've entered the secure area of a Web site. You should always look for this icon when in the checkout area of an e-tailer, in the account area of your bank, or other online service where money is exchanged or private, sensitive information is being sent. If you're unsure . . . stop. Call someone and verify you're on the site you think you're on and that it's okay to hit the "Send" button.

▶ What Is an Evil Twin, and How Can I Avoid It?

An evil twin is a wireless network set up by cybercrooks to capture any personal and financial information you send over it. The easiest way to avoid falling victim is to be extra vigilant when you're using a public wireless access point.

When you're out in public, at the airport, coffee house, or library, it's a wonderful convenience to find so many open wireless access points (a.k.a. "hotspots"), many of them free (see page 239 for more about wireless Internet access). But there's a growing danger in using these open networks, especially in dense urban areas and other heavily trafficked places such as airports. It is easy for thieves to set up a hotspot (they need little more than a laptop and a wireless card), lure you onto it, and then record everything you send through it to the Web. Later on, they sift through the traffic they've captured, looking for passwords, credit card numbers, etc. The main thing you can do to combat this is to make sure you're extra vigilant when accessing the Net over wireless away from home. Only log on to networks where you have some knowledge of who's behind it (e.g. if you're in a hotel, find out the name of the hotel's access point and use that, even if there are other hotspots with stronger signals). Be very wary of sending your credit card numbers over wireless on the road. If you have a choice of a wired connection (such as Ethernet in your hotel room),

DEEPER

Pharming woes. Unfortunately, pharming is likely to be a growing form of cybercrime. To find out more about it and to keep abreast of developments, both from the guys wearing the black hats and those wearing the white, go to pharming.org.

use that instead. Pay attention to dialog boxes that may be warning you to something fishy (those boxes that you usually find annoying and dismiss when safe and sound at home), the padlock icon on your browser (which tells you you've accessed a legitimately secured Web server), and the "https:" in the Web address box which also assures you that you're on a secured/encryption-enabled page (the "s" stands for "secure"). And pay closest attention to your internal "skeezy meter." If something doesn't look or feel right, if you're not certain that your online data transactions are secure, don't continue. We've gotten so used to paying bills, checking our accounts, and transferring funds electronically, that we sometimes forget that we can always pick up the phone and do some of our business that way.

▶ How Can I Prevent My PC from Becoming a "Spam Zombie"?

Arm yourself with software tools and commonsense to avoid losing control of your computer to spammers

A "spam zombie" is a personal computer (hopefully not yours) that's been turned into a spam-mailing monstrosity. It commandeers its host PC and Net connection to secretly heap mountains of spam on other unsuspecting users. You don't see the workings of this (its processes are hidden), but you sure feel its effects, as your system becomes pokier than a four-foot granny driving home from church.

To ward off the zombies to begin with, you should follow the general rules of healthy computing:

1. Don't ever open an attachment to an email unless you're absolutely certain the sender meant to enclose it. Just because the email is from somebody you know doesn't mean the mail and attachments are legit. If in doubt, email and ask them.

2. Don't ever open a file on your computer that has the extension .exe, .bat, .scr, .vbs, .pif, or .reg if you don't know exactly what it is and where it came from. In fact, make that any file with any extension, if you're not 100 percent confident about it.

DEEPER

Stay on top of the mal-ware. You can keep abreast of the latest spam-filtering and anti-virus apps by going to CNet's download.com and searching on "spam filters" and "anti-virus." There you'll find reviews and ratings by CNet's staff as well as reader reviews. From there, you can download free applications and demos of the latest commercial anti-spam tools.

3. If the offer sounds too good to be true, it probably is (e.g. "Free porn for life. Click *here*!").

For ongoing spam protection, see box, left. For anti-virus software on the PC, I like BitDefender Anti-Virus ($40 from bitdefender.com) and Kaspersky Labs' Internet Security 6.0 ($70 from usa.kaspersky .com). While the latter product costs more, it includes a spam-fighting program and updates itself hourly (to protect against any new outbreaks).

On a Mac, the free program ClamXav (clamxav.com) is good and free. The good news for Mac users is that, because the Mac userbase is so much smaller and OS X is more secure by default, spam zombie and virus-makers rarely target it, and even if you open a viral file by mistake, it probably won't execute under the Mac OS. (But don't let this fact make you complacent. If that smug hipster yutz in Apple's PC vs. Mac commercials doesn't motivate evil computer zombie creators to target Apple products, I don't know what will!)

MAINTENANCE

▶ How Can I Back Up My DVDs?

How to make copies of your favorite shiny plastic discs

Making backup copies of video DVDs on your computer requires special compression software. That's because video DVDs are 9 GB and most computer DVD drives can only write 4.7 GB disks.

For Macs, the easiest software is Roxio's $50 Popcorn (roxio.com). However, before you can copy your DVDs with Popcorn, you first need to decrypt them. Popcorn is not allowed to decrypt DVDs because it is illegal to make software that decrypts scrambled copyrighted material without the permission of the copyright holder. The data on commercial video DVDs is scrambled to prevent piracy.

(This is a joke, if you ask me, because pirated DVDs are sold all over the world for $1 to $5 per disk. The pirates already know how to unscramble DVDs, and they don't care about laws preventing them from making illegal copies. The only thing DVD encryption does is make it more difficult for honest people to make legal backup copies of DVDs they own.)

To unscramble DVDs, download a copy of MacTheRipper (mactheripper.org), which not only descrambles the encrypted movies on a DVD, but also removes region restrictions. (As the Web site for MacTheRipper states: "MacTheRipper is intended to backup DVDs you have legally purchased for personal use. Any copyright-infringing activity you choose to perpetrate using this application is illegal, immoral, and beyond our control." It's good advice.)

Once you install and launch MacTheRipper, insert a DVD into your computer's DVD drive (the drive must be capable of writing as well as reading DVDs, of course), wait for the program to scan the DVD, then click "Go." It will place a decrypted copy of the DVD on your hard drive. Now launch Popcorn and select "Read From: VIDEO_TS Folder." Select the copy of the DVD and then press the large circle in the lower-right corner of the Popcorn window and let it do its thing, which ought to take a little less than an hour. Then you can run Popcorn to compress and burn the unscrambled movie onto a blank DVD.

To make a backup of a movie DVD in Windows, you need a similar pair of programs. To decrypt and compress your DVD, you need to download the free utility DVD Shrink (dvdshrink.org). Insert the DVD you want to copy, launch DVD Shrink, and click "Open Disc." Select the DVD drive from the pull-down menu (it's usually Drive E) and click OK. It will take a few minutes to scan the DVD. When it's finished, click "Full Disc" at the top of the window, then click "Backup!" In the resulting dialog box, select "ISO Image File" from the "Select backup target" menu, and then click "OK."

To burn the resulting compressed file, use an application called Nero (nero.com), which costs $79.99.

CHAPTER 11

TIPS FROM MY FAVORITE BLOGGERS

If anyone has good ideas about how to make the best use of the online world, it's bloggers. They spend a lot of time online, and are constantly experimenting and searching for better Web techniques. I've asked my favorite bloggers to share their indispensable Web sites and hard-earned tips for getting the most out of the Web.

>COOP's Design Advice for the Aesthetically-Challenged Blogger

No white type on black backgrounds, please.

In fact, never using a type color that is lighter than the background color would make me even happier.

It should be enough that I read your crappy blog on my laptop screen; do I have to continue to read it on the inside of my eyelids when I go to sleep at night?

And while we're on the subject of eyeball-abuse: no artwork behind the type, *especially* not animated artwork. (Let's refer to this as the "MySpace Rule" in future.)

Seriously, I know that you think all that stuff looks really badass, like a Motorhead album cover or something, but all you're doing is giving all your poor readers a headache. And unless your URL is excedrin.com. that's probably a bad idea.

COOP is a world-famous artist, and he has no idea how computers actually work. Seriously. He thinks they are filled with Smurfs or something. He sells crappy geegaws at www.coopstuff.com and writes about selling crappy geegaws at positiveapeindex.blogspot.com.

>Mark Hurst's Favorite e-Card Service

My favorite way to send e-cards is to use Delivr (delivr.net), a free e-card Web site. Several times a year I send out e-cards—for birthdays, anniversaries, and other important dates—but for a long time I couldn't find a good selection. Amazon (amazon.com) and Hallmark (hallmark.com) only offered cheesy or maudlin designs, and other sites did who-knows-what with your email address. I was happy to find Delivr, a free service that uses publicly available photos from Flickr (flickr.com). Best of all, the photos are always different, so if you don't like the selections, just click "Next" for another page of photos.

Mark Hurst is the founder of the Gel conference, the consulting firm Creative Good, and several other projects at goodexperience.com.

>Cory Doctorow's Tip for Hard-to-Find Phone Numbers

Lots of old-school Net users put their cell phone, home phone, or other preferred numbers in the contact info for their personal domains. It never hurts to do a WHOIS when you're looking for an unlisted or hard-to-find number. Go to internic.net/whois.html and enter the personal domain of the person you want to call.

Cory Doctorow is a science fiction writer and co-editor of Boing Boing (boingboing.net).

>Kevin Kelly's Tip for Currency Conversion

For travel, research, or online shopping in a global village, you need a fast, easy way to convert foreign currency amounts into dollars, or vice versa. I use The Universal Currency Converter (www.xe.com/ucc). In "Full" mode it will convert any currency in the world to any other. It's free, easy, and conspicuously bookmarked on my desktop. I use it often.

Kevin Kelly is editor-at-large for Wired, publisher of Cool Tools (kk.org/cooltools) and author of Out of Control.

>Mister Jalopy's Tip for Using Gmail as a Travel Wish List

I use Gmail (gmail.com) to keep track of restaurants I want to visit, vacations I want to take, movies I want to see, article ideas I want to explore, things I want to see, and books I want to read. Use a tag in the subject line to drop tips into broad categories (e.g. Restaurants: Chung King: Paris: Musee National Gustave Moreau, etc.) and then save them as drafts. At such time they are not relevant, I discard with

Mister Jalopy breaks unbreakable machines and occasionally fixes them at Hoopty Rides (hooptyrides.com).

a flourish. Assuming Google remains a viable concern, I will be able to track these tips until I die from any computer in the world.

>How Jesse Thorn Gets Cheap Magazine Subscriptions

As a public radio host, I am required by contract to have a subscription to *The New Yorker*, the weekly magazine of Things the Media Elite Should Know. Unfortunately, as a public radio host, I am barred by circumstance from making more than $18,000 a year. Given that *The New Yorker* is kind of an expensive magazine, at least by my standards, I was kind of in a bind. A year or two ago, though, a listener to my show emailed me a tip that has changed my life forever: you can buy magazine subscriptions on eBay. Not only can you buy them on eBay, but they are unbelievably cheap. Now—let it be said that this is only the case for mass-market magazines that make their money from advertising. As much as I love *The Believer*, for example, there are no discounts to be had there. But *Wired*? Three years for $2.99. *Vogue* for the lady friend? $5.99 a year. I even picked up *Guitar Player* for my eleven-year-old rock star brother—and it was four bucks.

You don't have to be a public radio host, living off government cheese, to appreciate that . . . but it does help.

>Jesse Thorn's Tip for Microphone Placement

The podcasting revolution has transformed everyone from eight-year-olds to grandmothers into audio creators. I've been making audio for years as the host of "The Sound of Young America," and I like to think I've learned a few things (example: when interviewing your favorite comedian ever, press record *before* you start). Here's something you should know about microphone placement if you've just started as a podcaster. Mic placement can't turn your voice into Howard Stern's or Carl Kassell's, but it can make a big difference.

The key consideration when placing a mic is this principle: you want the mic to point towards your mouth, but you don't want your mouth pointing towards the mic. Think of it this way: if you imagined an arrow shooting out of the business end of your microphone, would it hit your lips? The answer should be yes. And if you imagined an arrow shooting out of your mouth, would it hit your mic? The answer should be no. Place your mic a little to the side and a little below your mouth, and point it towards your teeth.

The reason for this: most mics sound best when they're quite close to your mouth, six inches or less. Many voice mics sound best when they're as close as two or three inches away (try yours at different distances and see what works for you). The catch is that when you're close, and speaking into a mic straight-on, the delicate sound vibrations of your voice can be overwhelmed by the big vibrations of the puffs of air coming out of your mouth—especially on plosive sounds like "p." The right microphone placement will keep the sound waves and ditch the air puffs.

Jesse Thorn is the host of "The Sound of Young America," a public radio show about things that are awesome, which is podcast for free at maximumfun.org.

>John Battelle's Tip on How to Deal with Email

My tip is pretty old-school. I won't rest until my email box is clear. Email has become my dashboard to my working life and my use of the Web, and more than 350 stream in each day. I find that if I am very focused on addressing the myriad issues that stream in each day, and don't stop work till I have ten or fewer mails pending each day, I force myself into work habits that keep me focused on the right things most of the time.

John Battelle is chairman of Federated Media and runs Searchblog (battellemedia.com).

>Jeff Diehl's Tip on Transcribing Your Podcasts

Putting aside the claims that you can charge money for podcast transcripts the way TV shows do (not true), there is a more basic reason for transcribing your podcasts. At first thought, a podcaster may resist this idea, thinking that a text version will compete with the podcast for an audience. On the contrary!

When author Neil Gaiman was on "The RU Sirius Show" podcast, we decided to also publish a transcript on our sister webzine, "10 Zen Monkeys" ("Neil Gaiman Has Lost His Clothes"). It got linked very widely as primary blog source material, so that eventually Wil Wheaton blogged it on Suicide Girls, and it also got ranked well on Digg. Our podcast downloads increased as a result.

The key is, of course, the link back to the podcast's original post. Make it prominent so that bloggers, famous for their "skimming" habits, take notice (it makes their own posts that much richer when they mention that an audio version is available). This guarantees "retro-traffic," traffic moving in the opposite direction as originally intended.

Some other benefits of transcripts are that you can display blog ads on transcripts. So, if you can, why not allow each episode you create to become both a new form of content and marketing for your audio shows?

[How do you transcribe your podcasts? You can do it yourself or hire someone to do it. Casting Words (castingwords.com) charges 42¢ per minute, and Idictate.com charges 2¢ per word. This can get pricey, though. An alternative is to post a "help wanted" notice at elance.com and let freelancers bid on the job. You might get a better rate this way. Elance.com charges 8.75 percent of the bid you accept.—Mark]

Jeff Diehl is an independent publisher and media producer. He edits "The 10 Zen Monkeys" webzine (10zenmonkeys.com) and is a co-founder of the Mondo Globo Network (mondoglobo.net).

>Douglas Rushkoff on Low-Bandwidth Web Browsing

I'm an Internet enthusiast, but I've always had problems with the Web. It's a slow, opaque interface on an otherwise fast and transparent network. Here in Brooklyn especially, we've been left out of the high-quality DSL and cable zones of our Manhattan neighbors, so the slowness of the Web compared with other, less visual Internet applications is really noticed.

So I spend most of my efforts trying to get away from the browser—and to use almost anything else instead. That means an RSS reader, like NetNewsWire (www.newsgator.com), instead of visiting blogs one page at a time. It means doing my Gmail from Eudora or Mail, instead of going onto the page. And waiting until I'm at a café with free Internet to do my big downloads and system upgrades.

When I do go on the Web, I'm mindful to avoid portal pages—or the pages on a site *before* the page I really want to visit. Sometimes that's as easy as setting preferences on a site, like a banking site, to make a certain page ("recent transactions") my preferred start page. On a high-security, highly encrypted site, this can save a whole minute of secure loading. Other times, like on discussion boards, I take the counter-intuitive step of "expanding" all the conversations at once. Even though that one page may take a while to download, I don't have to click open each of the particular posts I might be interested in.

Another trick is to tell your email program not to accept attached files. This filters out pretty much *all* of that new, image-based spam, and gives you the ability to choose which attachments to waste the bandwidth to download. Plus, you have the added advantage of not filling up your mailbox data files with unnecessary bulk.

On particularly slow days, I've even resorted to going into my browser preferences and turning off images (usually listed in preferences under "content"). Then, I can even visit a friend's Flickr or other photo site and choose which pictures I want to bother to download based on their captions.

Douglas Rushkoff (rushkoff .com) is the author of books such as Get Back in the Box, *comics such as* Testament, *and* Frontline *documentaries including "The Persuaders."*

It's a miserly approach to bandwidth, for sure, but it's an interesting set of habits to develop. Because when I'm at a workplace or somewhere else with a *real* broadband connection, I end up getting in and out a lot faster than I would otherwise. And for me, the best part about being on the Web is getting off it.

>Todd Lappin's Two Essential Web Sites

Typetester (typetester.maratz.com): What font should I use? How big? And how will it look? Typetester is a handy little screen type demonstration tool that allows you to experiment with different fonts, sizes, and colors to instantly see how they'll really look when released into the wilds of the WWW.

Todd Lappin is the fleet management officer for Telstar Logistics (telstarlogistics .com), a leading provider of integrated services via land, air, sea, and space.

Bay Area Ship Positions (boatingsf.com/ais_map.php): Loose lips used to sink ships. But what about open APIs? This is so fun to watch; it's a real-time "air traffic control" view of all ship traffic coming and going from San Francisco Bay—think LoJack for Popeye. In my perfect world, I'd have a giant wall-sized projection of this, refreshed constantly, in my office or living room.

>Mr. Bali Hai's Tip on Blocking Image Hotlinks

I maintain several very large online galleries of scanned images that used to be a frequent target of "hotlinkers": lazy bloggers and forum users who linked directly to an image in my gallery, thus using my ISP to host the image and stealing bandwidth that I was paying for. If your ISP uses the Apache Web server, hotlinking can be stopped by setting up a file called .htaccess on your Web site. Now, I'm not a great programmer, so I was very happy to find the Htaccess Disable Hotlinking Code Generator (htmlbasix.com/disablehotlinking .shtml), which creates .htaccess files automatically: all you have to do is enter the URL of the sites that you want to block, then upload the file to the main directory of your Web site.

Mr. Bali Hai develops training courses for high-end computer systems and travels all over the world sampling potent cocktails and collecting vintage tiki ephemera. His Web log is Eye of the Goof (mrbalihai.com/goof).

>Mangesh Hattikudur and Will Pearson's Headline-Writing Helper

RhymeZone (rhymezone.com): It's a little shameful, but when brain-power's running low and we're desperate for clever headlines, my last resort has always been poetry. And, despite the fact that I spend most mornings in the shower doing bad freestyle rap, the last thing I want to do when my brain's that exhausted is play the alphabet game with strange words. So RhymeZone ends up being a lifesaver. Simply stated, it's just a rhyming dictionary with a thesaurus attached, and it's helped me out in plenty of pinches. A bland title on homeless parades suddenly became "The Fragrance of Vagrants." An awful headline on fortunate mistakes turns into "It's a Blunderful Life." And while the solutions aren't all winners, when it's 3 AM and trying to be funny makes your brain hurt, RhymeZone always seems to understand.

Mangesh Hattikudur and his friend Will Pearson co-founded mental_floss magazine and they blog daily at mentalfloss.com.

>Hanan Levin on Getting Ideas with Random Google Searches

Even though I surf the net a lot, I am pretty unsophisticated, technically speaking. I use only simple Web tools and lean toward the basic applications.

On my blog, I like to introduce eclectic links before they appear on the mega-link-hubs: the Boing Boings and Metafilters

Hanan Levin is a realtor-blogger from Riverside, California. His link-blog, Grow-a-brain (growabrain.net), is the "Original Real Estate Blog."

and Reddits of the world. So I do a lot of random Google surfing to pick up unusual items. Once I discover a blog-worthy obscure topic, I find that a good place to uncover additional info is through Google Image Search (images.google.com). After seven-plus years of extensive Google usage, I still cannot fathom how rich this resource is.

>Scott Rosenberg on the Incredible Opera Web Browser

I live in my Web browser, and typically have four to six windows open, each of which have anywhere from five to twenty tabs open. Open tabs are like my "to-do" list: pages that I need to read, or that represent work in progress, or that are reminders of things I want to buy or correspondence I need to send. I never, ever want to lose my set of open tabs to a system crash or browser crash.

My answer for years now has been Opera (www.opera.com). It has never lost a tab set. Opera is great about storing the state of your windows and tabs and keeping that information absolutely current, so that even if another application crashes your system, you'll never lose your tabs. You can also manually store sets of tabs that represent important project areas or "what I was reading on such-and-such a date."

Other Opera advantages: It's the fastest Windows browser I know, and those fractions of seconds add up! It's now free. And it's never targeted by virus writers because so few people use it. Firefox is a fine thing in many ways—I love its extensibility and the fact that it's an open source. It also has its own version of tab-saving. But I find the handling of this feature more intuitive and foolproof in Opera. (Until very recently, of course, Internet Explorer didn't even offer tabs, so forget that.)

Scott Rosenberg is the author of Dreaming in Code, *co-founder of Salon.com, and a blogger at Wordyard (wordyard.com).*

>David Pescovitz's Tip on Buying Used Books Online

As a lifelong bibliophile, I'm concerned about the digitization of almost everything. What fine books will be forgotten or dumped in the recycling bin of history? What beautiful texts will be protected from eternal preservation in the name of "copyright"? What obscure, esoteric, and outré information will be lost to time? Fortunately, the

Internet also makes it easy to locate the lonely books that will almost certainly be left behind during the scanning rapture when all of the "worthy" pages will ascend into cyberspace.

AbeBooks.com is like the Akashic Record of used bookstores, a searchable catalog of more than 100 million books for sale by 13,500 independent booksellers around the world. AbeBooks.com has yielded me countless "scores": a 70's paperback thriller about a magician that had inexplicably ended up in my elementary school library; a pristine 1963 copy of *Barney Beagle Plays Baseball*, the first book a dear friend of mine ever read on his own and hence a perfect birthday present for him; an obscure Italian book about Wunderkammern that I just had to have, even though I don't know a word of Italian; a biography of Daniel P. Mannix, himself a pulp nonfiction author whose rarest 1960's works I've nabbed on AbeBooks; and, perhaps most joyfully, *Terra II*, a thin paperback plan for space colonization penned in 1974 by Timothy Leary, Joanna Leary, and L.W. Brenner. Copies of *Terra II* are so scarce that even Leary's dearest friend Michael Horowitz, himself a psychedelic book dealer, couldn't help me score, and the Web was no help. But finally, three years after adding *Terra II* to my "Want" list on AbeBooks.com, I woke up one morning to an automated email informing me that a copy had turned up, a signed one no less.

Eventually, I'll try to scan *Terra II* for the world to enjoy. Of course the aura of the book, and the smell of its yellowing pages, will be lost in the translation. And that's why even if every book in the world were scanned, AbeBooks.com would never become obsolete.

David Pescovitz is the co-editor of Boing Boing (boingboing.net), editor-at-large of MAKE, and a research affiliate at the Institute for the Future.

>Bonnie Burton's Self-Promotion with LiveJournal

Though this tip isn't really a techie trick or tweak, it does come in handy for those of us DIYsters wanting to promote our writing, music, art, or anything to the online masses. LiveJournal (livejournal.com) and other blogging sites offer multiple communities where everyone from Sherlockians to rogue taxidermists can discuss topics to their heart's content. This is a prime spot to start promoting your writing, music, or art in a very easy way.

Since most blog community sites like LiveJournal are free, it's easy to plug and play. Just register and get going. I've notified potential readers about my own magazine articles on such topics as growing carnivorous plants, sewing costumes for Flaming Lips concerts, and drawing droids. When I published my book *You Can Draw Star Wars*, I found myself interacting with thousands of potential readers and fans on fifteen different *Star Wars* community blogs! It's an essential tool for doing grassroots marketing and helping your content become virally linked from blog to blog. With hundreds of people in each community, it's a fantastic way to instantly market all your projects without having to hire a PR lackey to do it for you!

Bonnie Burton is a content developer for Lucasfilm, Ltd., and runs GRRL.com.

>Cyrus Farivar's Top Three Greasemonkey Scripts

NYT Links (userscripts.org/scripts/show/782): as both a journalist and a responsible citizen of the world, I often turn to *The New York Times* on a daily basis for news of the world, reading about everything from the latest happenings in Iraq to whatever the latest Manhattan cultural trends are. As such, the NYT Links Greasemonkey script is probably one of my favorite scripts on the Web. This script will open all *Times* articles in the printer-friendly version. This has two effects: it makes each article much easier to read on-screen with clear and straightforward formatting, and it also strips out the ads. I do appreciate that the *Times* makes money off of online ads and know that they contribute to paying for the articles that I love so much. Still, my enjoyment of an on-screen article is directly related to whether or not I'm jarred by an ad disrupting the flow of text, which is an effect that often does not happen in print. Thus, I have no qualms about installing this little script. For me, it's hard to imagine reading the *Times* any other way.

Better Maps (userscripts.org/scripts/show/2416): while Google Maps (maps.google.com) certainly wasn't the first online mapping service, it stands head-and-shoulders above its competitors—as a result, I rely on it exclusively when looking for a particular location or for finding directions. But when friends give me directions, they sometimes choose to use Yahoo! Maps (maps.yahoo.com) or

Mapquest (mapquest.com). This requires an extra few seconds on my part copying and pasting the address into Google Maps. However, there's a Greasemonkey script that will do it for me. With Better Maps, any Yahoo! Maps or Mapquest URL automatically gets transferred to Google Maps without my having to think about it.

NPR Embedded (userscripts.org/tag/npr): when I'm not reading *The New York Times*, I'm often listening to National Public Radio. Unfortunately, NPR makes it a little difficult and annoying to listen to archived stories and shows online. Listening requires the launching of a separate application (RealPlayer or Windows Media), which is totally unnecessary given that the audio can be included right there in the browser. NPR Embedded solves this problem. When I want to listen to a particular story, it's right there, and I don't have to spend the extra time or processor power to launch a separate application.

Cyrus Farivar is an Oakland, California–based freelance technology journalist who writes for The Economist, *National Public Radio,* Wired News, *and others. He blogs at cyrusfarivar.com.*

>Gina Trapani on Synchronizing Firefox's Bookmarks

You've spent a good amount of time saving, pruning, and organizing your Web browser bookmarks on your home computer. But when you get to the office, all that work's for naught—unless you use Firefox with the Foxmarks Bookmarks Synchronizer (addons .mozilla.org/firefox/2410).

The Foxmarks add-on automatically syncs the must-visit sites and favorite bookmarklets you've saved on any computer you use to every other computer you use, automatically—even if you're logged onto more than one at the same time.

To set up Foxmarks, download and install the add-on. Once you restart Firefox to complete the installation and register for a free Foxmarks account, you're on your way to synchronized bookmark bliss. You'll have to install Foxmarks on every computer that you use and enter your username and password in order to access your synced bookmarks.

Foxmarks is most useful for anywhere access to private bookmarks you'd rather not store on a social bookmarks service like del.icio.us, as well as to favorite bookmarklets that only work within your Web browser.

Also, Foxmarks is perfect when you want to "drop off " a Web site from one computer to another. For example, if you bookmark a link at the office that you'd like to post to your blog later on in the evening from home, add it to your "to blog" bookmarks folder. Similarly, if there's a URL you find on the weekend that might come in handy at the office on Monday, place it in the "at work" bookmarks folder. Foxmarks will automatically make that bookmark available on all your computers so you can process it wherever and whenever you need it.

Gina Trapani is a freelance Web programmer and editor of Lifehacker (lifehacker.com), a blog on software and productivity.

>Andrew Michael Baron on Generating Subtitles for Online Video

DotSUB (dotsub.com) is a great free service for generating subtitles and closed captions in almost any language (Klingon is not supported).

While watching a video, the viewer can opt to contribute to the translation by entering text into form fields as video play.

Once the translation is submitted, it is published instantaneously, like a wiki entry. This is useful for a closed-captioned audience. Then, for example, if another audience member notices a spelling error, that person can simply update the translation, which is also published immediately.

Because the Flash captions are just text stored in a database, the video is never re-rendered, and thus any change to a translation can happen dynamically.

Just as exciting is the idea that other bilingual audience members will translate the video into even more languages. By simply selecting the desired language from a list of hundreds of supported character types, videos can thus be made accessible to an international audience by the audience themselves.

You can see an example here: Cueteboom (cueteboom.com).

Andrew Michael Baron is the producer of Rocketboom (rocketboom.com).

I have everything set up now with this Spanish Rocketboom site and just need to find a translator who will do it daily for a few weeks while I get the word out, in hopes that people will start to translate it each day on their own.

>Gareth Branwyn's Two Essential Web Sites

Jeteye (jeteye.com): There are so many Web-based blogging, journaling, organizing, and social bookmarking tools out there. I have a tendency to try each one as they come out and then drop them in turn, going back to old, ingrained habits and trusted tools. Few such technologies and services become part of my everyday work life. Jeteye is such a tool. It allows you to quickly assemble and neatly organize disparate Internet content into Web pages called Jetpaks. You can then access your Jetpaks from any browser and make them either public or private. You can assemble links to sites, include graphics, make notes, search your 'paks, use and search on tags, and more. I'm currently working on a book that has a lot of moving parts. I can't imagine how jumbled my research would be if I didn't have it all organized in Jeteye.

GTDTiddlyWiki (shared.snapgrid.com): most wikis are designed for public access and community-wide contributions. GTDTiddlyWiki is a bit different. It uses wiki technology, built on top of TiddlyWiki (tiddlywiki.com), to create a personal organizer that lives inside of your Web browser. All of the tools to organize your life (to-do lists, dated journal entries, calendars, notes, and shopping lists) are contained within a single HTML document. You use the easy-to-learn wiki mark-up language to style your content. And you can customize the look and feel and categories of your organizer. The "GTD" in the name refers to "Getting Things Done," the wildly popular personal organizing book and system by David Allen. You don't have to be part of the GTD cult to use GTDTiddlyWiki, but if you are part of the Borg, I mean, a user of GTD, you'll definitely want to add "Evaluate GTDTiddlyWiki" as one of your "Next Actions."

Gareth Branwyn is a writer, editor, and media critic who covers technology and cyberculture for Wired, Make, Esquire, the Baltimore Sun, and other publications. He is cyborg-in-chief of Street Tech (streettech.com).

>Steve Lodefink on the Web Developer Extension for Firefox

If you're going to rule the Web, then chances are at some point you will find yourself poking around under the covers a bit to find out what makes a site tick. Sure, Web 2.0 has brought us so many easy ways to publish our content that most of us don't bother to build our own custom Web sites anymore.

But if you happen to be a Web developer, or the sort of proud individual who demands a custom WordPress (wordpress.org) blog theme or the cleverest MySpace (myspace.com) page, then you are going to have to spend some time figuring out how HTML and CSS page layout works. This is where Chris Pederick's Web Developer extension for Firefox comes in (chrispederick.com/work/webdeveloper). Upon installing the extension, you will see a new toolbar with options to dissect and examine every aspect of a Web page from right there in the browser. Some of the handiest features for me are:

Instant CSS and HTML editing. You can edit the CSS and HTML on the fly and. see the effect instantly without having to save any files or copy anything to your server.

Outlining. Quickly toggle colored outlines of DIVs, tables, headings, or just about any other HTML element. This is a huge help when troubleshooting a layout.

There are tons of other features and, although geared towards the serious developer or page designer, this tool set will really help the casual Web tinkerer quickly figure out what is what on the code side of the Web.

Steve Lodefink is a Web designer with the Walt Disney Internet Group in Seattle.

ACKNOWLEDGMENTS

First and foremost, I want to thank Sir Tim Berners-Lee for inventing the World Wide Web and changing my life. I don't know what I'd be doing if the Web never appeared, but I'm sure it couldn't be better than the life I live now. I work from a home office and communicate with my clients via email, instant messaging, and Skype. If I had to commute every day in LA traffic I'd go insane. So thanks for maintaining my sanity, Sir Tim!

This book wouldn't have happened without St. Martin's Lisa Senz sending me an email. My early email and phone brainstorming sessions with Lisa and Tom Mercer were exciting and inspiring.

David Moldawer's editorial direction was paramount in shaping the structure and content of the book. Thank goodness I got to know David, otherwise I might never have learned about his freaking hilarious podcast, Moldawer in the Morning (moldawer.com).

My agent, Byrd Leavell of the Waxman Literary Agency, was at my side every step of the way, offering encouragement and words of wisdom. Thank you all.

I also want to offer my heartfelt thanks to my friends and fellow bloggers who provided ideas and inspiration for the contents of *Rule the Web*. My friend Gareth Branwyn of streettech.com provided priceless research and writing assistance during crunch time and I can't begin to express my gratitude.

Most of all, I want to thank my wife, Carla, and daughters, Jane and Sarina, for the nights and weekends I used to write this book. I owe you trips to every Disneyland on the planet.

INDEX

Please note "i" is appended next to page references to designate relevant images or charts.